NUMBER

5

FOREIGN DIRECT INVESTMENT

INTERNATIONAL FINANCE CORPORATION
Member of the World Bank Group

FOREIGN INVESTMENT ADVISORY SERVICE
A Joint Service of IFC and the World Bank

WASHINGTON, D.C.

The International Finance Corporation (IFC), an affiliate of the World Bank, promotes the economic development of its member countries through investment in the private sector. It is the world's largest multilateral organization providing financial assistance directly in the form of loans and equity to private enterprises in developing countries. The Foreign Investment Advisory Service (FIAS) is a joint service of IFC and the IBRD.

Distributed by the World Bank
All IFC publications in print are shown in the World Bank's annual Index of Publications. This index contains an alphabetical list by title; indexes of subjects, authors, countries, and regions; and complete ordering information. The latest edition is available free of charge from the Distribution Unit, Office of the Publisher, the World Bank, 1818 H Street, N.W., Washington, D.C. 20433, U.S.A.; from Publications, the World Bank, 66 Avenue d'Iéna, 75116 Paris, France; or at the online publications site: http://www.worldbank.org, and click on "publications."

Principal authors: Dale R. Weigel, General Manager, FIAS; Neil F. Gregory, Policy Analyst, IFC Corporate Planning and Financial Policy Department; and Dileep M. Wagle, Manager, IFC Corporate Planning and Financial Policy Department

LIBRARY OF CONGRESS CATALOGUING-IN PUBLICATION DATA

Weigel, Dale R., 1938-
      Foreign direct investment / International Finance Corporation.
Foreign Investment Advisory Service.
            p. cm. — (Lessons of experience series ; no. 5)
      Principal authors, Dale R. Weigel, Neil F. Gregory, and Dileep M. Wagle.
      1. Investments, Foreign. I. Gregory, Neil F. II. Wagle, Dileep M.
III. International Finance Corporation. IV. Foreign Investment Advisory Service.
V. Title. VI. Series: Lessons of experience ; 5.
HG4538.W35 1997
332.67'3—DC21   97-35907
                                                        CIP

ISBN 0-8213-4050-6

CONTENTS

GLOSSARY

ASEAN	Association of South East Asian Nations
BIT	Bilateral investment treaty
EPZ	Export Processing Zone
EU	European Union
FDI	Foreign direct investment
FIAS	Foreign Investment Advisory Service
GATT	General Agreement on Tariffs and Trade
ICSID	International Centre for the Settlement of Investment Disputes
IBRD	International Bank for Reconstruction and Development
IFC	International Finance Corporation
IMF	International Monetary Fund
MAI	Multilateral Agreement on Investment
Mercosur	Latin American Southern Cone trade bloc (Argentina, Brazil, Paraguay, Uruguay)
MIGA	Multilateral Investment Guarantee Agency
MNC	Multinational corporation
NAFTA	North American Free Trade Agreement
OECD	Organization for Economic Cooperation and Development
PFA	Project financing agreement
PPA	Power Purchase Agreement
SMEs	Small and medium enterprises
TRIM	Trade-related investment measure
UMA	Union du Maghreb Arabe
UNCTAD	United Nations Conference on Trade and Development
WTO	World Trade Organization

PREFACE

Foreign direct investment (FDI) has been soaring in recent years. This spectacular growth has been fed by increasingly close integration of national economies, driven by worldwide competitive pressures, economic liberalization, and the opening up of new areas to investment. Developing countries have shared in the growth in FDI inflows, and quite a few of them have become a source of outflows.

Building up strong private enterprises in member developing countries has been a focal point of the International Finance Corporation's economic development work. By supporting local entrepreneurs directly and assisting the evolution of domestic capital markets, the Corporation has promoted domestic private investment as well as its complement, foreign direct investment. Over four decades, the IFC has invested in more than 500 companies that have foreign investors. In the process, IFC has gained unique insights into ways of structuring projects for success. Since its establishment by IFC in 1985, the Foreign Investment Advisory Service (FIAS), now a joint IFC-World Bank Group agency, has conducted more than 230 advisory assignments in 100 countries. Through this process, FIAS has learned much about the nature of policy and regulatory impediments to foreign investment in many parts of the developing world.

Three principles guide IFC's work: the business principle, the catalytic principle, and the principle of special contribution. Following the business principle, IFC focuses on promoting competitive and dynamic private enterprises by taking on a partnership role and by accepting the same market risk as project sponsors. The catalytic principle focuses on the demonstration effect of individual transactions, a key to extending the

Corporation's real developmental role. The special contribution principle directs IFC to complement the market, and hence focus on projects and places where it can provide special value added. IFC's involvement with FDI shows how these principles interact.

The increase in FDI flows does not mean that they are easy to attract. Flows to emerging markets are still heavily concentrated among a relative few developing countries and play a minor role in the economic growth of many others. The good news is that difficulties can be surmounted, and with sound policies even countries the markets consider risky can attract foreign direct investment. Attracting FDI, however, is only the beginning. It does not guarantee that host countries will capture the full economic benefits of FDI. Only appropriate policies to promote open and competitive markets can do that.

This report presents some of the lessons IFC has learned from its investment and advisory experience in the developing world. They show interactions between policy frameworks and the volume and structure of FDI. Case studies of difficult as well as successful projects show how the Corporation promotes successful project structures and regulatory changes as it tries to get the strongest development impact for investments.

The report was prepared jointly by IFC's Corporate Planning and Financial Policy Department and FIAS. The principal authors were Dale R. Weigel, Neil F. Gregory, and Dileep M. Wagle, with research support from Tracy Rahn and Felina Danalis. As with the other volumes in the Lessons of Experience series, the authors have drawn upon a full range of operational experience with FDI transactions from across the

Corporation. The report has also benefited from comments from staff of the World Bank. An earlier version of the report was discussed by IFC's Executive Directors in July 1997. Data used in the report reflect IFC's operational position through June 30, 1997.

Jannik Lindbaek
Executive Vice President
International Finance Corporation

September 1997

EXECUTIVE SUMMARY

Foreign investment in the form of loans or equity is an important source of capital for growth in developing countries. Equity investments can be either indirect (portfolio) or direct, known as foreign direct investment (FDI). FDI does much more than provide developing countries with financing for their growth. It brings them new technologies, management techniques, and market access as well. FDI may be stimulated by exploitation of proprietary technology or natural resources or by access to markets.

THE ROLE OF FDI IN DEVELOPING COUNTRIES

Foreign direct investment in developing countries has a long history. It has fluctuated over time, as investors have responded to changes in the environment for investment, including government policies toward foreign direct investment and the broader economic policy framework. Hence, trends in FDI have reflected changes in policy stances by developing countries, from import substitution in the 1950s and 1960s through natural resource-led development in the 1970s, structural adjustment and transition to market economies in the 1980s, and an increased role for the private sector in the 1990s.

FDI in developing countries has flowed mainly into manufacturing and processing industries. It has traditionally been concentrated in a small group of countries, which partly reflects the size of their economies and partly their attractiveness as a location for FDI. In the past, attractiveness has been closely linked to possession of natural resources or a large domestic market. With the shift toward globalized production and trade, competitiveness as a location for investment and exporting has become the main determinant of attractiveness.

The largest developing-country host for FDI is China, but Eastern Europe has emerged as an important new location for FDI. FDI has also reached the poorest countries. Although the actual amounts invested are generally low, reflecting the small size of their economies, FDI flows relative to GDP in poorer countries are as high as in richer countries. Countries in South Asia and Sub-Saharan Africa, however, lag behind in the volume of FDI flows relative to GDP.

For a long time, FDI came almost exclusively from the major industrial countries. Recently, the sources of FDI in developing countries have widened, and many developing countries have emerged as sources in their own right, particularly for their own regions. Regional links are also important for FDI from developed economies.

Recent trends toward globalization of production and consumption patterns have led to a sharp increase in global FDI. At the same time, trade and investment liberalization has brought more developing countries into the globalized economy. This has led to a dramatic surge in FDI flows to developing countries, which increased fivefold from 1990 to 1995, and exceeded $100 billion in 1996. This increase went mainly to 12 large developing countries, in part reflecting their economic size. Thus, China alone received $167 billion between 1990 and 1996 (1996 prices). Already a significant part of the economy in many developing countries, FDI is likely to continue at high levels for the foreseeable future.

Policies have also played a role in this increase. India, the next largest developing country after China (measured by population), received only 0.2 percent of GDP in FDI inflows, compared to China's 5.4 percent of GDP. Since both are populous, low-income countries, differences in population or income level do not explain this disparity. Prior to 1982, India had received more FDI in relation to GDP than China. What changed was China's policy stance toward foreign investors. After years of strictly regulating FDI, China began to see that it could make a welcome contribution to modernization and integration into the world economy. This was reflected in a changing policy framework, to which foreign investors responded quickly. Since 1992, however, India's steps toward economic liberalization have also had a positive impact on FDI flows and are indicative of its future potential.

FDI is not just attracted to the economic giants, with large domestic markets. Countries of all sizes at different stages of development from all over the world have attracted FDI worth more than 5 percent of GDP, including Czech Republic and Malaysia. What they had in common was an evolving policy framework that was attractive to foreign investors.

PROMOTING FDI THROUGH POLICY ADVICE

IFC was established to promote private investment in developing countries, including FDI. It was one of many international initiatives that promoted FDI, including bilateral trade agreements, bilateral and multilateral financial institutions, and investment promotion programs.

Together with other members of the World Bank Group, IFC set up the Foreign Investment Advisory Service (FIAS) in 1985 to advise developing countries on policies to promote FDI. Since then, it has assisted more than a hundred countries in various ways. Its advice takes many forms, from diagnostic studies giving an overview of constraints to FDI, to investment policy studies giving specific solutions for specific issues or sectors or for building institutions to accompany policy change and promotional strategies. Dialogue on the policy framework for FDI also occurs in the context of other IFC advisory work and project financing.

GETTING THE POLICY ENVIRONMENT RIGHT

Many factors influence the flow of foreign direct investment to developing countries, but the most obvious one is often overlooked: namely, the willingness of developing countries to allow it. Historically, many countries have placed onerous limitations on the scope for FDI, even when seeking to promote it. Inevitably, this has acted as a deterrent.

Restrictions on inflows of FDI have taken many forms, including limits on entry to certain sectors, complex approval mechanisms, high taxes and complex incentive regimes, restrictions on share of foreign ownership, and restrictions on use of land and expatriate labor. Restrictions have been imposed for many reasons, including concerns over excessive foreign influence and loss of national wealth, desire to promote indigenous entrepreneurship and workers, and desire to achieve transfer of technology and management techniques. Only fairly recently have a number of developing countries reduced their restrictions.

Wider policies also matter. A liberal trade and payments regime encourages FDI. Often, imports lead to investment and production for the world market. Liberal payments systems allow foreign investors to take advantage of these opportunities. A number of other administrative barriers, often long unrecognized, have deterred FDI. Important barriers include the exclusion of foreign investors from land ownership, restrictions on the use of expatriate labor, and requirements for sundry permits and approvals.

A large state role in the economy can also deter FDI, whether through price controls, methods of capturing rents from natural resource exploitation and monopolies, or through the presence of a large state enterprise sector. Privatization methods can have a large direct impact on FDI inflows, as can the structure of direct sales and the sales process. Privatization can have positive indirect effects on FDI, too. Although very high effective tax rates can deter FDI (and some investments are particularly sensitive to tax rates), selective incentives can be both costly and ineffective in attracting FDI. Attempts to foster domestic linkages with foreign enterprises have generally been counterproductive, too.

Finally, getting policies right may not be enough; active investment promotion may be required as well, unless the domestic market is sufficiently attractive to FDI. Effective promotion involves image building, investment generation and investor servicing to influence investment decisions. Needless to say, promotion without good policies will not work.

PROMOTING FDI THROUGH PROJECT FINANCING

IFC has invested in developing countries in every part of the world since 1958, in more than five hundred companies that have foreign investors. IFC's investments have been spread broadly among countries, even the poorest countries. The Corporation has been an early investor in new and risky locations for FDI and has worked with investors from many different countries supporting FDI in a wide range of sectors. Sometimes, even the largest multinationals have found benefits in cofinancing with IFC, and developing-country governments have often welcomed IFC's presence in a venture.

IFC's projects have been largely successful and profitable, despite sometimes difficult investment conditions. Two thirds of the projects financed have been

foreign sponsored, and nearly two thirds of them have been structured as joint ventures with local partners. In these, the foreign sponsor is usually responsible for day-to-day management or technical support. A fifth of the projects have local sponsors, who bring in foreign partners to provide access to technology, management expertise, or marketing support. Projects with equal stakes between foreign and local partners have done relatively poorly.

Until the 1980s, most IFC foreign direct investment projects took place in highly regulated economies, which influenced the relative attractiveness of production for domestic and export markets. As a result, few FDI projects were based on international competitive advantage. Instead, they were oriented toward producing for protected domestic markets or exploitation of developing countries' natural resources. There were no investments in nontradables such as infrastructure. The policy environment also influenced the ownership structure of projects, with few wholly foreign-owned ventures. These patterns are reflected in the types of product and the country locations and affect the pattern of project performance. Projects have done better in open than in protected markets and better still with contractual marketing arrangements.

Since 1980, a marked shift has occurred in the composition of IFC's foreign direct investment portfolio, one that has accelerated in the 1990s. Projects are increasingly based on production for global markets or provision of nontradables, and reliance on contractual marketing arrangements has grown. Foreign control has increased, with more projects majority owned by foreign investors, and more wholly foreign-owned projects. Privatization has brought foreign investors into many previously local enterprises. This is reflected in the changing country composition of the portfolio, the changing sectoral composition, and the improved performance of the more recent portfolio.

GETTING PROJECT STRUCTURES RIGHT

The structure of IFC's foreign direct investment projects reflects the policy constraints under which they were formed, with most taking the form of joint ventures. Though a common form of business organization, joint ventures are inherently fragile. Forced partnerships are more difficult to implement, particularly when they are with public enterprises, and equal partnerships have been problematic.

Limits on foreign ownership have impeded effective project structures, too. They have sometimes had the effect of reducing sponsor commitment to meet additional costs or to resolve management problems. They have also encouraged foreign sponsors to find alternative means to profit from the venture. FDI project structures are also affected by restrictions on capital transfers. FDI projects have been vulnerable to delays and cost overruns, including those generated by extensive government regulation. Close regulation of FDI projects reduces their flexibility to respond to developments.

With careful project design, however, joint ventures can be implemented successfully. It is important to ensure appropriate management arrangements through, for example, a management contract; clear financing arrangements; and careful handling of each partner's interests as a contractor with the enterprise or as a holder of related assets.

GETTING MORE FROM FDI

Governments have been eager to maximize the benefits from FDI and minimize harmful side effects. Restrictive economic policies have reduced the benefits and increased the costs of FDI through deadweight costs of regulation, economic costs of protection, inefficient project structures, encouragement of the use of transfer pricing to repatriate profits, and fiscal losses from tax incentives. Recently, countries that have liberalized have benefited more from FDI. This process is expect-ed to be sustained without major reversals, as more and more countries see the benefits of more liberal policies toward FDI.

Global integration will continue to drive FDI flows, wherever the economic environment is open to it. Globalization will increasingly blur the distinction between foreign and domestically owned enterprises, and between developed and developing countries. Countries that are open to foreign investment stand to share in the rising global prosperity that globalization brings.

Nevertheless, to create an enabling environment for FDI, a large unfinished agenda of policy reform remains. Some of the countries that have made progress in reducing restrictions, including some already receiving large amounts of FDI, still have some way to go toward providing a fully open environment for FDI. Many more countries have only begun to reexamine their policies toward FDI or the impact of their general economic policies on FDI flows. Yet these countries have not missed their chance to participate in global FDI flows. The rapid increase in FDI volumes in recent years has shown that this is not a zero sum game. As more countries open up to FDI, global integration will increase, leading to an increase in overall FDI flows. The challenge for the future is therefore to open more economies and sectors to foreign direct investment, thereby bringing opportunities for economic development to a larger part of the developing world.

INTRODUCTION

Foreign direct investment (FDI) has played an important—if at times controversial—role in the growth of emerging economies. From time to time, developing countries have expressed serious misgivings about the economic, social, and political consequences of foreign investment. Most commonly, they have feared losing control to foreigners over important parts of their economies and excessive drains on profits as foreigner investors, exercising "oligopolistic powers," make off with excessive profits. Developing nations, perceiving a conflict between national and foreign corporate goals, have imposed a variety of restrictive policies in an effort to protect themselves. Some of these policies may have captured a larger part of the economic rents, but at the expense of reducing the investment's overall benefits.

Restrictions notwithstanding, the volume of FDI flows has swelled, from an average of $77 billion in 1983-87 to $318 billion in 1995. Developing countries, with average inflows of only $18 billion in 1983-87, received nearly $100 billion by 1995, a more than fivefold increase. Fundamental changes in the structure of the global economy over the period explain much of this increase: a strong movement toward the market, especially among the former socialist economies, and a liberalization of trade and investment regimes in many developing countries. Above all, global economic integration increased enormously, and developing countries participated in it (albeit unevenly).

FDI has given the global integration process a major boost by helping link markets for capital and labor and raise wages and capital productivity in recipient countries. With newly liberalized trade and investment regimes and new technologies lowering transport and communication costs, multinational firms have espoused increasingly global strategies to capture the large savings arising from specialization and dispersion of activities. As a world network of multiple linkages has developed, intra-firm trade across national boundaries has increased sharply between parents and their affiliates in developing as well as developed countries.

The developed countries have been the driving force behind the surge in FDI flows, with outflows rising from an average of $72.6 billion in 1983–87 to $270.5 billion in 1995. Though small in comparison, outflows from developing countries also rose enormously: from $4.2 billion in 1983–87 to $47 billion by 1995. This activity signals their growing integration into the global economy—and the still-untapped potential.

Recognizing the costs of being locked out of the global economic expansion, many developing countries have changed their attitude toward FDI over the past decade. As a result, they have been pursuing much more open policies on industry entry and exit conditions, factor and product market regulation, and barriers to trade. Liberalization has led to significant increases in FDI flows—in some cases spectacular. In China, Poland, Czech Republic, Vietnam, Hungary, and the Russian Federation, FDI inflows have risen more than tenfold in the four or five years preceding 1995. In Mexico, India, Brazil, and Malaysia FDI has grown twofold or more.

In 1995, 74 percent of flows went to only 10 developing countries. The skewed nature of this distribution reflects differences in some countries' economic size, but also in their progress on the policy front. As important as the investments themselves, the influx of FDI has led to significant improvements in the efficiency of production in the more liberal countries, where globally competitive industries operate in a variety of export markets.

A CHANGING FRAMEWORK

From a look at FDI's evolving role in emerging markets in the past three or four decades, two distinct phases stand out. In the first phase, the 1960s and 1970s, closed-economy models of development were in vogue, and foreigners often made direct investments to reach lucrative opportunities inside tariff walls to exploit natural resources or take advantage of trade quotas.

As a result, efficiency gains from FDI were often limited not only by the adverse effects of protectionism but also by the impact of many developing countries' restrictive investment frameworks. These included controls on investment size, direction, location, and extent of ownership. Host-country insistence that foreign subsidiaries take on local partners, whether they wanted them or not, was another limiting factor. Though intended in part to promote rapid transfer of skills and technology to the local economy, such structurally weak joint ventures usually did little to maximize competitive efficiency. In addition, they often deterred the very types of foreign investment developing countries would have welcomed, for example, those involving high-technology products.

Restrictive frameworks were an outgrowth of developing countries' assumption that the supply of FDI resources was inelastic and therefore unresponsive to the nature of the investment-incentive framework. Recognition that this assumption was erroneous and carried economic costs provided strong motivation for subsequent economic liberalizations.

In the second phase, the 1980s and 1990s, the role of FDI has changed noticeably. With integration of international production and cross-border markets by multinational corporations (MNCs), the key ingredients of growth—created assets, technology, intellectual capital, learning experience and organizational competence—have become much more mobile across national boundaries and increasingly housed in MNC systems.

GOVERNMENT OBJECTIVES

On the whole, government policies toward foreign investors have been based on straightforward objectives: maximizing economic gains while minimizing any socioeconomic and political costs. The problem has been that in practice, costs and benefits have been closely intertwined. They have therefore involved a choice of trade-offs, so that seldom have there been any clear-cut means for implementing these objectives. In the 1960s and 1970s, but to some extent now, too, governments in developing countries have faced a series of dilemmas in shaping their policies toward foreign investment. For instance, permitting multinationals to repatriate most of their profits could be taken as allowing them to siphon off much of the newly created wealth. Forcing multinationals to reinvest their profits locally, however, would in effect allow them to increase their control over the national economy. Similarly, if multinationals paid local wage rates they would be "exploiting local labor." If they paid higher than average wages, they would skim off the best labor to the disadvantage of local firms.

Resolving these dilemmas entailed a variety of constantly shifting policies. Their impact was sometimes perverse, resulting in unnecessarily weak project structures and sponsor commitment. This diluted the expected benefits and frustrated the object of the exercise. The more liberal policies of later years were partly due to a recognition that there were different and more practical ways of achieving the same objectives and capturing the efficiency gains associated with FDI. IFC's experience over this time period illustrates the impact of these policies, particularly on project structure and competitive efficiency.

PURPOSE OF THE REPORT
IFC has had a long association with FDI at both the investment and advisory levels. From its first FDI project in 1958 to the present day, IFC has supported (through equity, loans, and mobilization of commercial finance) more than 500 companies involving foreign direct investment in more than 100 countries in the developing world. In addition, through its Foreign Investment Advisory Service, IFC has provided a range of advisory services to governments seeking to promote foreign investment in their countries. In consequence, the Corporation's role in facilitating the flow of FDI to developing countries has grown over the past four decades.

The breadth of the Corporation's experience with direct investment transactions provides a unique opportunity to examine FDI's evolving role in economic development, even though IFC's population of FDI projects is not wholly representative of global trends in FDI to developing countries: foreign project sponsors looking for financing support from the Corporation are rarely major multinational corporations seeking to establish wholly owned subsidiaries abroad. Instead, they are usually sponsors who may be concerned about country risk because of their own size and financial strength or because of project structures with which they are not fully comfortable, particularly joint ventures involving local partners. Nevertheless, IFC's project experience provides a window into the manner in which the investment framework has changed in developing countries and its implications for the success and efficiency of FDI ventures. While analysis of project performance has not been the main purpose of this report, these results have been valuable in highlighting the very real link between policies and project performance. Improvements in policies the world over have been reflected in improvements in project results, and hence gains from FDI.

This report attempts to:
- put IFC's project lending and policy advice (through FIAS) into the context of global trends in FDI
- describe IFC's experience as a policy adviser and project financier
- draw lessons from IFC's experience in these roles.

In the light of developing countries' still limited share in global flows of foreign direct investment and the huge potential for increase, these lessons may prove interesting to policymakers wrestling with the challenge of attracting FDI as well as to investors looking toward emerging markets for profits. Policymakers may find pointers for identifying and eliminating barriers to foreign investment. Prospective investors may gain insights into ways of working effectively within the confines of the economic and regulatory frameworks they are likely to encounter.

THE ROLE OF FDI IN DEVELOPING COUNTRIES

Foreign investment in developing countries has soared over the last ten years, overtaking official finance as a source of external funding for economic development.

FDI BRINGS MORE THAN JUST FINANCE

Foreign investment can take two forms. Foreign equity investors can simply buy a stake in an enterprise or take a direct interest in its management. The first, indirect form of investment, is called foreign portfolio investment. Foreign direct investment (FDI) involves more than just buying a share or a security. It is the amount of financing provided by a foreign owner who also is directly involved in the management of the enterprise.[1] For statistical purposes, the International Monetary Fund (IMF) defines foreign investment as direct (FDI) when the investor holds 10 percent or more of the equity of an enterprise. As a rule of thumb, this is usually enough to give the investor a say in the management of the enterprise. Sometimes an investor with a smaller share plays an active role, or a larger investor may remain passive.[2] Both foreign portfolio and direct investment were quite small until the mid-1980s, but have grown rapidly since (Figure 2.1).

Figure 2.1. Real Foreign Direct Investment and Foreign Portfolio Investment to Developing Countries, 1970–96 (1996 $ billion)

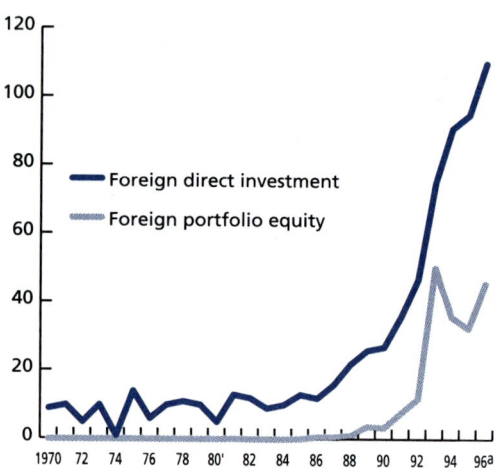

Source: World Bank Debtor Reporting System.
a. Preliminary data.

With portfolio investment, the enterprise benefits from the finance, and (in the case of equity) a sharing of risk. Direct investment can bring additional benefits to improve investment productivity:

■ Involvement in management may provide access to better management techniques.

■ Access to technologies: technology owners are often unwilling to make technology available to a partner unless they can retain some degree of management control, which FDI provides.

■ Access to marketing expertise and market links: the FDI partner may be a customer for the products or may have better access to export markets or better marketing skills.

Thus FDI can provide more than just a finance flow. It can also provide an operational link between an enterprise and a foreign partner. A foreign partner that has investment expertise, technology, or market access not available in the host economy can raise the productivity of the enterprise. For example, the Turkish government exploited its copper resources in Cayeli/Rize in partnership with domestic and foreign mining companies (Box 2.1).

Box 2.1. Cayeli Copper Mine, Turkey—Drawing on FDI to Develop a Natural Resource

The Cayeli copper/zinc underground deposits are located in northeastern Turkey, close to the Black Sea. The orebody's potential had been known for many years, and small-scale mining had taken place at the surface and with short tunnels since Roman times. The Cayeli orebody is, however, unusually complex. ETiBANK, the State-owned mining enterprise which held the mining rights to the orebody, shared the financial and investment risk by seeking the participation of a foreign investor with mining experience and also domestic investors.

A joint venture (JV) was established in 1983 between ETiBANK, PHELPS DODGE (an American Company, which sold its shares to INMET of Canada in 1987) and GAMA (a Turkish private company). ETiBANK leased its mining rights to the newly formed JV in return for a royalty fee. The company is overseen by a board of directors constituted of representatives from INMET, ETiBANK, and GAMA. Most major decisions require 60 percent support, so the sponsors must reach consensus. INMET established and operates the mine under a technical assistance agreement. The operator has maintained sufficient freedom to run the mine successfully, and the shareholders have provided consistent financial support as required. INMET has performed effectively, completing the project on time and on budget.

Since this project began, at least two other private sector mining projects have been developed, and mining has the potential to become a major contributor to the Turkish economy.

The host economy benefits from the additional economy activity, creating employment and tax revenue. Entry by foreign firms can also increase competition in domestic markets, reduce monopoly profits, and stimulate quality upgrades of products and services by all firms in the sector. Thus, investment in Mauritius by a textile company from Hong Kong, China, helped take the Mauritian textile industry upmarket (Box 2.2).

A 1995 study of 69 developing countries found that FDI stimulates economic growth, and has a larger impact than domestic investment. It also found that far from crowding out domestic investment, FDI seems to supplement it.[3]

Operational links often provide the impetus for FDI.

Box 2.2. TIL Textiles, Mauritius—FDI Takes the Textile Industry Upmarket

The textile industry in Mauritius benefits from good infrastructure and supportive government policies, including an Export Processing Zone (EPZ) that provides generous incentives and stability in labor relations. Focusing on value added, labor intensive products, the industry has grown rapidly. Textiles and manufacturing account for about 90 percent of employment in the EPZ, and 53 percent of Mauritian exports.

When IFC invested in Textile Industries Limited (TIL), the company had been established in Mauritius for 18 years. It is a wholly owned subsidiary of Esquel of Hong Kong, China, which supplies its inputs, and markets its products. With support from IFC, it developed new production facilities using CAD-CAM technology which enabled it to move its products upmarket, while saving labor. This was necessary, because Mauritius had exhausted its potential for further economic expansion through labor-intensive manufacturing, and TIL had had to import scarce unskilled labor.

After implementation of the project, TIL increased exports to such private labels as Ralph Lauren, Yves St. Laurent, Tommy Hilfiger, and Nautica. It has become one of the world's leading high-quality shirt manufacturers. About 80 percent of its production is now for the top-end customers.

TIL offers an in-house training program for all employees. The quality of its products confirms the high skill level of its work force. Trained Mauritians hold most senior management and supervisory positions. Productivity has been particularly high at TIL because it is one of the few EPZ companies that has been able to upgrade its product line and invest in technologically advanced, capital-intensive equipment.

Although most of the direct returns to the enterprise accrue to the foreign investor, the company's success has helped raise the standards of the whole EPZ textile industry. It has established the reputation of Mauritius as a source of high-quality textiles and has encouraged other companies to emulate its move upmarket.

Although management, technology, marketing, and other know-how can be supplied under contract, such arrangements normally involve less control. Nor are they immune from risk, particularly since contracts are difficult for foreign partners to enforce in many countries. With increased concern about retaining control over intellectual property, obtaining technology under contract has become more difficult. Suppliers of know-how and technology may prefer to take an equity stake (FDI) so they can exercise some control over the use of their inputs and share in the financial rewards for taking risks. For example, production of auto components in India has been fostered by FDI (Box 2.3).

Marketing advantages cut both ways. The foreign partner can be expected to have superior access to international marketing channels or more experience in international markets. For its part, the local partner may be able to provide access to the local market. FDI may occur so that a foreign partner shares in the domestic partner's market advantages, or vice versa. Again, the partnership may involve equity holdings by both partners (i.e., involving FDI) as a means of sharing control, risks, and rewards.

FDI'S LONG HISTORY

The story of development almost everywhere includes foreign direct investment, from the Persian Gulf's oil fields to India's tea plantations and Malaysia's rubber plantations. Early in the twentieth century, a large part of the world's infrastructure was developed through foreign direct investment, including electric power in Brazil and telecommunications in Spain. British firms invested in consumer goods manufacturing abroad from an early date. German chemical companies were expanding outside Germany before World War I as were U.S. auto manufacturers. Swedish, Swiss, French, and Japanese firms had established foreign subsidiaries at an early date as well.

These investments were based on new technologies and management and organizational practices. By 1914, the world stock of FDI was estimated at $15 billion, about one third of all international investment at the time. The United Kingdom was then the largest source of investment, followed by the United States and Germany. The United States was the largest recipient of FDI.

The stock of world FDI had risen to $66 billion by 1938, with U.K. firms still the largest investors. More than half of this investment had been made in developing countries, mainly in Latin America and Asia. Much of it was in agriculture and mining, but a significant part was also in infrastructure.

Box 2.3. UCAL Fuel Systems, India—Strong Sponsor Relations with Technical Partner Underpin Auto Parts Industry Development

In 1989, Mikuni of Japan formed a joint venture with Carburetors Limited (CL) of India to manufacture carburetors and fuel pumps, based on Mikuni technology. The main customer for these products was Maruti, an Indian car maker, which was a 60-40 (now 50-50) joint venture between the government of India and Suzuki of Japan.

UCAL currently buys components from 120 suppliers. Through regular meetings, UCAL enforces the same discipline and high standards in these relationships that Maruti does. Most UCAL suppliers have had to expand capacity and many have successfully reduced their reliance on UCAL as a single customer. The project has enabled Maruti to increase the level of domestic component sourcing in an efficient way, and lowered its exposure to yen-rupee parity changes. UCAL's carburetor now costs Maruti about 30 percent less than the Mikuni import and about 15 percent less than European substitutes.

These patterns shifted after World War II as U.S. firms became the main source of FDI, and manufacturing investment became most prevalent. As mentioned in Chapter 1, during the 1950s and 1960s, most developing countries pursued "inward-oriented" development strategies, which emphasized the growth of domestic industry behind trade barriers. Production for the domestic market was encouraged over exports, and imports were discouraged or restricted. Governments played an active role in regulating and directing private business. In doing so, many policymakers were concerned about possible adverse consequences of FDI such as creation of economic dependency, political interference, and weakening of domestic companies.

Such policies generally deterred FDI. The creation of domestic markets protected from imports gave foreign producers an incentive to shift production into the country, instead of trying to export to it. Thus, FDI was concentrated in import-substitution industries through a process known as tariff-jumping. This incentive was strongest in countries with large internal markets such as Brazil and Mexico in Latin America, which attracted large volumes of FDI to industries protected from imports.

FDI also continued unabated to countries that were rich in natural resources and locations that gave products preferential access to export markets. For example, textile production shifted to developing countries such as Mauritius that had unused quotas for export to industrial country markets under the Multi-Fiber Agreement. However, there was disinvestment in infrastructure sectors during this period as many developing governments took over control of firms from foreign (and domestic) private investors.

Escalating commodity prices in the 1970s had two effects on FDI. First, high prices encouraged increased FDI in extractive sectors, particularly oil and gas. This benefited countries such as Congo, Ecuador, Indonesia, and Nigeria, which saw sharp increases in FDI in the early 1970s.[4]

Second, the balance of payments surpluses of commodity-exporting countries provided an abundant source of investable capital. This money was recycled to developing countries through large-scale sovereign lending by commercial banks. Thus, developing countries became more reliant on sovereign borrowing and less interested in attracting FDI. In addition, some developing countries benefited sufficiently from commodity price increases to meet their own investment needs from domestic savings, without FDI. The economic buoyancy of many developing countries in this period encouraged policymakers to pursue inward-oriented approaches, often expressly aimed at delinking from the global economy. A number of countries tightened policy restrictions on FDI.[5] Investors responded to the apparent lack of interest, or even hostility, of host governments by reducing their FDI in many developing countries. Colombia, Kenya, and Pakistan were among countries where FDI fell sharply in the early 1970s. The second trend proved stronger than the first: Chile, Egypt, Venezuela, and Zambia saw massive disinvestment, despite abundant natural resources, as a result of deliberate policies favoring domestic, public investment in extractive industries. Several countries used the additional resources generated by higher raw material prices to buy out foreign owners of mining and petroleum ventures. As a result, FDI to developing countries stagnated in the 1970s (Figure 2.1).

This stagnation continued into the first half of the 1980s, as developing countries struggled to restore economic stability in the face of falling commodity prices, recession in industrial countries, and high global interest rates that together triggered a debt crisis. Furthermore, the consequences of inward-looking, state-oriented economic policies became apparent in low investment productivity and public enterprises' mounting losses. Insulation from the global economy led to a collapse in exports and massive balance of payments deficits in many countries.

In response to deep-seated balance of payments and fiscal deficits, many countries embarked on structural adjustment programs, designed to reorient their economies toward private sector production, international trade, and competitiveness. This involved reducing tariffs and other restrictions on trade, making currencies convertible for current transactions, and liberalizing the business environment, including deregulation of FDI. Nowhere were these trends more marked than in the former socialist economies, which by the end of the 1980s began the transition to market economies.

FDI flows to developing countries began to increase in the second half of the 1980s in response to these changes (Figure 2.1). These flows were more focused than in the past on export-oriented industries, attracted by low operating costs and market links.

As private enterprise proved more effective than the public sector at mobilizing investment and providing efficient services in many countries, governments continued to open up more areas of economic activity to the private sector in the 1990s. Infrastructure, once the preserve of the public sector in most countries, became increasingly open to private investment. FDI in infrastructure grew accordingly.[6]

Privatization provided a direct means to transfer economic activities from the public to private sector.[7] Where the privatization process was open to foreign direct investment (as in Argentina, Chile, and Colombia), it attracted FDI, both directly and indirectly. Privatization accounted directly for $38 billion in FDI to developing countries in 1988–1995 (Chapter 4).

Liberalization of FDI policies by developing countries continues into the 1990s, hand in hand with liberalization of trade policies, both unilaterally and as part of the Uruguay Round of multilateral trade negotiations. Indeed, it would be difficult to find a developing country that has not enacted more liberal investment laws in the 1990s. In Ghana for example, changes in invest-

Box 2.4. Gold Mining, Ghana—Developing an Important Export Industry Through FDI

In the early 1960s, Ghana was producing over 26 tons of gold a year. By 1984, output declined to less than 8 tons as a result of lack of private investment, which was discouraged by government interference in the sector. Lack of capital and technical expertise that foreign direct investment can provide were binding constraints on the expansion of mining. In 1986, the government took decisive steps to reverse the decline, with advice from IFC and the Foreign Investment Advisory Service (FIAS). It created a Minerals Commission that acted as a focal point to interact with foreign investors; revised the mining code; and allowed the use of offshore forex accounts to guarantee repatriation of earnings. The effect of these measures was dramatic as foreign direct investment rehabilitated the sector.

IFC financed the rehabilitation of Ashanti Goldfields Corporation, which now ranks among the world's top 10 gold producers. It also financed new investments in new gold producers Bogosu and Iduapriem. IFC invested $330 million for its own account and through mobilizations. It advised all three companies on the application of state-of-the-art technologies. Because of the significant improvements in Ashanti Goldfields' performance, government has divested 17 percent of its shareholding with an offering on the London and Accra Stock Exchanges.

Gold production increased three and a half times, from 8 tons in 1984 to 28.5 tons in 1992, and an estimated 45 to 50 tons by 1996. Since the reforms of 1986, exports have more than doubled, to more than $416 million in 1993. Ghana has become Africa's second largest gold producer.

Source: IFC, Building the Private Sector in Africa (Washington, D.C.: IFC, 1995).

ment policies paved the way for a resurgence of the gold industry through FDI (Box 2.4).

The number of bilateral treaties on the promotion and protection of investment have increased almost three-fold during the 1990s. Multilateral agreements on investment have also been developed, mainly as part of wider multilateral agreements such as the North American Free Trade Agreement (NAFTA). The industrial countries are negotiating a Multilateral Agreement on Investment (MAI) treaty to govern investment flows into these countries and World Trade Organization (WTO) members are increasing the idea of a global investment agreement. The thrust of these treaties and agreements is to continue the liberalization of the policy framework for FDI.

FDI AND ECONOMIC GLOBALIZATION

Economic liberalization, combined with advances in communications and transport, has led to growing integration of world markets for goods, services, and capital. This process has emerged in the 1990s and is expected to continue for some time to come.

FDI has given the global integration process a major impetus by helping link markets for capital and labor and raise relative wages and productivity of capital in recipient countries. Multinational firms have adopted increasingly global strategies based on greater special-ization and dispersion of activities and have aimed to capture the substantial economies to which they give rise. The growing multiplicity of linkages is reflected in a sharp rise in intra-firm trade across national bound-aries, between foreign affiliates in developing countries and parent companies in developed (and sometimes other developing) countries as well as between foreign affiliates within developed countries.

To illustrate, between 1983 and 1993, the share of intra-firm exports in total exports of U.S. parent firms rose from 34 percent to 44 percent, and for imports from 38 percent to 49 percent. At the same time, the share of intra-firm exports among U.S. foreign affiliates increased from 55 percent to 64 percent, and of imports from 83 percent to 86 percent.[8] Excluding exports from parent firms to affiliates, the share of exports by affili-ates to other affiliates rose from 37 percent in 1977 to 60 percent in 1993. Multinational corporations now sell more goods through foreign subsidiaries than they export from their home countries. Provision of long-

distance commercial services is also growing fast and promises to become a large segment of world trade.

Increasingly, the ingredients of economic growth—cre-ated assets, technology, intellectual capital, learning experience, and organizational competence—are housed in company systems. To gain access to these ingredients developing countries need these companies to participate in the domestic economy. For example, sale of Chilean telecommunications to a foreign investor brought Chile's telephone services up to global standards (Box 2.5). The role of FDI in global eco-nomic activity, as measured by the ratio of FDI inflows to gross domestic fixed capital formation, has doubled in the past two decades to 4 percent in 1995.

The newly industrializing countries of East Asia and other countries that are well integrated into global trade and investment flows have benefited from these trends, exhibiting sustained high rates of growth. This has encouraged other developing countries to recognize the benefits of greater integration into the global econ-omy. A fear of being locked out of the expanding glob-al economy and the globalization of firms has spurred developing countries to change their approach to FDI, in some cases dramatically.

The criterion by which developing countries measure the value of FDI has shifted from its direct contribu-tion to local value added to its longer term conse-quences for the competitiveness of domestic resources and capabilities. This has in turn resulted in a greater acceptance of the need for deregulation, market liberal-ization, and removal of a variety of control and regula-tory impediments, all of which—by adding to transac-tion costs—have created serious disincentives for FDI in the past. As a result of policy changes, developing countries have increased their share of FDI from 12 percent in 1990 to 36 percent in 1995.

Together, these changes have led to an almost revolu-tionary change in the sources of foreign capital for developing countries. The growing importance of resource flows from private sources to developing countries is evident, accounting for over 85 percent of the total in 1996, compared with only 44 percent in 1990 (Figure 2.2). FDI has become the largest single source of external funds for development, exceeding official development finance by a large margin.

Box 2.5. CTC, Chile—Bringing Telecoms up to Global Standards Through FDI

Compañia de Teléfonos de Chile (CTC) provided 95 percent of Chile's local telephone services. In 1988, government privatized CTC, with IFC help. The Bond Corporation of Australia bought a controlling share, but due to financial difficulties, it sold its stake in 1990. It was bought by Compañia Telefonica de Espana (CTE), which now controls 43.6 percent of CTC. The management team is mostly Chilean but has some senior managers from CTE.

IFC helped finance a major investment program by CTE, which modernized and expanded the wireline network and introduced a cellular telephone service. This doubled the number of lines in service, and increased the number of payphones by half. By end-1993, the network was fully digitized and automated, placing CTC among the world's most modern systems. CTC's services were brought up to international standards. Staff productivity has increased 27 percent between 1990 and 1993, when its level of 176 lines per employee put it on a par with the best international players.

By 1993, CTC had 34,000 cellular subscribers, using a network of 56 sites. Since then, the company has continued to expand local services, and move into long distance services, cable television and other communication services. It is now undertaking foreign investment in cellular services in cooperation with CTE.

Source: Privatization: Principles and Practice, *Lessons of Experience 1, Washington, D.C.: IFC, 1995.*

Figure 2.2. Aggregate Net Resource Flows to Developing Countries, 1990–96 ($ billion)

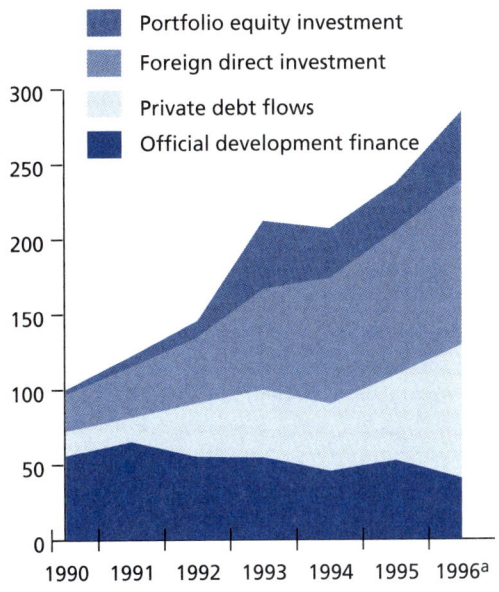

Source: World Bank Debtor Reporting System.
a. Preliminary data.

Figure 2.3. External Finance Flows to Developing Countries, 1996ª

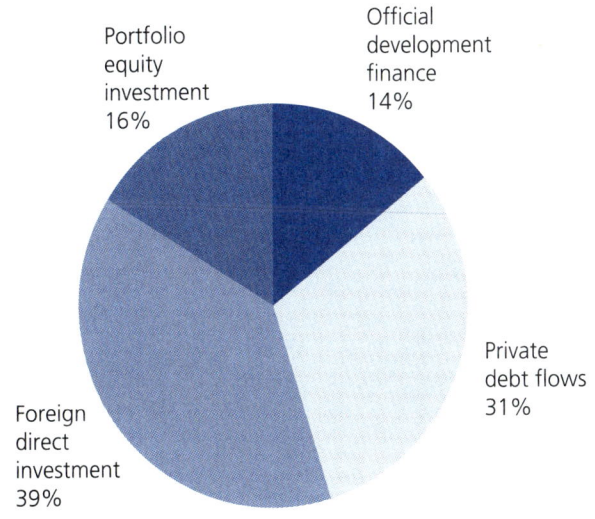

100% = $284.6 billion

Source: World Bank Debtor Reporting System.
a. Preliminary data.

FDI to developing countries has grown rapidly, especially since the mid 1980s. In 1970-96, these flows grew by 10 percent a year in real terms. Real FDI in 1980-89 was 50 percent more than in the previous 10 years, and two fifths of that in the next 7 years. FDI now averages 1.7 percent of developing countries' GNP and accounts for nearly 40 percent of all global FDI flows to developing countries (Figure 2.3). Developing countries now receive one third of global FDI (Figure 2.4).

Figure 2.4. Real FDI Flows to Industrial and Developing Countries, 1970–95 (1996 $ billion)

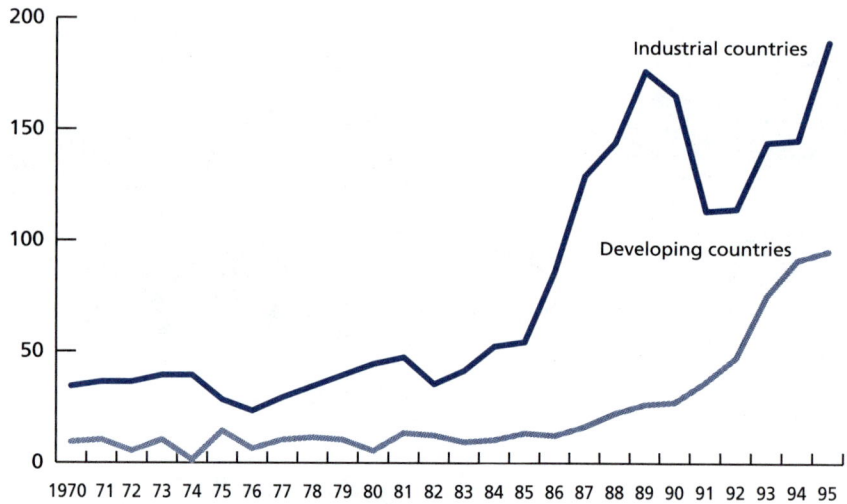

Source: IMF, International Financial Statistics, and World Bank Debtor Reporting System.

The rapid growth in FDI in the past few years partly represents a stock adjustment. In other words, assets are being transferred from public to private ownership, and investors are rebalancing the global composition of their portfolios as barriers to FDI fall. This process is just beginning, because developing countries still have room for further policy liberalization. At the same time, the accelerating trend toward global integration will create further opportunities for rebalancing investments and greater involvement of developing countries in global production patterns, thus providing further stimulus for FDI.

THE PATTERN OF FDI FLOWS TO DEVELOPING COUNTRIES

Information on sectoral distribution of FDI is available for only 16 developing countries, but these account for 68 percent of developing-country FDI. For these countries, secondary activities (manufacturing and processing) account for over 40 percent of FDI. However, between 1975 and 1990 a shift occurred from secondary toward tertiary activities such as services (Figure 2.5).

A fairly stable group of countries have been the largest hosts for FDI (Table 2.1). Brazil, Indonesia, Malaysia, Mexico, and Thailand have been among the top 12 recipients in the three successive 10-year periods from 1970 to 1996. This largely reflects their positions as

among the largest developing countries but conceals important changes in the composition of FDI.[9] For example, FDI in Indonesia has shifted from the oil and gas sector in the 1960s and 1970s to manufacturing in the 1980s and 1990s.

Figure 2.5. Sectoral Distribution of FDI Stock in Major Host-Developing Countries (percent)

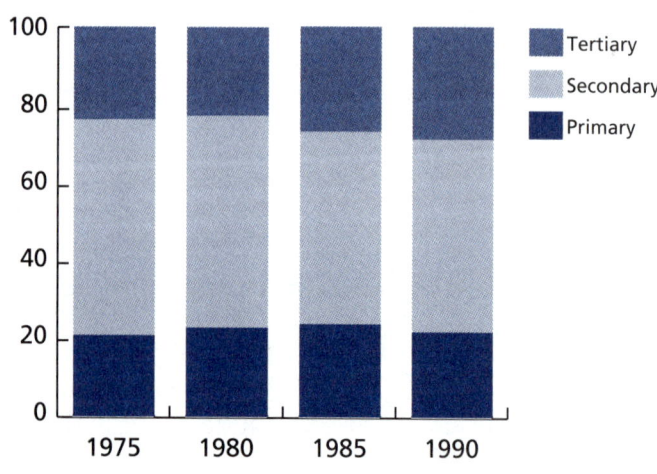

Source: UNCTAD, World Investment Report 1993, New York, N.Y., 1993.

Table 2.1. Top 12 Developing-Country Recipients of FDI

Rank	1970-79	1980-89	1990-96
1	Brazil	Mexico	China
2	Mexico	Brazil	Mexico
3	Nigeria	China	Malaysia
4	Malaysia	Malaysia	Brazil
5	Indonesia	Egypt	Indonesia
6	Greece	Argentina	Thailand
7	South Africa	Greece	Argentina
8	Iran	Thailand	Hungary
9	Egypt	Colombia	Poland
10	Ecuador	Nigeria	Colombia
11	Thailand	Indonesia	Chile
12	Algeria	Chile	Czech Republic

Note: Excludes countries with 1994 population below 5 million.
Source: World Bank Debtor Reporting System.

Table 2.2. Top Developing-Country Recipients of FDI, 1996

Rank	By value	By percentage of GNP
1	China	Angola
2	Mexico	Vietnam
3	Malaysia	Malaysia
4	Indonesia	Cambodia
5	Brazil	Czech Republic
6	Poland	China
7	Colombia	Tanzania
8	Czech Republic	Bolivia
9	Thailand	Peru
10	Peru	Colombia
11	India	Ghana
12	Chile	Mozambique

Note: Excludes countries with 1994 population below 5 million.
Source: World Bank Debtor Reporting System.

Measuring FDI as a percentage of GNP takes account of country size: larger countries offer larger domestic market for labor, materials, services, and other inputs and for sales of output. On this ranking, in 1996, Malaysia maintained its prominence, and China, Colombia, and the Czech Republic featured among the top 12 by either measure (Table 2.2.). Although the low-income countries' economies are too small to attract large amounts of FDI in absolute terms, in relative terms they do quite well: half of the top 12 recipients of FDI as a percentage of GNP are low income. Similarly, Africa, with its preponderance of small, poor countries, does not make the top 12 in absolute terms, but measured against GNP, a third of the top 12 are African countries.

The big story of the past 15 years has been the rise in FDI in China (Figure 2.6). With changes in economic policy since 1979, China's FDI rapidly caught up with its size and rate of economic growth. Between 1990 and 1996 China received some $167 billion (1996 prices). Measured in relation to GNP, however, it ranked sixth in 1996. By contrast, the next largest developing country, India, remains way down the list, with FDI of only 0.6 percent of GNP, against China's 4.8 percent. This reflects India's relatively slow progress in restructuring growth and orienting its policies to encourage FDI.

Figure 2.6. Real FDI to China and India, 1980–95 (1996 $ billion)

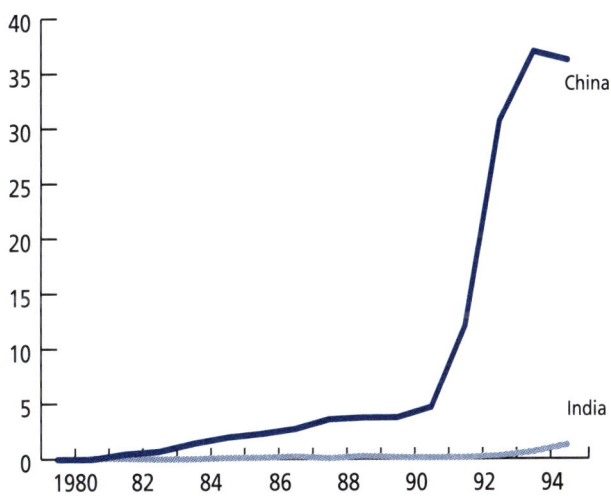

Source: World Bank Debtor Reporting System.

Eastern Europe and the Central Asian republics of the Former Soviet Union have emerged as important FDI hosts during their economic and political transition, driven in part by privatization. Poland, Hungary, and the Czech Republic, the farthest along toward becoming market economies, have attracted the most FDI.

Figure 2.7. Real FDI by Income Group (1996 $ billion)

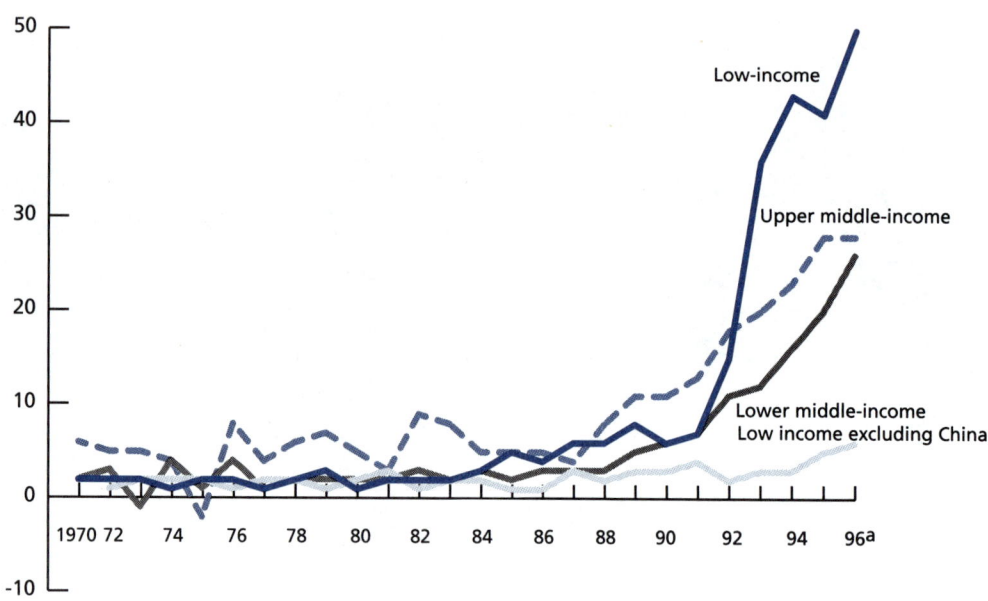

Source: *World Bank Debtor Reporting System.*

a. *Preliminary data.*

For example, FDI in Poland has risen from $11 million in 1980 to $4.2 billion in 1996 (1996 prices). Countries with slower transitions (for example, Bulgaria and Romania) have seen a smaller FDI response. In the Central Asian republics, most FDI has been in the oil and gas sector. The share of FDI in Europe tripled from the 1970s to the 1990s (Figure 2.9).

Regional patterns are influenced by the relative attractiveness for FDI in each region as well as by income level. Using FDI to GNP ratios again to normalize for economic size, from 1990-96 East Asia received the highest flows at 3.5 percent of GNP. At the other end of the range, South Asia had the lowest ratio at 0.3 percent, followed by Sub-Saharan Africa with 0.7 percent of GNP.

Low FDI in South Asia reflects a long history of restrictive policy environments, which has only recently begun to change. In Sub-Saharan Africa, low FDI in the 1990s reflects the aftermath of the economic crisis of the 1980s and continuing civil unrest as well as restrictive policies. This contrasts with the 1960s and 1970s, when investments in resource extraction made Africa the second largest host region for FDI to developing countries, despite restrictive policies. Africa has recently only begun to see renewed FDI flows, in countries that have achieved a measure of economic stability and liberalization.

Ghana illustrates Africa's changing fortunes. It received an average of $62 million a year (1996 prices) between 1970 and 1979. Over the next 10 years (1980-89), government pursued inward-looking, public-sector oriented policies, and the economy weakened. As a result, FDI dwindled to only $9.6 million annually. After the initial rigors of economic stabilization and reform, however, strong economic growth and a liberal economic environment led FDI to surpass the levels of the late 1960s and early 1970s, averaging $95.1 million a year (1990-96).

Excluding China, absolute FDI flows to low-income developing countries remain far below flows to middle-income countries. However, when account is taken of the smaller size of low-income countries, the disparity is much less. Low-income countries (excluding China) received FDI flows equivalent to 1 percent of GNP in 1996, compared to 1.4 percent and 1.5 percent in lower and upper middle-income countries, respectively (figures 2.7 and 2.8).

Measured in relation to country size, FDI flows are significant for a wide range of countries. Excluding offshore finance centers and countries with population under a million, some 57 countries received FDI flows greater than or equal to 1 percent of GNP in 1996 (Table 2.3). For 24 countries, it was worth more than 3 percent of GNP, and for 6 countries it was over

Figure 2.8. Real FDI as Percentage of GNP, 1996ª

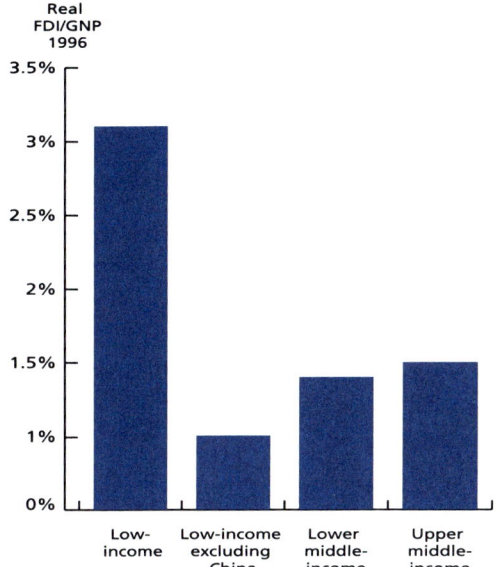

Source: World Bank Debtor Reporting System.
a. Preliminary data.

Figure 2.9. FDI by Host Region, 1970–96 (percent)

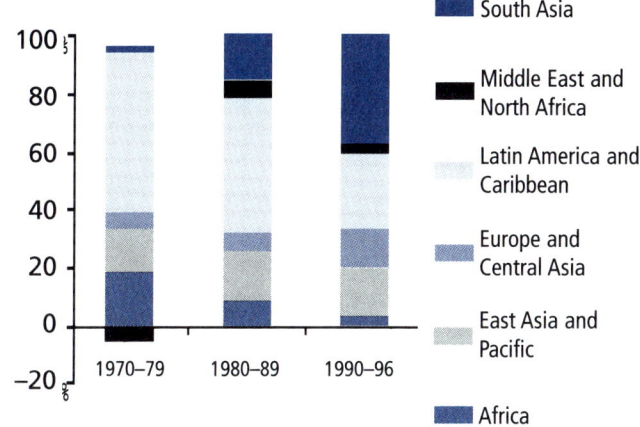

Source: World Bank Debtor Reporting System.

5 percent of GNP. This means that FDI is already important for all these countries, and shows how important FDI could become for other developing countries.

SOURCES OF FDI

Until the 1970s, the United States and the United Kingdom were the largest sources of FDI to developing countries. Since then, Germany and Japan have become important investors in developing countries. Today, the group of source countries is wider than ever before, and includes developing countries themselves. Improvements in developing countries' economic policies have created a climate for strong international businesses to emerge. Multinational enterprises are no longer found only in industrial countries. Developing-country businesses are growing in importance as outward investors. Comparing 1990-95 with 1984-89, the

Table 2.3. The Importance of FDI Flows to Less Developed Countries, 1996

FDI > 5% of GNP	FDI 3%-5% of GNP		FDI 1%-3% GNP		
Angola	Albania	Hungary	Azerbaijan	Kazakhstan	Philippines
Cambodia	Bolivia	Jamaica	Botswana	Latvia	Romania
Czech Republic	Chile	Laos	Bulgaria	Lebanon	Slovak Republic
Malaysia	China	Mozambique	Cameroon	Lesotho	Slovenia
Trinidad and Tobago	Colombia	Nicaragua	Dominican	Macedonia,	Thailand
Vietnam	Costa Rica	Papua New Guinea	Republic	FYR	Tunisia
	Ecuador	Peru	Egypt	Mexico	Uganda
	Estonia	Poland	Gabon	Morocco	Uruguay
	Ghana	Tanzania	The Gambia	Oman	Venezuela
			Guinea	Namibia	Zambia
			Honduras	Nigeria	
			Indonesia	Paraguay	

Note: Excludes offshore finance centers and countries with population less than 1 million.
Source: World Bank Debtor Reporting System.

share of FDI from developing countries in world FDI doubled from 6 percent to 12 percent.[10] East Asia accounts for 90 percent of FDI outflows from developing countries; Hong Kong, China, has become the largest single outward investor among developing countries, with 80 percent of it going to China. Some of this may represent "round-tripping" of Chinese investment through a foreign partner to take advantage of incentives for FDI, or investment by firms from Taiwan, China. Brazil, China, Chile, and Thailand are the other main outward investor countries. One motivation for this has been to seek a supply of key raw materials (such as minerals and logs). Another has been to seek lower labor costs in less developed economies, as domestic industries in the home countries become technology intensive, and labor costs rise.

FDI flows between developing countries are mainly intra-regional and are greatest in East Asia. In 1994, 57 percent of FDI flows from developing countries were invested in the same region. Excluding Japan, some 60 percent of FDI in East Asia comes from within this region; for example, Indonesia is the fourth largest foreign direct investor in Malaysia. This partly reflects the influence of regional economic groupings such as Association of South East Asian Nations (ASEAN) in lowering barriers to intra-regional trade and investment and partly the importance of business ties between ethnic groups in different countries.

Regional links are also important for FDI from developed economies. The European Union accounts for most FDI flows to Eastern Europe and Central Asia. The United States has historically directed the largest share of its FDI to Latin America. This partly reflects the importance of physical proximity as a factor in determining the location of FDI for manufactured exports. With a shift away from manufacturing, the strength of regional links may diminish. However, the prospects for regional integration will continue to encourage regionalization of production and marketing, and hence FDI.

With appropriate policies, FDI flows to a wide range of countries and sectors. The increasing diversity and volume of FDI flows between countries of all income levels show that policy restrictions, not any basic characteristics of FDI, limit the distribution of FDI flows. What the preceding examples suggest is that with appropriate policies, many different types of economies could attract much larger FDI flows. Thus, the current concentration of FDI in a few developing countries could well dissipate as other developing countries take steps to reduce their own economies' obstacles to FDI.

LESSONS OF EXPERIENCE

A review of historical trends in FDI to developing countries shows that:

1. Countries at every stage of development can attract FDI across a wide range of sectors from developing countries as well as industrial countries.
2. The largest economies naturally attract foreign direct investment, but experience shows that it can be an important part of even the smallest, poorest countries' economies.
3. The volume and direction of FDI flows respond to the national and international policy environment.
4. Current trends toward integration of the global economy provide a stronger impetus than ever toward FDI in developing countries for those countries open to it.

Notes

1 *Financing can include loans by the foreign owner as well as equity investment.*
2 *Foreign portfolio and direct investment may represent only a transfer of assets, not necessarily an economic investment in the host country.*
3 *E. Borenzstein, J. de Gregorio, and J. Lee, "How Does Foreign Direct Investment Affect Growth?"* NBER Working Paper *5057, Cambridge, Mass., 1995.*
4 *The oil price increase itself raised the value of inventories held by foreign subsidiaries, which increased the companies' net worth. This in itself resulted in a recorded FDI inflow, to account for the increase in net worth.*
5 *However, Malaysia, Chile, and a few other developing countries began to liberalize their FDI policies during the 1970s. This set the stages for an early resurgence of FDI in them.*
6 Financing Private Infrastructure, *Lessons of Experience 4 (Washington, D.C.: IFC, 1996).*
7 *The evolution of privatization methods in developing countries is discussed in depth in* Privatization: Principles and Practice, *Lessons of Experience 1 (Washington, D.C.: IFC, 1995).*
8 *All data from United Nations,* World Investment Report 1996: Investment, Trade and International Policy Arrangements, *New York, N.Y., 1996, Chapter 4, especially Table IV.2.*
9 *Data on gross FDI flows to developing countries are not widely available. The FDI flows reported in this chapter therefore refer to net flows (inflows minus outflows). Because FDI overflows are small for most developing countries, there is little difference between net and gross FDI. However, for countries such as Brazil, Chile, and Thailand, gross outflows are between a quarter and a half of gross inflows. Thus, net FDI data significantly understate the importance of FDI inflows to these countries.*
10 *All data from* World Investment Report 1996: Investment, Trade and International Policy Arrangements, *United Nations, New York, N.Y.,1996.*

PROMOTING FDI THROUGH POLICY ADVICE

3

Since the end of World War II, the industrial countries have encouraged international private capital flows as a prime policy objective. As a result, barriers to private capital flows among industrial countries have been reduced, and institutions and policies have been developed to facilitate private capital flows.

INTERNATIONAL SUPPORT FOR FDI

Increased flows of private capital and technology to developing countries have been seen as a key to economic growth in the less developed regions of the world. This led to the establishment of the World Bank and its affiliates, including the International Finance Corporation. IFC's mandate encompasses both investing in productive private enterprises and advising member countries on ways to establish policies and institutions that would help create a welcoming climate for foreign and domestic private investment.

IFC was one of the international community's first initiatives to channel the flow of foreign direct investment (FDI) to developing countries. To improve the policy framework for FDI, including investment in developing countries, bilateral and multilateral legal agreements were also implemented. To protect investors against loss from political risks in developing countries, bilateral and multilateral investment guarantee programs were established. Individual industrial countries set up financial institutions alongside bilateral and multilateral investment promotion programs.

Countries have improved the legal and policy framework for foreign direct investment through a series of bilateral investment treaties (BITs). Most of these treaties have been between an industrial country and a developing country, but recently, some have been between two developing countries. Altogether, 155 countries have been involved in one or more BITs.[1] These treaties aim to improve the conditions for investment by firms of each signatory country in the other. According to the International Centre for the Settlement of Investment Disputes (ICSID), the number of BITs has expanded steadily, reaching nearly 1,130 by May 1997.

In addition to bilateral agreements, a series of multilateral instruments have been approved that help improve the frameworks for international investors, including those from developed countries investing in developing countries. These include both multilateral treaties binding on all ratifying countries and non-binding instruments. Several of the most recent multilateral treaties contain closely similar provisions to those of BITs. In this way, BIT practices are being brought into a multilateral framework.

Some binding agreements deal with settlement of disputes between investors and host countries. One of the most important agreements established the ICSID, a multilateral institution, part of the World Bank Group, that provides a mechanism for arbitrating investment disputes. Another important treaty is the Convention on the Recognition and Enforcement of Foreign Arbitration Awards, which provides uniform standards for mutual recognition and enforcement of arbitration awards and dispute settlements made in participating countries.

Still another agreement, establishing the Multilateral Investment Guarantee Agency (MIGA), also part of the World Bank Group, provides political risk insurance to investors in developing countries. In addition, several agreements reached during the Uruguay Round trade negotiations limit aspects of host-country policies toward foreign direct investors that would adversely affect international trade. The North American Free Trade Agreement (NAFTA) treaty is an example of a regional treaty between developed and developing countries. Like some of the most recent BITs, this treaty enumerates investment liberalization obligations and establishes high standards of investment protection. Other new multilateral treaties with similar provisions on investment include the Investment Protocol of Mercosur, the G-3 Free Trade Agreement, and the Energy Charter Treaty.

Several other non-binding models, guidelines, and other instruments have influenced the international investment environment. These include:

- guidelines on investment and bribery by the International Chamber of Commerce, a private group
- the United Nations model double taxation convention and set of principles for controlling restrictive business practices
- the World Bank/International Monetary Fund Development Committee guidelines on the treatment of foreign direct investment.

The potential for discrimination from inconsistencies in investment policies, as well as the desire to harmonize and improve investment rules in general, has led to attempts to negotiate stronger binding rules governing investment in a multilateral framework. Some progress was made in this direction in the Uruguay Round, with the negotiation of the three agreements mentioned above on trade-related investment measures (TRIMS), trade in services, and trade-related aspects of intellectual property rights. A Multilateral Agreement on Investment (MAI) is now being negotiated among the OECD countries. Efforts also are being made to initiate multilateral negotiations on investment matters among a larger number of developed and developing countries within the World Trade Organization (WTO).

Nearly 15 of the OECD countries have established national financing institutions with mandates to support national firms' investments in developing countries. Some of these institutions can also invest with firms from other countries. These financial institutions have at their disposal the same instruments as IFC, including the ability to make equity investments and loans in private sector projects in which a company from the sponsoring country also invests. Some of these institutions operate with restrictions such as a preference for investing with small and medium-sized national firms instead of large multinational corporations.

Besides the national financial institutions, groups of OECD countries have established other multilateral institutions. The European Union supports International Investment Partners to promote FDI in developing countries. The Inter-American Development Bank has its Inter-American Investment Corporation whose activities parallel those of the IFC.

Many industrial countries operate investment promotion programs to encourage their national firms to invest in developing countries. These programs try to help firms secure information about investment opportunities. The techniques used include providing general information about the host countries, sponsoring missions of potential investors to specific countries, matching a potential investor with a specific project, and giving financial support for feasibility studies, project development, and start-up. Table 3.1 shows the programs offered by 13 OECD countries.

Many of these programs are targeted to a specific group of investors in the sponsoring country. When used, targeting is usually aimed at small and medium-sized firms, which are assumed to lack the resources needed to seek out investment opportunities, particularly in developing countries. Hence, as in all the programs to encourage investment in developing countries, the use of public funds is justified by a market imperfection, in this case the cost and difficulty of securing information about investments in developing countries.[2]

IFC'S ADVISORY ROLE

As one of the first attempts to facilitate private capital flows to developing countries, IFC has always dealt with investment policy issues that come up while arranging financing for specific projects. If left unresolved, these issues could derail the projects. Examples include dividend repatriation restrictions, regimes governing imports of equipment, or employment of expatriate managers and technicians.

IFC also has a long history of advising on the legal and institutional framework for capital markets and more recently on privatization methods and the content and administration of environmental regulations. Advice in these areas is given under advisory assignments and in the context of project financing.

Several characteristics set IFC-sponsored advisory activities apart from those of other private and public advisory agencies:

■ Advice provided by IFC-sponsored units is informed by IFC's considerable experience as a lender to, and investor in, private sector projects in a wide range of developing countries. This practical experience with the problems of investing, combined with its economic development mandate, makes IFC an almost unique source of hands-on advice on creating a friendly environment for private investment.

■ IFC policy advice is demand driven. These demands often arise in the course of project financing, a privatization program, or other efforts to improve a country's investment climate. Because IFC responds to a client's needs instead of trying to convince a

Table 3.1. FDI Promotion Programs of Industrial Countries

Country	Information	Matchmaking	Missions and seminars	Sectoral studies	Feasibility studies	Project development and start-up
Austria	■	□	■	□	□	■
Belgium	■	■	■	■	■	■
Canada	■	■	■	□	■	■
Denmark	■	■	□	□	■	■
Finland	■	□	■	■	■	■
France	■	□	□	□	■	■
Germany	■	■	■	■	■	■
Italy	■	■	■	■	■	■
Japan	■	■	■	■	■	■
Netherlands	■	■	■	■	■	□
Sweden	■	■	□	□	■	□
Switzerland	■	■	■	■	■	■
United States	■	■	■	■	■	■

Source: OECD and FIAS.

developing country to change its ways, its advice is more likely to be accepted.

■ As a member of the World Bank Group, IFC draws on, and contributes to, the Group's expertise and involvement in client countries. Together, the Group can cover the full range of issues involved in investment policies.

■ Because IFC's advice reflects practical experience with investments, it is usually specific, detailed, and pragmatic—designed to correct flaws. IFC seeks workable solutions to problems, not optimal policies, to get investment moving. The World Bank Group and other agencies are better equipped to focus on the broad economic policy issues.

■ Advice from IFC-sponsored units is oriented toward opening up opportunities for private sector initiatives. The aim is to reduce or eliminate government restrictions on private activity and government interference in the market so that markets can function. At the same time, IFC advice is also intended to promote the host country's welfare. For example, it often advises against tax incentives because they are unlikely to be cost-effective.

■ IFC advice usually aims to promote competition and ensure transparency in regulatory processes—principles that will help the host developing country to obtain the best outcome.

As IFC and other investors appraise a project financing opportunity, policy issues often arise. In these cases, IFC raises the issue with the host-country government and suggests a range of solutions that will allow the project to go ahead.

Policy issues have come up in the context of financing activities since IFC first began operations. Because dialogues with government on such issues were rarely documented, the magnitude of such assistance over the years cannot be measured. However, some examples of topics covered illustrate the range. Lessons learned in such cases can also be incorporated in the policy advice given by the Foreign Investment Advisory Service (FIAS).

Policies that distort market prices often affect the viability of projects in developing countries. Output prices may be controlled and input prices may be distorted in various ways. The distortion may be due to general

---

Box 3.1. Some Common Policy Issues in Project Financing

■ Cotton price controls (Uzbekistan)

■ Fertilizer price controls penalizing efficient plants—usually private—and subsidizing inefficient plants—usually in the public sector (India)

■ Price controls on hotel rooms during inflation, making new hotel investments unprofitable and causing losses in established hotels (Kenya)

■ Establishing a system for setting the price of electric power from independent power producers so as to facilitate private investment

■ Setting natural gas prices to make investment in gas-using industries viable, while providing adequate return (Thailand and other countries)

---

policy—for example, taxes, tariff protection or environmental issues—or may be project specific (Box 3.1).

Taxes of various kinds have raised issues affecting project viability. In the Russian Federation, multiplicity of taxes, the resulting tax level, and the instability of the tax system have impeded IFC investments with foreign oil companies. In an African country, assessing the same tax on ethanol as on gasoline made the ethanol production unviable.

As a development institution, IFC has played an increasing role in promoting good environmental standards including attention to the social impact of investments. IFC has helped governments set environmental codes for private sector including FDI, in a number of sectors. For example, it helped the government of Egypt set environmental standards for development of tourism along the Red Sea coast, so that the ecology of the area is not threatened by development. In the context of individual projects, IFC ensures that potential environmental and social impacts are assessed, and seeks appropriate mitigation and avoidance measures before investing.

Aspects of the legal framework are often addressed in the context of a project appraisal. IFC helped Ghana, Kazakhstan, and Uzbekistan draft mining codes when it became apparent that existing codes were not adequate for prospective new investments. In the Russian Federation, IFC helped set up an institution and a system for registering shares. IFC helped Uzbekistan draft a bankruptcy law. Because as a lender, IFC has to be concerned about the security of its loans, it helps to perfect security instruments such as land mortgages and the transferability of oil and mining concessions to the lenders in case of bankruptcy.

Specific issues affecting foreign investors are often raised in the context of IFC projects. For example, IFC itself is generally considered a foreign investor under many countries' ownership laws. Mexico, the Philippines, and some other countries, however, have been willing to regard IFC as a local investor, or at least not foreign, in calculating ownership shares. This has enabled IFC to give comfort to minority foreign owners who feared loss of control over a venture. IFC has also persuaded some countries to loosen ownership restrictions on a trial basis to facilitate specific foreign investments. Examples may be found in the banking and insurance industries.

Restrictions on the access of foreigners to land are not uncommon in developing countries. IFC raised these issues and sought specific solutions in India and Indonesia, for example, to facilitate investment in agro-industry projects.

Raising policy issues in the context of project financing and privatization has both advantages and disadvantages. The advantage is that the issue is concrete, and the consequences of not resolving it are usually clear (that is, the project will not go ahead). The disadvantage is that solving one case may not solve the problem generally for other investors. That is why free-standing advisory services (that is, not associated with individual projects) have a role to play. IFC has provided such free-standing advice affecting FDI mainly through FIAS.

THE FOREIGN INVESTMENT ADVISORY SERVICE

In the mid-1980s, developing-country governments, increasingly aware of the benefits of foreign direct investment, began to ask IFC for assistance in structuring policies and institutions to attract more of it (Chapter 2). Governments went to IFC for such assistance because it was the only multilateral development institution that was itself an equity investor and was thus expected to know what kinds of policies and institutional arrangements would be good or bad for investment.

In response to this interest, IFC established the Foreign Investment Advisory Service, which it now sponsors jointly with the World Bank. The mandate of FIAS is to advise member countries on policies, programs, and institutions that would enable them to attract more beneficial FDI. This is free-standing policy advice, independent of project financing, that draws on IFC experience in its project financing as one of the sources of information on policy and institutional issues in the host developing countries.

FIAS advises developing-country governments on specific policies, programs, and institutions that affect the amount and the quality of foreign direct investment that a country receives. This includes general diagnostic studies, specific investment laws, sector-specific studies, institution building, and promotional strategy development. The World Bank and other institutions advise on general economic policies that may affect FDI flows.

In its 12 years of operations (through FY97), FIAS has completed 231 advisory projects in 100 countries and every part of the developing world. Asia and Africa have each been the locale of about one third of the advisory projects. Europe and Central Asia, Latin America, and the Middle East and North Africa together make up the other third.

Two thirds of the projects dealt with policies, about one third concerned investment-related institutions, mainly investment promotion agencies and promotion strategies. Policy work (diagnostic studies, specific work on investment policies, and sector work) was most prominent in Europe and Central Asia and Africa. This emphasis makes sense in light of Eastern Europe's transition to market-based economies, and Africa's undeveloped policy structure for foreign investment. Development of institutions received more emphasis in Latin America reflecting that region's more open policy environment for foreign direct investment.

FIAS undertakes diagnostic studies to identify a country's main policy impediments to productive foreign direct investment. The issues typically identified include prohibitions on foreign investment in many sectors or locations; restrictions on the share of foreign ownership in the equity of domestic companies; difficult administrative approval processes; restrictions on repatriation of dividends and capital; taxes; the charac-

Box 3.2. Some Common Issues in Diagnostic Studies

■ A requirement that foreign firms generate through exports all of the foreign exchange they would need for imports, royalties, and repatriation of dividends and capital (China, 1986)

■ Different legal systems in West Bank and in Gaza after the peace agreement

■ Inadequate functioning of the legal system, which made enforcement of contracts almost impossible for both foreign and domestic private businesses (Bangladesh, 1993)

■ A multiround approval process for foreign investors (Bahamas, 1992)

■ Foreign investors' difficulty in gaining access to land (Lesotho)

ter and functioning of legal systems; and problems foreign firms have in gaining access to land and bringing in technical and managerial staff (Box 3.2).

A diagnostic study may identify a wide range of issues. A report on the Russian Federation, completed in 1992, identified eight broad areas for improvement to create an acceptable environment for foreign direct investment. These areas reflected the transition of the Russian economy at the time the study was done, and included stability of laws, acquisition of foreign exchange, the legal framework for private businesses, and laws on land ownership and leasing. A diagnostic study of Zimbabwe in 1993 was much more narrowly focused. It identified problems due to the investment approval process, policies governing the availability of foreign exchange for dividend and capital repatriation, foreign ownership restrictions, and the extent of government involvement in the economy.

Diagnostic studies identify issues, but few go far in designing solutions to the problems identified. Investment policy studies explore specific issues in detail and make detailed recommendations to the gov-

ernment. This advice follows guidelines developed by the World Bank Group in 1992.[3] FIAS advice gets into much more specific details than are contained in the guidelines. Among the issues treated have been restrictions on foreign ownership share, investment incentives and taxes, legal guarantees, and dispute settlement mechanisms (Box 3.3).

Box 3.3. Some Examples of Investment Policy Studies

■ FIAS helped the government of Honduras prepare a new investment law that applied to all investors, domestic and foreign; guaranteed equal treatment to all investors; set out the principle that foreign investment was open in all sectors except those prohibited by specific negative lists; and provided guarantees, including access to foreign exchange.

■ Poland was advised in 1990 to provide more certain access by foreign investors to foreign exchange, and to circumscribe the authority of the Foreign Investment Agency to screen new investments, impose ownership structures, and review business decisions after enterprises were established.

■ The Philippines revised its investment law to expand sectors open to foreign investors and allow up to 100 percent foreign ownership where not prohibited in the constitution. Projects and sectors eligible for tax incentives were reduced, and administration of incentives was made more automatic.

■ Malawi was advised to eliminate industrial licensing except for a short negative list of activities that would be regulated for reasons of public health and safety. Regulations that delayed company registration, land acquisition, duty drawbacks, local borrowing, and access to foreign exchange were targeted for simplification or elimination.

■ Trinidad and Tobago was advised to simplify its investment incentives, reducing the number, moving away from discretionary incentives to those that are more automatic and part of the general tax system. It was suggested that corporate taxes be decreased, thus reducing the need for discretionary incentives.

FIAS has also helped governments identify—and fix—the policies that affect FDI in specific sectors of interest, most frequently agriculture or infrastructure sectors. The investment policy issues in these sectors have usually resulted from specific sectoral policies such as land ownership policies or commodity pricing policies in the case of agriculture.

As policies toward foreign direct investment open up, institutions have to evolve. Once policies have been eliminated, parts of government that administered them have to be cut or reoriented. At the same time, institutions to promote investment in newly opened areas have to be developed. FIAS has assisted developing countries in both aspects of this transition (Box 3.4).

The most difficult part of this work has been getting existing organizations to reorient their activities and staff from investment approvals to investment promotion as policies change. In some cases, this change has been successful, as in the Philippines, while in others it has not, as in Bangladesh.

With the liberalization of investment policies, several countries have become interested in promotion programs of another kind: namely, promoting linkages between foreign investors and domestic firms. Such programs were first introduced in developed countries such as Ireland and in some of the newly industrialized economies such as Singapore and Taiwan, China. FIAS has drawn on this experience to help Indonesia, Mexico, Philippines, and Thailand develop linkage programs.

Finally, FIAS has been involved in helping several countries build institutions to collect data on foreign direct investment. This work has been both conceptual, involving transfer of the concepts and techniques of investment data collection, and institutional. The institutional work has helped governments develop the organizations necessary to collect data and, perhaps more important, methods of intra-agency cooperation.

Strategies for promotion agencies can be specified at two levels. At the "grand strategy level," the agency has to allocate resources among the three major aspects of investment promotion: image building, investor servicing, and targeted investment generation. When an investment promotion agency reaches the stage of doing targeted investment generation, a more specific strategy

> ### Box 3.4. Some Examples of FIAS Institutional Development Work
>
> - In Venezuela, CONAPRI was created, a new promotion institution owned jointly by both the public and private sectors, with a Board of Directors dominated by private companies.
>
> - In Tunisia, a new Foreign Investment Promotion Agency was created, drawing staff from an existing government industrial promotion agency.
>
> - In Malaysia, MIDA, an established and successful promotion agency, reoriented its activities away from approval of investment incentives to more active investment promotion and facilitation.
>
> - After major policy changes, the Ghana Investment Center and the Board of Investments in the Philippines reoriented their activities from investment approvals to investment promotion.
>
> - Croatia created a new investment promotion agency.
>
> - Sri Lanka converted an Export Processing Zone authority for a region into a national board of investments.

is needed. Direct "selling" of the country to specific investors has proven the best way to promote new investment. This means that the agency must decide on which sectors, countries, and specific firms to contact. FIAS has helped Tunisian, Sri Lankan, Moroccan, and Costa Rican promotion agencies, among others, to devise such strategies.

OTHER IFC ADVISORY WORK
In addition to its work with FIAS, IFC has provided developing countries with free-standing policy advice on privatization and capital markets development. Though not specifically directed at FDI, these advisory activities have helped generate FDI flows to these countries.

IFC has advised developing countries on capital markets policies and institutions since the early 1970s. Covering a wide range of subjects, including securities market development, policies affecting banking and other financial institutions, and specialized financial services such as leasing, the capital markets advisory program assisted 90 countries in almost 800 separate advisory projects through fiscal year 1997.

Free-standing advice on privatization is of more recent origin but covered more than 80 projects in 30 countries.[4] An important part of this work has been in designing and implementing small-scale privatization (shops, transport equipment) that can be replicated in many localities. Of more interest to foreign investors are mandates given to IFC by governments for developing and implementing the privatization of a single, generally large enterprise.

The objective of capital markets advice has been to aid the growth of domestic capital markets, but the program has helped to attract foreign direct investment as well. Establishing a viable policy framework for financial institutions of all types has enhanced their opportunities for FDI. IFC's work in facilitating the development of leasing industries in many countries is the most obvious example of this positive impact.[5] Of course, a vibrant, competitive capital market also helps foster FDI flows: direct investors like to rely on local capital markets for some financing needs, even including the sale of shares.

The privatization mandates have dealt with several issues that concern foreign investors. One of these is the share of equity that foreign investors are permitted to hold. A common goal of many privatizing countries has been to ensure a wide distribution of ownership of privatized enterprises. This goal often conflicts with the need to attract FDI where it will enhance the viability of an enterprise. Foreign investors are most concerned about maintaining control of their investments, either through majority ownership or through other means such as management contracts.

In its privatization advisory work, IFC has tried to overcome these conflicting goals. Sometimes, IFC suggests combining foreign investment with employee share-ownership plans. The privatization of Peru's electric company, Electrolima, an Argentine integrated steel producer, and several Polish cement companies were all based on this model. In other cases, management agreements give a minority foreign investor, for example KLM in Kenya Airways, an effective voice in management.

These are pragmatic solutions that can work in some situations. But both the advisory and investment experience of IFC point to some key policies that can allow developing countries to make the most of their potential for FDI.

LESSONS OF EXPERIENCE

In conclusion, review of IFC's role as a policy adviser shows that:

1. IFC's role has been part of a larger international effort to encourage greater flows of private capital and technology to developing countries.
2. IFC's policy advice has been unique, drawing on IFC's experience as an equity investor, and in providing detailed and specific advice as a financier of projects.
3. IFC's advice has helped shape the environment for FDI in the context of projects, through FIAS advisory work, and through other advisory assignments.

Notes

1 *International Centre for the Settlement of Investment Disputes*. Bilateral Investment Treaties *(Washington, D.C.: ICSID, 1997), p.1.*

2 *T. Belot and D.R. Weigel, "Programs in Industrial Countries to Promote Foreign Direct Investment in Developing Countries,"* FIAS Occasional Paper *3, IFC and MIGA, Washington, D.C., 1992.*

3 Legal Framework for the Treatment of Foreign Investment: Guidelines, *vol. 2, (Washington, D.C.: World Bank, 1992).*

4 Privatization: Principles and Practice, *Lessons of Experience 1 (Washington, D.C.: IFC, 1995).*

5 *Lessons from IFC experience with leasing is treated extensively in an earlier volume in this series:* Leasing in Emerging Markets, *Lessons of Experience 3, (Washington, D.C.: IFC, 1996).*

4 GETTING THE POLICY ENVIRONMENT RIGHT

Many different factors affect the type and volume of foreign direct investment (FDI) flows to developing countries. These include: conditions in the investors' home countries; market size in host countries; their macroeconomic policies; and structural changes leading to globalization of industry.

Factors of this kind lie beyond IFC's reach in either its investment or policy advisory roles. IFC is much more involved in microeconomic policies, which have a direct impact on investment projects. Microeconomic policies encompass investment restrictions, taxes and incentives, pricing, specific trade and payments restrictions, privatization procedures, and other more specific policies that immediately affect an investment's feasibility and profitability. At this level, IFC has identified a number of important links between specific policies and flows of direct investment.[1]

RESTRICTIONS ON ENTRY BY FOREIGN DIRECT INVESTORS

Many developing countries spent decades building barriers to foreign direct investment. These have included restrictions on the proportion of equity a foreign investor may hold in an enterprise, and restrictions on the types of enterprise that foreign investors may undertake. Though commonly designed not to block FDI but to promote domestic enterprise, these restrictions have nonetheless deterred FDI and impaired the quality of FDI flows. Restrictions on foreign ownership have forced foreign investors to form joint ventures with local investors. Although these arrangements often make commercial sense, legal limits on FDI have led to commercially weak joint ventures, sometimes because of the quality of the local partner, sometimes because of the inherent difficulty of managing joint ventures, especially those between local and foreign partners.

Limits on foreign investor ownership have also had the perverse effect of reducing the investor's incentive to make a success of the project. Where the potential returns from equity were small, the investor could choose to earn profits through the contractual relationship with the company instead (for example, as a supplier of technology). Where the equity at stake was limited, a foreign investor was likely to be less committed to the project and less likely to invest money and effort in making a success of it. Where the investor was in a joint venture with a local partner with limited resources, agreeing on arrangements for injecting additional finance was likely to be difficult. IFC's experience of these shortcomings is discussed in more detail in Chapter 6. The point here is that restrictions on foreign ownership have weakened the quality of FDI.

Systems for controlling inflows of FDI have included the following elements: outright bans in selected industries, requirements for official approval, vague criteria for approval, heavy taxes requiring relief through investment incentives, limitations on the foreign firm's equity, and local content requirements.

Outright ban. Many developing countries excluded foreign direct investment in a number of "important" sectors. The forbidden industries were specified by either a positive list, specifying sectors open to FDI, or a negative list, specifying the industries closed to FDI. Negative lists are considered the more open of the two methods because of the practical difficulty of specifying in detail a vast array of sectors where investment is banned. The sectors permitted (positive list), or banned (negative list), were sometimes specified in concrete terms (for example, by using a Standard Industrial Classification, as in Korea) and sometimes imprecisely (as in Poland's 1988 law banning investments that threaten "the economic interests of the state"). Positive or negative lists have also been expressed in terms of geography: that is, foreign investment may be permitted only in certain regions, or FDI may be banned in certain regions, usually the main metropolitan areas or on coasts or borders.

Official approval. Investments in the nominally open sectors or regions were, nevertheless, often subject to official approvals. If no approval was required, the investor may still have had to register the investment.

For a few years in the early 1990s, Mexico operated a system that allowed foreign investors meeting certain conditions (location, size, employment creation) to establish without approval. A check was made after the firm was established to see that the investor had complied with the criteria for establishment. Some countries have provided for "automatic" approval of investments not on a negative list (Indonesia) or on a positive list (India). These "automatic" approvals were really simplified approvals with a time limit and relatively objective criteria.

Vague criteria. Sometimes clear and objective criteria governed the approval decisions (for example, sector, size, employment, location). More often, decisions were based on vague criteria such as those used by Poland (above) or approval was denied because the investment might "disrupt markets" (Korea, Philippines). Many countries were willing to approve investments that would "contribute to the economic development of the country." Such criteria were not sufficiently transparent for potential investors to know in advance whether or not their investments would qualify for approval.

Taxes and incentives. In some countries, taxes and tariffs were so high that only investment incentives could make a project viable, and obtaining incentives often constituted an additional approval. For example, in countries with high import tariffs on capital goods and raw materials, a tariff exemption may have been required to allow an investment to compete in world markets. In many such cases, approval of the exemption constituted an approval of the investment. In Thailand, for example, no investment approval was required, but tariff exemptions were important to investors. These were given based on a positive list of "promoted industries."

Equity limits. Restrictions on the share of a firm's equity that a foreign investor could own were another important barrier to FDI. Many developing countries, until recently, did not allow 100 percent, or even majority foreign investment. Most countries in the Persian Gulf still do not allow majority foreign ownership. It was only in 1991 that India allowed majority (51 percent) foreign ownership in 33 industries with "automatic" approval. Some of the countries that generally restricted foreign ownership allowed it in return for certain performance such as exporting a large part of output (perhaps from an Export Processing Zone), or bringing advanced technology to the country.

Investments under these conditions, of course, were subject to an approval process.

Local content rules. Local content requirements restricted foreign investors' flexibility to make efficient use of domestic and local resources, and to use established suppliers of inputs. Similarly, restrictions were often placed on the proportion of foreign staff employed (discussed below).

Where investment approvals were required, additional complications often arose from dispersal of authority. Some countries centralized their approvals in a single agency, at least for the entry decision (although other decisions could involve additional agencies). Ghana, Indonesia, and Mexico had centralized decision making. Many other countries required multiple approvals. Sometimes, several ministries had to approve investments, as in Kenya. In other countries, a hierarchy of decision makers culminated in approval by a minister or a prime minister. In one Persian Gulf country in the early 1990s, prospective investors had to obtain approval from the Ministry of Industry to apply for an application to make an investment. The licensing department and a foreign capital investment bureau in the ministry reviewed the application and made recommendations to an interministerial committee. That committee, in turn made recommendations to the Minister of Industry, who had the power to make the final approval.

Where multiple approvals were required, governments sometimes established a coordinating body to help investors secure the necessary approvals. The Board of Investments in the Philippines has been such a body. Some coordinating bodies only did legwork for investors; others had some influence and authority in their own right. Though sometimes thought of as "one stop shops," often they were simply "one more stop." Navigating through the approval process could take months, even years, and the uncertainty of the outcome, or even the route, dissuaded potential investors from applying.

In some cases, a seemingly opaque and complex approval process actually operates in a way that facilitates investment, as in China, for example. On paper, the process is multilayered; the criteria for approval, opaque. Nonetheless, the system operates in such a way that tens of thousands of even small investors have secured approvals. The secret in this case has been del-

egating decisions to provinces and cities, coupled with a desire at the local level to encourage investment. In some cities, it is said, an approval can be secured over dinner. Of course, it helps that potential investors are willing to put up with a lot to gain access to China's resources and markets. It also helps that many, perhaps most, of the investors are ethnic Chinese who are better able to operate in the system than investors from North America, Europe, and Japan.

MOTIVES FOR RESTRICTIONS

Why have developing countries built such barriers to foreign direct investment when most developed countries today have few restrictions? The reasons cited usually involve fear of foreign control, a desire to build up domestic industries, and anxiety over division of profits.

Risk of foreign control. A link is perceived to exist between the share of an enterprise's equity owned by a foreign firm and the control that foreign investors can exercise. Developing countries that had just achieved political independence from colonial powers did not want to substitute economic control by foreign firms for foreign political control. Governments feared that these firms' broader objectives would lead them into decisions that were not in the best interests of the host country. For example, when the world nickel market weakened, it was feared that the Canadian company INCO would close a mine in Panama rather than one at home, in Canada.

Possible inhibitions on local enterprise. Another reason for controlling foreign investors was to keep open opportunities for local firms. Paralleling the infant-industry argument for trade protection was the fear that foreign direct investors, if allowed free rein, would take over markets and prevent domestic entrepreneurs from emerging. This was the main reason for excluding foreign investors from some sectors such as retail trade. It was also a reason for preventing 100 percent ownership by foreign firms in other industries: in joint ventures, local firms presumably could learn from foreign firms, while still exercising control in the national interest.

Capturing rents. A desire to bargain over the division of profits was another reason for ownership restrictions. One way for a host country to capture the economic rents from exploiting its natural resources was to share ownership with foreign investors. Bargaining also may have been possible when the source of profits was in the technology or management skills of the investing firm. In these cases, restriction of foreign ownership may have enabled a local partner to share in the profits from the foreign firm's capabilities.

In many developing countries, government-created market distortions have opened the gates to high profits. Import restrictions enhance the attraction of producing import substitutes, and in banking, interest rate controls can raise profitability. In those circumstances, it is rational for developing countries to limit the entry of foreign firms, for the profits they capture from such distortions constitute a pure loss to the host country. If a local company's profits increase because local consumers buy a product for more than the international price, that is a transfer within the country. If the extra profit accrues to a foreigner, it is a loss to the host country.

The economic success of countries such as Singapore, which welcomed foreign direct investment instead of restricting it, prompted other countries to loosen their policy framework for FDI. In 1979 China's opening up to foreign direct investment for the first time in the postwar period gave the liberalization process a real boost. Since then, it has gathered speed (Box 4.1). It was aided in the early 1980s by the world debt crisis, which cut off foreign capital from commercial banks for many countries. A further impetus came in the late 1980s, with the collapse of communism in Eastern Europe and the disintegration of the Soviet Union.

The process of liberalizing entry regimes has generally followed a certain pattern. First, governments have tried to make the existing system work more efficiently by setting time limits for various approvals and appointing a single agency to coordinate the approval process. Then, the sectors open to FDI have been increased, perhaps by shifting from a positive list that specified what was allowed to a negative list that specified what was banned. Ownership restrictions might then be liberalized, permitting majority foreign ownership in some sectors. The stages of liberalization are illustrated by a case study of Indonesia (Annex 4A).

Giving up approvals has been the big decision in this process. The first step might be to move to a system of "automatic" approvals for many investments. These are streamlined approvals according to set criteria. Once broad classes of investments are free from restrictions, approvals can usually be eliminated.

Box 4.1. Liberalization of Foreign Direct Investment Policies

Korea, Mexico, Poland, and India are among the countries that have liberalized their investment policies.

■ **Korea.** Moving through the liberalization process, Korea switched from a positive to a negative list of open sectors, liberalized ownership restrictions, and progressively reduced the number of investments subject to approval. Now, most manufacturing and service industry sectors are open to 100 percent foreign ownership on the basis of a simple notification rather than an approval procedure.

■ **Mexico.** By allowing majority ownership in enterprises that met specific criteria, Mexico modified its approval process for majority foreign ownership in 1989. These changes were made in the implementation of the 1973 Investment Law. Subsequently, the law itself was changed as a result of the North American Free Trade Agreement treaty. The changes opened more sectors to majority foreign ownership without any approval. Recently, Mexico has moved a step backward, putting secondary petrochemicals back on the negative list of industries where majority foreign ownership is not allowed.

■ **Poland.** Moving rapidly through the liberalization process, Poland passed its first foreign investment law in 1976, allowing small private investments by foreigners of Polish descent. In 1988 before the fall of Communism, Poland enacted a liberal foreign investment law that allowed FDI, even 100 percent foreign ownership in all sectors, but subject to approval according to vague criteria. This law was quickly amended to eliminate the approval process, and now Poland is open to all foreign direct investment.

■ **India.** In 1991, India began a liberalization process. The government opened 33 sectors to majority-owned foreign investment (up to 51 percent) with "automatic" approval by the Reserve Bank of India (rather than an inter-ministerial committee managed by the Ministry of Industry). In addition, a cabinet-level Foreign Investment Promotion Board (FIPB) was established in the Prime Minister's office to approve higher levels of foreign ownership in the 33 industries, as well as in other industries. Up to 1997, India has made no further liberalization moves and the FIPB has been put back into the Ministry of Industry.

INTERNATIONAL FINANCE CORPORATION

Today, there are still plenty of restrictions on foreign ownership of enterprises in developing countries. Yet virtually every developing country has reduced the number of sectors where FDI is banned, has eliminated approval processes or made them more transparent and less bureaucratic, and has increased the share of equity that foreign firms can own. Countries such as Indonesia, the Philippines, and the Andean countries that had phase-out requirements have largely abandoned them.

Liberalization of entry and ownership policies has been one of the main factors underlying the dramatic growth in FDI in the 1990s (Chapter 2). China's policies since 1979 were, of course, essential for the subsequent growth of FDI: before 1979 FDI was banned in China. India began to receive significant amounts of FDI only after entry restrictions were liberalized in 1991; remaining restrictions in India still keep FDI below potential. Indonesia and the Philippines likewise saw a surge in FDI after liberalizing entry restrictions.

TRADE AND PAYMENTS REGIMES

A liberal trade regime and international payments system are important factors facilitating increased flows of efficient foreign direct investment. Liberal trade policies are important both to allow firms to develop markets and to produce goods and services efficiently once an investment is made (Box 4.2). Liberal payments systems allow investors to repatriate dividends and capital so as to realize benefits if an investment is successful.

Of course, trade restrictions have motivated much foreign direct investment in developing countries. In the 1950s, 1960s, and 1970s, import substitution was a primary force behind most manufacturing FDI in Latin America. Much of the FDI motivated by trade restrictions was not beneficial to the host country, however, because these investments often resulted in operations that were too small and too isolated to produce efficiently. Furthermore, the trade restrictions themselves reduced economic welfare by raising prices and reducing competition in the domestic market.[2]

Moreover, FDI motivated by trade restrictions was significant mainly in the larger developing countries and for manufacturing industries. Even in those countries, the process ran out of steam by the mid-1970s, after the easier import substitutions had been achieved. The relatively recent liberalization of trade and payments systems established the conditions necessary for the rapid post-1980 growth of FDI.

Box 4.2. A Liberal Trade Regime Opens Opportunities

In the mid-1950s, the government of Turkey decided that Turkish farmers needed protection from the possibility of importing poor quality foreign seeds that might also bring in plant diseases. As a result, the government established a state enterprise to produce seeds and to develop new seeds for Turkish farmers. It also set up restrictions on seed imports and decreed that any seed sold in Turkey had to be tested for several years by the Ministry of Agriculture to establish the seed's productivity under Turkish growing conditions.

This system had the expected effect of closing off Turkey from modern seed development. By the late 1970s, Turkish agriculture was falling behind other countries, with stagnant and falling yields, and a black market in modern imported seeds. A Turkish agricultural attache at the time remarked that he could make his fortune by filling his pockets with tomato seeds when he went home.

Seeing this situation, the World Bank concluded that Turkish agriculture needed an infusion of new technology from foreign seed companies. The Bank enlisted IFC in an effort to promote FDI by these firms in Turkey. The promotion effort found, however, that Turkish seed policies precluded any investment. The foreign firms wanted to enter the market by first importing seeds to test varieties, while building a marketing infrastructure. Only after ascertaining what types of corn, tomato, or soybean seeds would work, and determining the size of the market, were the firms willing to consider investing.

IFC and the Bank at this point switched their emphasis from promotion to policy. A new government with a private sector orientation had just come to power in Turkey and made the necessary changes in policy. The process leading to FDI began to unfold: a number of companies began to export seeds and established marketing networks in Turkey. Many of these firms later established seed production and research facilities, after testing the market and developing the marketing infrastructure. Ultimately, more than 20 foreign firms established operations in Turkey. These firms did not need protection in the Turkish market. In fact, besides serving the domestic market, many began to export to other countries in the region and beyond. Hence, imports ultimately led to FDI and exports.

IFC has invested in a wide range of projects that began with exports into the country, and led eventually to an investment as the market developed. A number of these investments originated in other developing countries (Box 4.3). This process has been aided by the reduction of trade barriers that has made exports possible. Domestic markets of many, perhaps most, developing countries are too small to support efficient operations in many manufacturing and even service industries. The growing possibility of exporting a part of the output makes investment a more realistic possibility.

Trade liberalization, of course, can create problems for operations that were established behind trade barriers. IFC has seen several of its investments with foreign sponsors in textile plants in East Africa fail, as barriers to imports of finished products fell even as other barriers continued to raise costs of other inputs. A study done for FIAS of foreign investment in Latin America showed that unilateral reduction of trade barriers had motivated many of the firms surveyed to rationalize production in the region. Some plants were closed, and production was concentrated in fewer plants, each with perhaps a narrower product range than before but serving a larger market area.

The opening of world markets has made it possible for all developing countries to attract foreign direct investment on the basis of local resources (natural, human, locational, or infrastructural) rather than on the basis of market size. Thus, Costa Rica recently attracted a major Intel semiconductor assembly and test facility to supply chips to the United States, Europe, and Latin America (Box 4.11). Exports of electronics products from Costa Rica can enter the United States duty free as a result of provisions in the Caribbean Basin Initiative. Costa Rica has also concluded a free trade agreement with Mexico. Tariffs and other trade restrictions on chips are not so high in other parts of the world as to preclude substantial exports from Costa Rica as well.

Export-oriented investments are still hampered by physical barriers and by poor infrastructure. And, because the world has not achieved universal free trade, export possibilities still constitute something of a patchwork. Intel can more easily export chips from Costa Rica to the United States, for example, than to Japan. Common markets and free trade areas are playing a greater role in determining the market area for foreign investments. Sometimes these market areas are

sufficiently large to allow efficient investments to be established. In other cases, they are less desirable since they lead to investments, both foreign and local, that divert trade from lower cost sources.

Box 4.3. A Case of Export-Led FDI

Brahma, a Brazilian brewery, began exporting to Argentina in 1986. Within eight years, it acquired about 4 percent of the rapidly growing Argentine beer market, despite relatively high transportation and handling costs. In 1995, in keeping with its overall Latin American expansion strategy, Brahma chose to undertake a greenfield investment and build a brewery, with IFC financing, near Lujan, about 70 kilometers outside Buenos Aires.

The investment decision was based on several factors. First and foremost, the venture was designed to replace the inefficient and costly practice of exporting to Argentina, which entailed transporting beer packaged in glass bottles 1,300 kilometers by train and truck, and then collecting and returning bottles to Brazil for recycling. By brewing nearer to the main market in Greater Buenos Aires, substantial cost savings would be realized.

The ready availability of agricultural inputs such as barley, rice, and sugar would also help control costs while ensuring a steady supply of inputs. In terms of market potential, too, Argentine beer consumption was steadily increasing and beginning to spread to the provinces. Finally, the project would further contribute to the integration of the Mercosur economies in a sector in which integration offered great potential for future growth as large national brewers recognized opportunities to capture relatively small market shares of growing markets in neighboring countries.

While it may be premature to speculate on the venture's success, some preliminary comments can be made. Brahma has successfully injected a healthy dose of competition into the formerly monopolistic Argentine beer market and has become the second largest beer producer, with a 13 percent market share. Sophisticated marketing and distribution methods have also been developed, with more efficient ways of distributing from plants directly to retailers. Brahma Argentina, in addition to serving the local market, plans to begin exporting to Uruguay and Paraguay in the near future.

Developing countries must establish conditions that allow foreign investment to produce for the world market. This includes trade liberalization that enables investors to get inputs of equipment, subassemblies, and raw materials at world market prices. General trade liberalization is the best way to do so. However, many developing countries have instead used free trade zones and investment-specific investment incentives to allow duty free imports of material and equipment. The Intel plant in Costa Rica mentioned above, for example, will be given free trade zone status.[3]

LIMITS ON FOREIGN EXCHANGE TRANSFERS

Liberal payments systems allow foreign investors to take advantage of opportunities created by liberal trade regimes. Foreign firms regard restrictions on repatriation of profits and capital as a nearly insurmountable barrier to direct investment. If they cannot get money out, they see little point in investing. Restrictions on profit and capital repatriation take many forms, from outright blocks to percentage limits.

Blocks. In an outright block to repatriation, the blocked currency might have to be held in a noninterest bearing account at the central bank awaiting repatriation. This kind of restriction has been applied in Kenya, for example, as well as in several other African countries. A less stringent arrangement of this type would allow reinvestment of the local currency at market interest rates while awaiting repatriation.

Repatriation delays. Long delays in repatriations, sometimes years after the dividend date, erode the rate of return on investment particularly where the currency depreciates in value. In effect, blocked dividends are a forced loan to the country at below market interest rates (if the market rate would incorporate exchange rate risk). As an equity investor, IFC suffered in earlier years from blocked or delayed dividend repatriations in Kenya, other African countries, and Turkey.

Limits on repatriation by net worth. A more sophisticated restriction of profit repatriation allows repatriation of dividends that are below a given percentage of a foreign investment's net worth. Here, net worth expressed in local currency may or may not be indexed for inflation or currency depreciation. Profits that cannot be repatriated can be reinvested, thus increasing the net worth basis for calculating allowable repatriation the next year. Brazil has used such restrictions for long periods of time, with the additional complication of allow-

ing repatriations over the limit, but subject to increasing tax rates. If these restrictions are binding (that is, if they cause firms to repatriate less than they would in the absence of the restriction), they effectively reduce the amount of direct investment that will be made.[4]

Limits on repatriation by foreign exchange earnings. Some countries limit use of foreign exchange—for all purposes, dividend repatriation as well as imports of materials—to all or part of a company's foreign exchange earnings. Ghana at one time restricted repatriation to less than 25 percent of a company's foreign exchange earnings. Until the late 1980s, China imposed a foreign exchange balance requirement on foreign investors that limited their foreign exchange use to the amounts earned (Box 4.4). Such a requirement, of course, essentially limits FDI to export-oriented investments. Such restrictions would limit direct investment in

---

Box 4.4. China's Payments Regime and FDI Flows

China did not begin to get large inflows of FDI until it moved away from a strict application of the foreign exchange balance requirement. The Foreign Investment Advisory Service and other advisers emphasized the central importance of a more market-based foreign exchange allocation system. In a 1986 survey by FIAS of almost 100 actual and potential investors in China, the foreign exchange balance requirement was named the number one impediment to investment.

In 1988, FIAS made proposals for improving the functioning of China's foreign exchange centers. The proposal was to establish more centers, increase access of private firms, and link the centers into something of a national market system for foreign exchange. China moved in these directions and, as a result, foreign investors were increasingly able to gain access to foreign exchange not generated themselves.

The result was a marked reduction in the importance given by investors to foreign exchange issues. In another FIAS survey of investors in 1991, foreign exchange issues were of less concern to investors than issues of administration, labor relations, and several other matters. Improvements in the foreign exchange allocation system helped to facilitate the subsequent rapid growth in FDI which began in 1991. Many investors found investment opportunities in China attractive only after a more liberal foreign exchange regime was established.

any country whose macroeconomic policies had an anti-export bias.

Many developing countries have improved foreign investors' access to foreign exchange, at least for current account transactions. This is shown by the fact that in 1975, only 29 developing countries had made their currencies convertible for current account transactions (including profit repatriation) by accepting the obligations of Article VIII of the International Monetary Fund Articles of Agreement. By July 1997, that number had increased to 111 developing countries.

Notable among the countries that have not yet accepted Article VIII obligations are Brazil and Nigeria. The fact that a country has not ascribed to Article VIII does not necessarily mean that it restricts profit repatriation. Still, Brazil even now bases approvals for repatriation of dividends on a 1965 decree limiting dividends to a percentage of net worth. The continuing possibility of restrictions on profit repatriation from Brazil may help explain why, until only recently, the real value of FDI in Brazil was no higher than in the early 1970s. Expressed in 1994 dollars, FDI in Brazil reached $3.5 billion in 1973 and stayed near that level until the debt crisis in 1982, when it began to fall to about $1 billion. Most of this amount probably was accounted for by (sometimes forced) reinvested earnings. FDI in Brazil did not surpass the 1973 level until 1995. Meanwhile, FDI in Malaysia increased tenfold over the same period. FDI in Brazil increased dramatically in 1996, after reduction of macroeconomic imbalances and further liberalization of restrictions on dividend repatriation.

OTHER RESTRICTIONS

The barriers to entry discussed above are only one of many impediments to FDI. Many developing countries spent decades developing wide-ranging regulation of private sector activities, including FDI. When a country decides that it wants more foreign direct investment, the liberalization process has to cover a wide range of subjects and deal with each in sufficient detail ultimately to create a conducive environment for foreign investment. As an example, Chinese officials estimated in the mid-1980s that more than two hundred laws had been enacted to create a framework for FDI that even then was still relatively primitive. Work on that framework is still a work in process. China, because it had to build from a starting point of no FDI at all, is an extreme example. However, many other countries had created such barriers that when they decided to seek more FDI they were not much better off than China was in 1979, when it opened up to FDI. Among the more important barriers found by FIAS in its work were difficulties investors had gaining access to land, difficulties in bringing in management and technical personnel, and requirements that investors obtain a myriad of other permits and licenses.

Inability to gain access to land. Foreign investors have faced many difficulties in owning or leasing land in a host developing country. These difficulties have discouraged FDI because no firm wants to invest without secure tenure of the land where its facilities are located.

In many countries land is communally owned, and mechanisms have not been developed to afford private companies secure access. In other cases, the state owns the land, and either policy or inadequate legal mechanisms have restricted access by private investors. Even where land was held privately, lack of clear conveyance and titling mechanisms has impeded acquisition by investors. Finally, government policies might enable local private landowners to monopolize land and hold it off the market for speculative reasons. Lack of title to land can make it difficult to raise finance domestically, as land is often taken as collateral.

Communal ownership has been prevalent in Africa, parts of Asia, and in the Pacific Islands. Governments in these countries have used various methods to make land available to private investors. Namibia has a mixture of freehold and communal land available. Freehold land has been in short supply, particularly in the main cities. Communal land is made available through a "permission to occupy," but this does not give investors enough security. Currently, the government is converting some communal lands to freehold. In Swaziland, most land is held by the Swazi Nation and has been allocated by local chiefs. Freehold land has been available to foreign investors, but restrictions on transactions have created potential difficulties for foreign investors.

The state controls allocation of land in many countries. Most of the transition economies of Central and Eastern Europe and the former Soviet Union are trying to shift to a system of private ownership of land but have been impeded by difficulties including inadequate surveys and title records. A unique difficulty in Central and Eastern Europe is the uncertainty created

Box 4.5. Gaining Access to Land in Indonesian Plantation Agriculture

Indonesia has a comparative advantage in the production of tropical tree crops such as palm oil, rubber, and coconuts. Prior to independence, these crops were developed on large plantations, usually foreign owned. Land for these plantations was leased by the colonial government for 99 years to private investors under provisions of an 1870 agrarian law.

This law was changed after independence to provide for several different types of land title: full ownership, the right of exploitation (basically the same as the old lease), and the right of use. Neither this law nor the 1870 law permitted full ownership to foreign companies.

In 1980, a presidential decree provided that the right of exploitation (the long-term lease) could not be held by a foreign company or by a joint venture in which a foreign company was a partner. In the case of a joint venture, only the Indonesian partner could secure a long-term lease to a property and convey a right of use to the joint venture company. Thus, foreign and domestic partners would have unequal rights in the joint venture.

Not surprisingly, foreign investment in Indonesian plantation agriculture practically ceased as a result of these measures. No investor was willing to commit to a venture to plant trees that would require at least eight years to mature without long-term control of the land on which the trees were planted.

The Indonesian government became concerned with the implications of its policy in the late 1980s, when it became clear that the state enterprise producing tree crops could not take advantage of opportunities in the sector. As a result, IFC was asked to help structure a project that might deal with the concerns of foreign investors, and FIAS was asked to review the overall policies that had brought foreign investment in the sector to a standstill.

The IFC project devised an innovative mechanism to get around the strictures of the law and the decree. The long-term land lease in this case was held by a subsidiary of an Indonesian development finance company (PDFCI) which, itself, was a small shareholder in the project. PDFCI was considered to be a creditable holder of the land-use rights because both the Indonesian government and IFC were shareholders. Moreover, Indonesia's Government Investment Agency (BKPM) guaranteed that the land use rights would not be transferred to another investor without BKPM's agreement.

While this project was being structured, the FIAS review raised the larger policy issue of secure access to land. FIAS recommendations summarized points made by others before, that Indonesia find ways to give foreign firms secure access to agricultural land. All of these recommendations became part of the government policy discussion.

The result was a change in policy in the early 1990s, subsequently amended in 1996. Under the new policy, joint ventures established under Indonesian law can obtain title to land for business operations for a period of 35 years, renewable for another 25 years. These titles are registered and can be used as collateral for debt. This change goes a long way toward eliminating the legal problems foreign investors had of gaining access to land.

by claims of prior owners on property confiscated by communist regimes. In Lesotho and Mozambique, too little land was made available, due in part to inadequate institutions to survey and process requests for leases. In Lesotho, leases were not transferable and thus could not be used as security for loans. In Indonesia, the government restricted foreign investors' rights to own and lease land (Box 4.5). Finally, in Morocco, land is scarce in the main cities because local investors hold potential prime commercial property as a speculative investment. These prime tracts were transferred to local investors by the government. There is no pressure to develop the land because land taxes are not based on potential best uses. The result is a scarcity of land available for new investments in Casablanca and Tangier, and substantially higher land costs than FIAS found in four other sites around the Mediterranean.

Box 4.6. Expatriate Worker Restrictions: Trinidad and Tobago, Estonia, UAE

Trinidad and Tobago. The restrictions on expatriate employment in Trinidad and Tobago were substantial according to a FIAS study in 1996. Person-by-person background checks were conducted for all work permit applicants. These were handled, first of all, by the Ministry of National Security, where the Department for Immigration is situated. They required the following:

■ evidence that no qualified national is available, normally in the form of advertising for the position
■ a police record showing no convictions from the current place of residence
■ character references, including one from current and previous employers
■ a completed application form in quintuplicate.

Applications were sent to a committee of representatives from the Immigration Department, the Ministry of Trade and Industry, and the Ministry of Energy, which met biweekly to review them, and were signed by the Minister for National Security. In recent years the process has been streamlined, with a reduction in committee representatives from 12 agencies to 4. The time required to comply, however, remained a number of months, if the time to generate all background materials is included.

Estonia. Residence and work permits posed a major difficulty for foreign investors in Estonia. As of 1996, laws designed mainly to stem the tide of immigration from surrounding countries were a drag on the activities of all foreign investors. According to the 1993 Law on Aliens, there is an annual immigration quota of 0.1 percent of the permanent population of Estonia (currently 1,000 per year). This includes foreign investors and expatriate employees as well as their families and dependents.

The application process for residence and work permits for expatriates was particularly onerous, requiring medical and psychiatric exams; medical histories of the applicant's

parents, siblings and children (including those who would not be joining the applicant in Estonia); photocopies of the applicant's entire passport; copies of diplomas and other evidence of qualifications; and a declaration that one was not an agent of the Russian Security Agency. This process was in addition to the requirement of proving that no Estonian was qualified for the same position, as evidenced by advertising in a local newspaper. No exceptions were allowed for this latter provision, serving as a particularly severe barrier to small firms and single proprietorships. The application for the work permit also had to be approved by the Ministry of Labor, which typically took at least two months. The Immigration Office frequently attempted to process residence permit applications within three months, but delays up to a year remained common. Both types of permits had to be renewed annually.

United Arab Emirates. UAE relies on expatriate workers at all levels, including highly skilled managerial, professional, and technical personnel. According to a FIAS study in 1993, the Ministry for Labor and Social Affairs issued expatriate work permits, normally for a period of three years. Unlike in other countries, the ministry did not limit the number of expatriate workers by quotas or targets. Instead, it responded mainly to private sector demand. The control which the ministry exerted was to limit, on a case-by-case basis, the numbers of expatriate workers to those it considered absolutely necessary for the operation of any given project. Based upon its view of the company's need, permits were issued. Given the government's tendency to issue the minimum number of permits possible (in keeping with the general policy objective of reducing or at least limiting the size of the large expatriate population), companies reportedly exaggerated the number of their applications to ensure they were granted the number necessary for their operations. The practice of rationing by administrative allocation was inefficient, largely because of the unclear criteria for rejecting applications and because it did not provide an efficient and market-oriented system for transferring surpluses of labor to sectors and firms in need.

Restrictions on expatriate labor. Most developing countries have restricted the right of foreign firms to bring in their own personnel to operate their investments (Box 4-6). Host countries hope to force foreign firms to train local labor for technical and managerial positions that otherwise might be occupied by expatriates. This kind of training is one of the benefits that developing countries hope to get from FDI.

The restrictions may take the form of an absolute ban on more than one or two foreign staff in a venture. In other cases, the proportion of foreign staff in different categories may be limited. A particularly onerous version of this kind of restriction is a requirement that a majority of the company's Board of Directors be local, regardless of the ownership of the company. Finally, each expatriate may be subject to a case-by-case

Figure 4.1. Administrative Approvals in Ghana, 1993

General Approvals, Permits, and Licenses	Specialized Approvals	Site Development: Land and Construction	Site Development: Utility Providers	Operational Requirements
• Registrar—General • Ghana Investment Promotion Centre • Bank of Ghana • Internal Revenue Service • Ghana Immigration Service • Local Assembly	• Ministry of Food and Agriculture • Ghana Standards Board • Ghana Tourism Board • Forestry Department • Timber and Export Development Board • Customs, Excise and Preventive Service	• Lands Commission • Town and Country Planning • Local Assembly (Engineering and Health Departments) • Environmental Protection Council	• Electricity Corporation of Ghana • Ghana Water and Sewerage Corporation • Posts and Telecommunications Corporation	• Bank of Ghana • Factories Inspectorate • Labour Inspectorate • Social Security and National Insurance Trust • Customs, Excise and Preventive Service

approval of visas and work permits. When such approvals are granted, they often have to be renewed at short intervals (for example, yearly). In Lesotho, for example, work permits are issued for only a year, and the delay in issuing the permits has been a year. Hence, foreign personnel receive permits that are ready to expire.

Restrictions on the use of expatriate personnel can constitute an important barrier to foreign investors. Investing firms are concerned about their ability to control the enterprise in the host-developing country through managers provided by the firm. Moreover, corporate, technical, marketing, and managerial know-how is usually embodied in personnel who have been with the parent company operations elsewhere in the world. When the use of such personnel is restricted, investors fear that the investment may not be able to perform up to the company's international standards.

Restrictions on foreign personnel by developing countries may not be needed, since investors usually have a strong economic incentive to substitute local for expatriate staff as soon as possible: expatriates generally cost two or three times as much as a local equivalent. Most of the benefits developing countries hope to get from foreign direct investment, for example, a transfer of

technical and managerial skill, can be realized only through people. By restricting the use of foreign staff, developing countries are reducing their potential benefits from FDI, as well as limiting the amounts of investment foreigners would be willing to make without the restrictions.

Recognizing these problems, some developing countries are liberalizing their treatment of expatriate staff. One approach, adopted by Malaysia a number of years ago, is to allow automatically a reasonable number (five in the case of Malaysia) of expatriate personnel for each investment, with the number increasing with the size of the investment. Other countries have streamlined the approval process for foreign personnel and have lengthened the time period for visas and work permits. Even with these changes, however, less liberalization has probably occurred in this area than in the case of entry restrictions.

Requirements for other permits and approvals.
Difficulties in gaining access to land and permits for expatriate workers, together with other permit and approval requirements, pose a formidable set of barriers to investment. Hernando de Soto, working in Peru, was one of the first to demonstrate the deadening effect of such administrative barriers on private invest-

ment.[5] As an example of the magnitude of these barriers, Figure 4.1 lists the administrative approvals of various types required to make an investment in Ghana in the early 1990s.

Formidable though this list is, it still gives only part of the picture. The magnitude of the problem becomes evident when the number of approvals is combined with complicated processes and, perhaps, inefficient or even antagonistic officials. Figure 4.2 illustrates the process in Ghana in the early 1990s to obtain just one set of the approvals listed in Figure 4.1: general approvals, permits, and licenses. The number of agencies involved and the number of back-and-forth steps made the process time-consuming and the outcome uncertain. The FIAS study of such barriers in Ghana concluded that an investor who followed all of the procedures would need a year and a half to two years to complete them.[6]

Many other developing countries have similar barriers that discourage investment, even if administered honestly and efficiently. Moreover, the existence of myriad approvals can give rise to corruption, which further distorts investment decisions.

An indicator of the height of administrative barriers is the ratio of implemented to approved investments. Investor-friendly countries target realization rates of 60 to 70 percent, and Singapore claims 80 percent. In Costa Rica, FIAS has interviewed relatively large investors who had plants up and running within one year after first visiting the country. At the lower end of the range, the implementation rate has been as low as 14 percent in Pakistan, and was around 30 percent in Indonesia in earlier years. Implementation in Vietnam has been similar, and Ghana has also been at the low end of the range.

Developing countries interested in attracting foreign direct investment have approached administrative barriers in much the same way they have approached entry barriers. First they have tried to make the existing process work better. Their smallest step in this direction is to centralize administration of the approval process by designating one agency to coordinate approvals.[7] Actually centralizing decision-making power is a more politically daring step, and hence more rare. But eliminating steps and improving the functioning of the institutions that administer the remaining steps is the most effective way of reducing administra-

Figure 4.2. General Approvals, Permits, and Licenses in Ghana, 1993

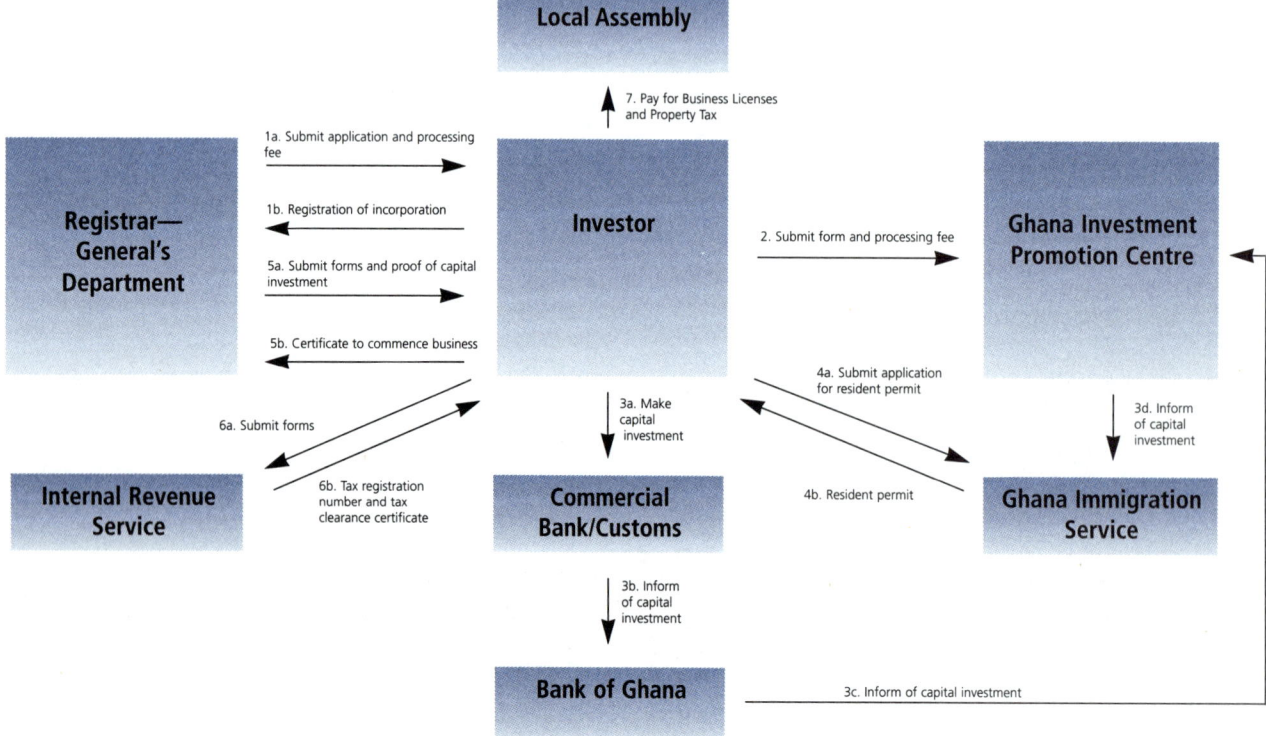

Source: FIAS.

INTERNATIONAL FINANCE CORPORATION

tive barriers. This is the route taken by virtually every country that succeeds in attracting and implementing large amounts of FDI.

THE ROLE OF THE STATE IN THE ECONOMY

Governments have played an active, often a dominant role in many developing countries' economies. They have taken action to influence prices to achieve social as well as economic objectives. They have directed and channeled private investment and have established state-owned enterprises in sectors where they thought private investment would be inadequate or undesirable. In some cases, governmental intervention has stimulated FDI, but its overall effect has been to deter it (Chapter 2).

Price controls. Price manipulation by developing-country governments has been a major inhibitor of investments by foreign firms. These manipulations have two effects. First, they can reduce the profitability of investments by reducing margins between inputs and outputs. Perhaps more important, pervasiveness and randomness of government price interventions increase risk, thus deterring investment.

Almost every government manipulates prices of agricultural products, food products, and agricultural inputs to some extent. These manipulations are widespread and of great magnitude in many developing countries. Although their intent is to protect farmers, extract surplus from the agricultural sector, or aid consumers, their effect has been to inhibit FDI in the agriculture and agribusiness sectors.

The Philippines offers an example of the problem. FIAS was asked to find out why more private investment, both domestic and foreign, had not been made to provide post-harvest services for rice farmers. Up to 25 percent of the harvest was being lost every year owing to inadequate drying, storage and transportation services. These losses could have been cut through investments in plant and equipment to dry and handle rice and ship it to processors.

But investment was not forthcoming for a simple reason: the margin between farm gate prices and retail prices left no room for service providers to make an adequate profit. The government had raised farm gate prices to give farmers more income. Consumer prices, on the other hand, were held down to reduce the cost of a staple food item to consumers. These objectives, by

themselves, seemed reasonable. Taken together, they precluded investment and perpetuated crop losses.

This example could be replicated over many crops and in many countries. The same kinds of distortions affect agricultural inputs. For example, India operated a fertilizer pricing scheme that established a uniform price for fertilizer across the country and penalized more efficient plants (usually privately owned) to provide subsidies to the less efficient plants (usually state enterprises). This arrangement left little incentive for an efficient foreign investor to establish a plant in India.

Many of the general policy issues IFC has raised with governments in the context of project financings have concerned price distortions. India's fertilizer pricing was one such case. Others have involved pricing raw materials and other inputs controlled by the host-country government.

Setting prices for natural resource exploitation. One of the more difficult issues concerns the pricing of natural resources controlled by the government. If the price set for extracting these resources is too high, investment in extractive activities will not take place. If the price is set too low, government loses some of the potential economic rents created by ownership of the resource. Furthermore, resources may be overexploited, forgoing future rents. This is particularly important for renewable natural resources such as timber, which could be sustained if the rate of exploitation is kept sufficiently low. Underpricing can lead to the permanent loss of such resources.

Regulating monopolies. Most governments regulate the prices of monopoly suppliers of services in the interests of consumer welfare. Again, excessive price controls will discourage investment, while lack of controls could lead to excessive prices. Many infrastructure services are regarded as monopolies and so treated. In some countries, the government owns, operates, and sets prices for all infrastructure services such as telecommunications, electric power, water, highways, and ports. In other countries, private investment in infrastructure is allowed, and the government regulates prices. In the case of infrastructure, it is not a question of whether governments will be involved in pricing, but how and at what level prices will be set.

Price levels and the mechanisms for changing them as conditions change are key factors in determining whether private investors, whether domestic or foreign, will be interested in investing in infrastructure projects. Countries such as China have opened infrastructure to foreign investment only to find that potential investors consider the government-set price or return levels too low. Other countries such as Pakistan and the Philippines have devised acceptable formulas and have received large amounts of investment. Pakistan is willing to buy power from independent power producers at a fixed price (but subject to adjustment periodically) and is not concerned about the producer's rate of return. China, on the other hand, seeks to regulate the rate of return, as do most U.S. state regulatory agencies.

Large state enterprise sector. Foreign direct investment will run into additional problems if the host country has powerful state enterprises in many industries that it wants to protect from foreign competition (Box 4.7). This protection is one important reason for the entry restrictions on foreign investors discussed above, particularly the sectoral prohibitions.

Even without such restrictions, a large presence of state enterprises will put a damper on FDI because foreign investors will not want to compete with government enterprises or rely on them as a source of inputs or as a market for outputs. These enterprises may enjoy advantages in input prices over private firms or they may be unreliable customers. FDI to produce electric power in India has been held back because the purchasers of power would be state power grids that are considered uncreditworthy. State enterprises that have access to government subsidies or preferential access to credit can also sustain pricing and marketing strategies that a private firm could not compete against. Furthermore, state enterprises' preferential access to credit can starve private enterprises of credit, including FDI ventures of credit.

Many developing countries have scaled back the state enterprise sector by selling or transferring enterprises to private parties, including local private firms, foreign firms, management and workers in the enterprises and the general public. This has had a large impact on FDI flows to certain regions, where these programs have been most prominent.

PRIVATIZATION

IFC's experience as an adviser and as an investor in privatization transactions has shown that the way privatization is handled can have a large effect on the direct par-

Box 4.7. Egypt: The Effect on FDI of a Large State Enterprise Sector

Dominance of state enterprises in Egypt's economy impeded FDI in a number of concrete ways, according to a survey by FIAS of actual and potential foreign investors in 1990. At that time, Egypt's public sector accounted for 70 percent of industrial value added, 98 percent of all exports, and nearly 90 percent of industrial exports. To protect important state enterprises, Egypt restricted private investment in some sectors. In industries where private investors were allowed to compete with public enterprises, they were at a disadvantage because they had to pay international prices for inputs. Public enterprises paid subsidized prices for domestic inputs such as energy and obtained imported inputs at the subsidized official foreign exchange rate. The following are some specific examples identified in the survey:

A U.S. investor in a glass bottling venture reported higher costs than the competing public enterprise. The competitor not only paid lower prices for energy and imported soda ash but also underpriced output because it was not under pressure to show profits.

Another U.S. company had to give up on a synthetic fibers venture because public enterprises producing textiles could buy cotton at subsidized prices. Domestic production of synthetic fibers would have freed more natural cotton for export at (higher) international prices.

French investors were reluctant to participate in joint ventures with Egyptian public enterprises because civil servant managers of these enterprises lacked business experience and ability to respond to market signals.

French investors complained about scarcity of small and medium private enterprises to be subcontractors and suppliers of inputs needed by their enterprises. The predominance of large public enterprises retarded the development of a private small and medium enterprise sector.

Foreign investors also complained about the dearth of private Egyptian business partners because of the predominance of state enterprises.

Box 4.8. Privatization and FDI

The wave of privatizations in the developing world since the late 1980s fed the explosive growth in FDI inflows. In 1988-95, developing countries received almost $38 billion in FDI inflows and another $21 billion in portfolio investments, together representing 45 percent of all privatization revenues. For many countries, privatization with foreign investor involvement presented a major opportunity to attract productive capital into their economies. For the economies of Central and Eastern Europe, for example, privatization is the centerpiece of the entire transformation process and usually involves foreign direct investors. During the particularly active period of 1988–95, these countries received slightly over 45 percent of their FDI inflows through privatization sales.

However, the effect of privatization on FDI inflows does not stop with a sale of assets to foreign investors. An econometric analysis for a cross-section of 36 developing countries in 1988-93 shows that privatizations have a strong secondary effect on FDI, attracting inflows independent from privatization sales themselves.* Each dollar in privatization sales attracts another 88 cents in additional FDI, according to estimates. A possible explanation for this result is that a strong privatization program sends an important signal to the investor community, that the government is willing to support private sector development and remove impediments and restrictions on foreign involvement. The strong attraction of infrastructure privatizations for additional FDI—$1 invested in infrastructure privatization results in another $2.4 in FDI inflows—seems to confirm this argument. Investors welcome improvements in infrastructure services for improving the business environment and reducing operational costs.

Thus, privatization can have a positive long-term impact on the availability of productive capital from abroad, enhancing the countries' development prospects. However, it depends very much how privatization programs are managed. The most successful privatizers during this period—defined by the relative size of the privatization program as well as their political stability—managed to continually increase their FDI inflows. Most important, these inflows continue to rise even after most privatizations have been completed. Other countries with smaller and less predictable programs, on the other hand, did not manage to send strong signals of commitment to the investor community, and FDI inflows remained unchanged.

Frank Sader, "Privatizing Public Enterprises and Foreign Investment in Developing Countries, 1988-93," Chapter 6, FIAS Occasional Paper 5, Washington, D.C., 1995, pp. 26-32.

FDI Inflows for the Most Successful Privatizers, 1988–93

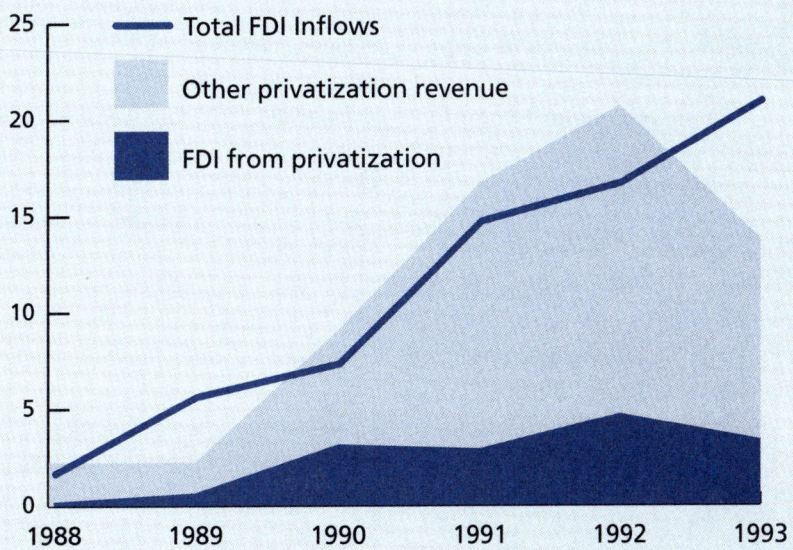

Note: Countries included are Argentina, Chile, Czech Republic, Hungary, Jamaica, Malaysia, Mexico, Philippines, and Portugal.
Source: Kathy Megyery and Frank Sader, "Facilitating Foreign Participation in Privatization," FIAS Occasional Paper 8, IFC and World Bank, Washington, D.C., 1996, p.6.

ticipation of foreign investors (Box 4.8). Privatization can be carried out in two basic ways: by direct sale of individual enterprises or by transfer of assets to the general public.[8] Clearly, direct participation of foreign investors is only possible in the case of direct sale: mass privatization of ownership is usually closed to foreign participation. This does not mean, of course, that foreign firms are forever excluded from ownership of enterprises transferred through vouchers and other arrangements. The new owners, whether individuals or funds, may at some point sell shares to foreign firms.

Direct sales of state enterprises have generated substantial flows of direct investment to developing countries in recent years. In 1988–95, $37.6 billion in FDI went into enterprises sold individually. This amounted to almost 10 percent of all flows of FDI to developing countries during the period. Flows were concentrated mainly in Europe and Central Asia ($16.4 billion, 45 percent of FDI flows to that region), and Latin America ($16.3 billion, 15 percent of total FDI flows). The flow to Africa, the Middle East, and Asia was much smaller, either because there were fewer privatizations (for example, in Middle East, North Africa, Sub-Saharan Africa, and South Asia), or because foreign direct investment provided a smaller share of total financing for privatization (as in Asia).

Even in direct sales, particular arrangements may affect the participation of foreign investors. Sometimes sale is reserved for local investors, including the firm's management, workers, or other local organizations. This was the case of a meat packing entity in Ukraine that was advised by IFC.[9] In other cases, some shares may be allocated to foreign investors along with other prospective owners. Sometimes the government is willing to sell only a part of the enterprise, often a minority position. The balance of political forces in the country usually drives these decisions.

Willingness of foreign investors to participate in mixed ownership structures depends very much on the specifics of the case. Foreign investors are very much concerned about being able to maintain control of enterprises in which they invest. Particular ownership structures that may result from a politically motivated division of shares may preclude the kind of participation foreign firms want. Direct investment may not be forthcoming in these cases, though sought by the privatizing government.[10]

Issues with ownership structures of enterprises being privatized seem to have been more prevalent in Central and Eastern Europe than in Latin America. Central and East European countries have relied more heavily on mass privatization techniques than have Latin American countries. Even in direct sales, Latin American countries seem to have been more willing to have control pass to foreign firms.

FIAS has also found that the process by which privatization is carried out affects the willingness of foreign investors to participate.[11] Attractive privatization programs share three important characteristics: political commitment, business orientation, and transparency. To implement a program based on these principles, moreover, the individual sales process should be separated from general policy decisions and political interference. The less privatization agencies are involved in the political process of privatization, the more effective they usually are.

Following these principles can maximize participation by foreign firms in the direct sale of state enterprises. These sales, in turn, can stimulate additional FDI. In 1988-93, FDI outside direct privatization sales increased almost dollar for dollar with FDI associated with privatization. Foreign direct investment in the privatization of infrastructure enterprises and industrial enterprises seems to have the greatest impact on other FDI flows.[12]

There are a number of reasons for this association. First, large-scale privatization tells investors something positive about the climate for other investments. Among other, more concrete links, poor infrastructure has discouraged investment in many developing countries, and privatization usually leads to capital infusions and improved operations. Moreover, privatization of industrial enterprises is usually followed by additional investments for rehabilitation and expansion. Thus, some additional FDI is relatively closely associated with investments in privatized enterprises.

Substantial privatization programs thus affect FDI flows in several ways: by providing a concrete vehicle for direct investment to participate in the country; by removing the impediments to investment due to a large overhang of state enterprises; by improving infrastructure and, finally, by sending a signal that the government is taking steps to create a favorable environment for private investment.

INVESTMENT INCENTIVES

Most officials of developing countries report that foreign private investors always seek all available investment incentives, and claim that without the incentives they would not make an investment in the country. At the same time, most surveys of investors show that incentives are relatively far down on the list of factors that influence investment decisions. How can these two seemingly contradictory bits of evidence be reconciled?

One explanation of this seeming contradiction can be found in the meaning of incentives, as used by business and government officials. A broad meaning of the term would include any governmental action that raises an investment's profitability above the levels that would be possible without the action or which reduces their risks. Stephen Guisinger, in a study of investment incentives sponsored by IFC in the early 1980s, identified 60 such actions that governments have used to either increase revenues, reduce costs, or reduce risk.[13]

Defined so broadly, incentives clearly have an impact on investments, including foreign investments in developing countries. For example, trade barriers, which both increase an investment's profitability and reduce risks, are known to have influenced direct investments in developing countries. Other more positive measures to improve profitability and reduce risk also are the essence of economic development, and no doubt influence private investment decisions.

The more generally accepted meaning of incentives, however, refers mainly to fiscal measures such as various ways of reducing taxes or providing other financial relief to an investment. Tax relief could come as "tax holidays," corporate tax rate reductions or tax waivers for a period of time. Tax relief also is provided by investment tax credits or accelerated depreciation. Other financial relief could be in the form of an up-front cash grant.

It is the impact of such fiscal measures on foreign direct investment that is debated. Business sponsors emphasize the importance of fundamentals such as market size, labor costs, and productivity. They downplay the effect of fiscal incentives in determining when and where they make investments. For their part, governments do not want to relinquish fiscal incentives because they find that investors seek every possible

type of fiscal relief and, moreover, many other countries give fiscal incentives.

As both investor and adviser to governments, IFC has seen both sides of this debate. From this perspective, tax levels help to determine whether an investment occurs or not, and the relative levels of taxation influence in some circumstances the location of investments. Therefore, developing-country governments have to decide whether to set effective tax rates at attractive levels for all investors or, instead, provide incentives for selected groups, or individual investments.

Clearly, taxes that are too high can deter foreign direct investment. FIAS worked with one country in Africa that taxed away 80 percent of income through a combination of income and dividend repatriation taxes. That rate would preclude most investments.

However, some kinds of investments generate huge economic rents, because of a monopoly position (for example, sole telecoms supplier) or ownership of a nonrenewable natural resource (for example, oil deposits). As an alternative to price controls, some governments attempt to capture such rents through special tax structures. This is economically efficient as long as the producer can still earn an acceptable rate of return. This is not easy to determine, and tax treatment can be a major factor influencing foreign investment in such industries.

As an alternative way of capturing a share of the rents, many governments insist on taking large equity stakes in enterprises in such sectors as mining and oil and gas production. In this way, rents distributed as dividends to equity holders will partly accrue to the government. This avoids the deterrent effect of high taxes but introduces the deterrent of limits on foreign ownership and the difficulties of running a business with government as a major shareholder.

A country's total tax burden is measured by the effective tax rate which is determined by the actual tax rate, tax holidays, depreciation schedules, tax credits and other features of the tax system (Box 4.9).[14] The tax rate a company actually pays also depends upon the rigidity of tax regulations and the quality of enforcement. In many developing countries there is ample room to reduce tax payments through alternative financial arrangements. For example, high taxes on profits can be reduced by using various means to lower a subsidiary's declared profits. One of the most common ways open to foreign investors is through the use of transfer pricing, whereby profits are transferred to related offshore companies by adjusting intra-firm pricing to reduce profits made in the high-tax country.

Some countries persist with permissive tax regimes, on paper or in practice, as a way to attract FDI, for fear that strict enforcement of high tax rates would deter FDI. While this may be true, an uncertain tax regime is a greater deterrent, as it increases the uncertainty of the economic environment. A low-tax, comprehensive regime that is enforced is therefore preferable to a high-tax regime that contains many loopholes, and is poorly enforced.

If effective tax rates are set at reasonable levels, research and practical experience suggest that FDI responds mainly to investment fundamentals such as market size, labor productivity, and infrastructure. These factors will determine the markets foreign investors will choose to serve and the possible investment sites from which these markets might be served.

Differences in effective tax rates, due to fiscal incentives or other features of the tax system, may influence the choice of one location over others with roughly similar basic attractions. For example, once a firm decides to invest in the United States or Southeast Asia, based on the attractions of the market and the availability of production inputs at favorable costs, incentives may determine the choice of one locality over similar locations within the United States or Southeast Asia. Whether fiscal incentives in any country will affect the basic decision to invest in the region is, however, doubtful.

Only heavily export-oriented firms are very sensitive to effective tax rates below the prevalent levels in most major advanced countries. Export-oriented firms such as garment manufacturers operate in highly competitive markets with very slim margins. Moreover, these firms are often highly mobile and sought-after because they generate jobs. Hence, taxes can be an important part of their cost structure, and the firms can easily move to take advantage of more favorable tax regimes. These are the companies that respond to Export Processing Zones, which usually offer benefits to firms that export a minimum share of total output, usually 70 percent, 80 percent, or more. Virtually all of these

Box 4.9. Effective Tax Rates

Effective tax rates vary widely among countries, and even among industries within a country. That is, the fiscal system has different impacts on different industries, usually because of the effects of depreciation rates on industries with different asset structures. The following table shows a range of effective tax rates at the end of 1994. In a few countries, the effective tax rate was negative because the fiscal system raised the financial return, usually by creating accounting tax losses that presumably were used to offset income in other businesses. The table shows that some countries may have had a problem because effective tax rates were relatively high. India was one such country. The Czech Republic also had higher effective tax rates than the more advanced countries of Western Europe. In the case of India, the high effective tax rate was reduced for those (relatively few) firms that could get a tax holiday.

Effective Tax Rates in Selected Countries (percent)

Country	Without tax holidays		With tax holidays	
	Manufacturing	Services	Manufacturing	Services
Argentina	12.8	13.7	—	—
Bangladesh	32.9	9.7	9.5	10.2
Chile	8.3	5.6	—	—
China	12.9	20.8	17.8	21.1
Czech Republic	37.4	25.9	22.2	19.8
France	23.3	21.5	n.a.	n.a.
Germany	25.4	29.8	n.a.	n.a.
Hungary[b]	4.2	−31.7	6.0	5.1
India	52.8	46.6	20.7	21.1
Indonesia	32.6	27.4	—	—
Korea, Rep. of	5.6	15.5	21.3	20.2
Malaysia	18.3	14.7	12.7	11.5
Mexico	15.9	16.8	10.4	17.3
Pakistan	37.6	2.3	11.2	13.9
Spain[a]	25.9	23.2	n.a.	n.a.
Thailand	28.5	28.9	8.6	8.2
Turkey[a,b]	−279.2	−307.4	n.a.	n.a.
United States	26.9	15.5	n.a.	n.a.

— not available
n.a. not applicable
Source: World Bank, IFC, FIAS, March 1995
a. These countries offer investment tax allowances or credits for investments in machinery and/or structures in place of tax holidays
b. The negative rate implies that the true value of deductions and credits exceeds the amount of taxes paid on income earned.

zones grant investors a lengthy tax holiday (often 10 years), a reduction or a waiver of import taxes on machinery and production inputs, and less cumbersome importing and exporting procedures than available nationally.

Among the different types of incentives that can lower a country's effective tax rate, investors prefer up-front incentives to those that are contingent on some outcome such as corporate profits. Hence, tariff rebates on imported equipment are among the most popular incentives, as are up-front cash grants, used by some European countries but rarely by developing countries because of the fiscal cost. Developing countries have used debt-equity swaps, a form of up-front incentive without a fiscal cost to governments. IFC has found that debt-equity swaps used by several Latin American countries did affect investment decisions.[15]

Countries with high effective tax rates can reduce them to more competitive levels by giving tax incentives only to a selected group of firms, while maintaining high tax rates for others. An alternative is to change the general fiscal system to lower the effective tax rate for all firms. Between these two extremes lie any number of options.

To lower effective tax rates for investors in selected sectors or industries, developing countries have used, besides Export Processing Zones, tax and import duty reductions. The Philippines, Thailand and other countries in Asia, for example, have established lists of promoted industries in which investments receive tax benefits. These "promoted" industries are often specified in great detail by size, location, and amount of foreign ownership required. One country, for example, included on its promotion list hotels with more than 200 rooms.

However, governments are not very good at targeting investments that are both sensitive to incentives and beneficial to the country. There is a great risk of giving incentives to firms that would invest without any incentive or would not benefit the country in any event. Moreover, giving tax incentives to some investors and not others introduces issues of discrimination between, for example, foreign and domestic investors,[16] investors in different industries, newcomers and established firms, and even between individual firms in the same industry. For these reasons, a moderate and transparent tax system for all firms is likely to be more effective than an extensive program of targeted incentives.

Another reason for caution is that certain types of "investment" incentives are not actually linked to investment. Tax holidays are based on the establishment of an enterprise, even if that establishment results in no new investment in the economic sense. In countries that give tax holidays, the motivation is strong to reconstitute an enterprise in a different form after the holiday period ends in order to get another tax holiday. The incentive given by an investment tax credit, on the other hand, is directly linked to the size of an investment. For this reason, the tax credit may be a preferable way of giving an investment incentive.

Despite these problems with use of selective incentives, developing countries are reluctant to give them up in favor of a general lowering of effective tax rates for all investors. In the experience of FIAS, client countries often reject recommendations in favor of low tax rates for all investors and against selective incentives. The selective approach to tax reduction is attractive to many countries because it may minimize the effect on fiscal revenues. Some countries such as those in Central and Eastern Europe traditionally have depended heavily on corporate taxes for revenue; and reducing the corporate tax rate for all firms to, say 15 percent, would have a major revenue impact.[17] Moreover, countries know that some types of investors do respond to especially low tax rates (such as those producing mainly for world export markets), and that other countries, including advanced countries, offer selective incentives.

Though difficult for most developing countries to give up the use of selective incentives in these circumstances, some developing countries have done so. For example, Indonesia gave up selective incentives in the mid-1980s, but has continued to receive growing amounts of FDI (Appendix A). Jordan and Lesotho are among countries that have adopted relatively low tax rates for most investors (without totally eliminating selective incentives). Malaysia and China have both moved to reduce incentives.

In conclusion, use of selective investment incentives presents a certain risk of needlessly forgoing tax revenues for little or no effect on investment. Before considering an incentive regime, first a modern and moderate general tax regime, conducive to investment of all types, must be put in place. Then countries can look at the few special cases in which selective incentives may be justified.

POLICIES TO ENCOURAGE DOMESTIC LINKAGES

Developing countries have been concerned that FDI-owned enterprises may not be connected closely enough to the domestic economy to transfer knowledge and skills to local companies. Host governments have perceived inadequate links between foreign and domestic firms, particularly for purchases of inputs from local firms. These backward linkages are thought to be particularly valuable for local firms, both as a source of demand and as a mechanism for transmitting technical and management know-how. As a result, policies to force domestic integration such as domestic value-added requirements were imposed, particularly on foreign-owned manufacturing firms.

These measures were aimed at increasing the return to the host economy by both reducing the drain on foreign investors (for example, by restricting foreign ownership shares) and by raising returns to local citizens (for example, through training required). The effect was also to reduce the financial return to foreign investors, often stifling foreign interest in the projects, excluding beneficial investments, and exacerbating problems of efficiency in investments that were made.

Rules on minimum domestic value added make it more difficult for firms to reach an efficient scale of operations, which make them less competitive on world markets and against imports. To the extent they can be operated at all, policies to force increased domestic value added have to be supported by direct or indirect subsidies such as protection of the domestic market.

Use of local content rules was recently proscribed by the international agreement resulting from the Uruguay Round of negotiations under the General Agreement on Tariffs and Trade (GATT). Called trade-related investment measures (TRIMS), these rules were considered to be barriers to trade. The TRIM agreement prohibited the use of these measures unless justified under GATT exceptions.

There are better ways than local content rules to encourage links between firms with foreign investments and domestic firms, according to research by FIAS and others.[18] A combination of market liberalization, including trade liberalization, and programs to help upgrade the technical and management capabilities of potential domestic and supplying firms can improve the prospects for links between foreign and domestic firms. In addition, a number of countries have found that active promotion programs also contribute to the formation of linkages between the upgraded domestic firms and foreign investors.

Market liberalization is important in this process because it creates the incentives that will lead some of the using industries to expand both in the domestic market and sometimes to supply the export market. This expansion, in turn, helps to create a market that is large enough for the local suppliers to reach an efficient scale of production. After the Philippines reduced tariffs on major appliances, for example, local appliance manufacturers had to consolidate models and upgrade production to compete with imports. By producing fewer models in longer runs, the appliance manufacturers found they could export, increasing scale still further. This opened up a large market for domestic suppliers to the appliance manufacturers who, in turn, were able to become competitive. Some of them began to export as they continued to supply domestic appliance manufacturers.

This process can open up opportunities for foreign investors in the supplying industries. For example, IFC has helped finance a large number of investments to produce auto parts, often with foreign firms.

Developing world-competitive local suppliers is as important for multinational companies producing in developing countries as it is for the host country. The most efficient producers in assembly industries such as autos and electronics rely on a close relationship with suppliers. Production processes that use just-in-time methods and supplier participation in product design often work best when suppliers and users are located near each other. Because of this natural interdependence, suppliers often coinvest with assembly firms. Thus, Intel's announcement of an investment in an electronic chip assembly and test facility in Costa Rica is expected to prompt other investors, domestic and foreign, to furnish inputs to the Intel plant.

Several advanced and developing countries have developed programs to support upgrading of potential supplying industries as part of broader efforts to help improve national firms. Korea, Singapore, and Taiwan, China, all have noteworthy programs to help upgrade local companies' technology and managerial capabilities. Sometimes this includes financing for investments.

Other developing countries have had local industry support programs that are less useful for fostering linkages with foreign firms. Usually operated as small and medium enterprise (SME) development programs, they often overlook the domestic firms that have the best chance of meeting the needs of foreign suppliers. The SME programs in the Philippines, for example, focus mainly on small firms outside metropolitan Manila. However, the firms that have the potential to meet the high standards international firms require of suppliers are usually larger and located in the Manila area. These firms need assistance, too, but cannot get it from the government programs.

To be effective, the host country's industry-support programs have to be designed with a sharp focus on the target market. They should nurture the best local firms, not the weakest. Only such hard-headed programs stand a chance of success.

Active promotion of linkages can also be useful. Just as promoting foreign direct investment makes sense in a world where information is not perfect, it is also true that foreign investors do not always seek out domestic suppliers. Governments could usefully support activities that help bring potential supplier and user firms together.

INVESTMENT PROMOTION

Some economists argue that, if countries would only get their investment policies right, investors would search out all worthwhile investment opportunities. This view is supported by investors' willingness to try new and challenging environments, such as China. The fact that even small oil companies seek out and identify oil exploration opportunities offshore of West Africa also supports the idea that potential investors are always looking for good opportunities, no matter how far away or how risky.

Nevertheless, prospective investors, even the largest firms, do not always conduct systematic worldwide searches for opportunities. The search for opportunities is a bureaucratic process whose initiation and direction may be swayed by many factors, including imperfect information and skewed risk perceptions.[19] Most companies consider only a small range of potential investment locations. Many other countries are not even on their map (Box 4.10).

Box 4.10. Many Countries Aren't on Investors' Maps

"Will the opening of Central and Eastern Europe to FDI divert investment from other developing countries?" Fearing that investment around the Mediterranean basin might be especially vulnerable, FIAS put this question to a group of corporate executives in 1990. The survey group came from a hundred West European, North American, and Japanese companies. They were from seven industries: apparel, autos and components, intermediate chemicals, electrical equipment, electronics, telecom services and tourism.

Except for firms in the apparel industries, developing countries of the Mediterranean basin were not on prospective investors' lists of possible investment sites, according to the survey. Companies that had any knowledge of these countries thought they were too risky to include in their corporate business strategies. Some East European countries were viewed as risky, too, but others were part of the European strategies of the companies interviewed.

The survey brought into stark relief the main question facing the Mediterranean basin countries: how do they get into the investment game? How do they get into investors' line of vision? Policy improvements and upgrades of infrastructure and labor quality might be part of the answer. Even after making such improvements, however, the investor community would have to be told about the changes in investment promotion campaigns.

Source: C.A. Michalet, "Investment Strategies of Multinational Corporations and the Attractiveness of Host Countries," FIAS Occasional Paper; forthcoming.

IFC has seen the effects of this imperfect search process in its own investment work, as it searches for potential foreign partners in developing-country projects. Many countries, developed and developing, as well as cities, counties, and states, are devoting resources to promoting investments in an effort to bridge the information gap. Companies also recognize the imperfections of markets and for this reason establish marketing programs, even for industrial products that will be sold to other firms. Some countries may not need to promote investment. China, for example, has never had a national promotion effort. But when the joint venture law opening China to FDI was implemented in 1979, businessmen flocked to China in droves. Policy change itself generated publicity and interest. China's huge population also inspired visions of huge markets, which was enough to induce a number of firms at least to look, even though the policy framework was still rudimetary. Russia has had similar advantages, but has not yet capitalized on them.

The same cannot be said for Morocco and Tunisia, two Mediterranean countries that have markedly improved their investment policies. Both countries need intensive promotion campaigns like Singapore's, Malaysia's, and Ireland's to get attention.

Successful foreign investment promotion campaigns share three main elements: image building, investment generation, and investor servicing, FIAS has found.[20]

Image building. Image-building techniques include general and specialized media advertising, participating in investment exhibitions; conducting general investment missions from source countries; and conducting general information seminars on investment opportunities. These techniques set the stage, helping convince prospective foreign investors that a certain country may be a good place to invest; no one expects them to directly generate investment. Image building is useful when the reality in a country is better than the perception held by the international investment community. Trying to create an image that is at variance with the facts is counterproductive.

Investment generation. Investment generation activities are designed to interest a specific investor in investigating opportunities and to make the investment. Direct mail campaigns, industry- or sector-specific investment missions, or informational seminars are effective tools.

But the best technique, one used by all successful investment promotion agencies, is direct presentations to specific targeted firms. This technique involves identifying opportunities in host-country industries and sectors. Firms that may want to invest in those industries are then identified and specific decision makers within the firm are targeted for presentations by the promotion agency. The presentations outline the investment opportunity and try to get the decision maker to investigate the opportunity on site.

When the investor visits the country, the promotion agency prepares an itinerary and provides whatever information is requested. The agency follows up with the investor to help the firm make an investment commitment.

Investor servicing. Investment service is the third element of a promotion program. Its techniques include counseling, expediting application and permit processing, and providing post-investment services. These techniques are designed to convert an investment commitment into an actual investment and, later, to ensure that the investor is pleased with the investment environment. This process is intended to make the new investor an "ambassador" who will influence other firms to consider the country as an investment site.

All these activities can influence the amount, character, and location of investment. A developing country will want to focus on different aspects of promotion depending on its circumstances. Investor servicing may need to be the focus if the investment environment has deficiencies that impede investment implementation. Image building will be useful when there is a good story to tell the international investment community. A country should not, however, try to convey an image that does not reflect reality. Prospective investors will find out the truth, to the detriment of the country's image. Finally, investment generation will be useful when the other elements are in place and there is a clear idea of the kinds of investment that offer potential in the country.

Success stories from investment generation efforts abound. One is the Intel Corporation's plan to locate a large assembly and test facility in Costa Rica (Box 4.11).

Generating investment is both time consuming and labor intensive. Some agencies have courted certain investors for years. Positive results do not come from one meeting or one investors' conference. They depend on the steady efforts of a professional organization, working over a period of time and building on an acceptable investment environment.

Promotion institutions can help the investment process as long as it is sufficiently independent of the government to have freedom in hiring and setting salary scales. After all, promoting investment is marketing, and salaries have to be high enough to attract skilled and experienced people from the private sector. At the

Box 4.11. How Governments Can Make a Difference: Intel's Decision to Invest in Costa Rica

Policies to attract export-oriented foreign direct investment have been an important part of Costa Rica's overall development strategy since the early 1980s. CINDE, an investment promotion institution established outside the government with financing mainly from the U.S. Agency for International Development (USAID), has been the main executing agent. The first sector singled out for targeting and promotion was the apparel industry, but by the late 1980s, focus was turning toward the electronics industry. This shift reflected the inherent attractiveness of the sector but also acknowledged that Costa Rica, with its relatively high per-capita incomes, would be increasingly hard-pressed to compete for the location of an industry driven mainly by cheap labor.

By targeting individual electronics companies, often beginning with no more than a "cold call," CINDE had been instrumental in influencing several electronics firms to locate in Costa Rica. Facilitation was an important part of this process. After helping to persuade a company to visit the country, CINDE took it as part of its brief to ensure that prospective investors met the right people, got the information they needed, and avoided unnecessary complications in applying for government licenses and permits. Thus, through the normal course of its business, CINDE enjoyed excellent working relationships with the country's public and private sector leaders.

Costa Rica was a late addition to the short list of Latin American countries Intel was considering as the location for a new $300 million semiconductor and testing facility. A presentation to Intel executives by CINDE showed that Costa Rica met the many threshold tests of the company during its rigorous site-selection process. Yet, on the eve of sending senior members of its site selection team to visit Costa Rica for the first time, some executives continued to have reservations about the whole enterprise.

A main concern was whether a small country like Costa Rica could accommodate an investment of this scale. Intel's 1996 sales, at $20.6 billion, were three times larger than Costa Rica's entire GDP. The investment itself would be about six times larger than the annual average of all other foreign direct investment entering the country. At full capacity, the factory's output, all of it for export, would be equal to the country's total current exports. As one executive remarked, putting Intel into Costa Rica would be like trying to put a whale into a bathtub.

CINDE recognized immediately that the size and strategic importance of an Intel investment placed it in a category by itself, although its needs for investor-facilitation services were not necessarily different in kind from those of CINDE's other clients. Consequently, a senior team was established to help Intel with its site investigation.

In this investigation, Costa Rica certainly did not "score" best by every measure Intel considered important. Some competing sites, for example, could offer cheaper labor; others a bigger pool of skilled technicians and managers; others still a more highly developed infrastructure and substantially cheaper electricity costs. In the final analysis, no small part of Costa Rica's "edge" in this intense competition came from the interest, direct involvement, and rapid response of senior members of government and officials working in tandem with a promotion agency and other parts of civil society.

same time, the agency needs connections with government that are strong enough to influence decisions affecting individual investments as well as investment policy. Because the promotion agency is the government's eyes and ears in the investment community, it should have a voice in the policy process.

The private sector should have a strong say in the promotion agency's operations to keep the operation lean and in tune with the mentality of private decision makers. Most of the funding, however, will have to come from the government, possibly with some support from international agencies. Investment promotion produces a public good for which private firms cannot be expected to pay, although local banks, utilities, and other private firms that will benefit directly from additional investment may contribute. However, most of the funding to support the operation of a promotion agency will have to be provided by the government.

The bottom line is that investment promotion will succeed only if the country is attractive to foreign investors. Promotion can supplement policy reform; it is not a substitute for it.

LESSONS OF EXPERIENCE

From its experience with foreign direct investment in the field, IFC has learned:

1. The national policy environment is a major factor in determining FDI flows to developing countries.
2. The policy environment can constrain FDI in many ways, some of them obvious, but some not immediately apparent to policymakers.
3. Liberalization of economic policies in general, and FDI policies in particular, can make a huge difference to the quality and quantity of FDI that a country receives.
4. Getting policies right may not be enough; active promotion may be required as well, but fiscal incentives are rarely worthwhile.
5. Attempts to promote greater linkages to the domestic economy are usually counterproductive.

Notes

1 Most of the examples used in this chapter reflect policies and practices in developing countries several years ago. Most of these policies and practices have now been improved, reflecting the general trend of policy liberalization.

2 In evaluating its investments, IFC has analyzed economic efficiency of prospective operations and avoided participating in those not promising to be economically efficient. Ex-post evaluations have shown that this effort was largely, but not totally successful.

3 This is not a special concession for Intel. Costa Rica's free trade zone legislation provides for individual plants to operate as a stand-alone free trade zone. There are many such plants in Costa Rica, in electronics and other industries.

4 See D.R. Weigel, "Restrictions on Dividend Repatriation and the Flow of Direct Investment to Brazil," Journal of International Business Studies (Fall 1970), pp. 35-50.

5 See, for example, H. de Soto, The Other Path (New York, N.Y.: Harper & Row, 1989), pp 131-35.

6 Ghana subsequently took action in response to this study to eliminate unnecessary barriers to investment.

7 See L. T. Wells, Jr., and A.G Wint, "Facilitating Foreign Investment," Chapter 3, FIAS Occasional Paper 2, Washington, D.C., 1991, pp. 20-29.

8 For a more detailed discussion of policy options in privatization, see an earlier volume in this series, Privatization: Principles and Practice, Lessons of Experience 1 (Washington, D.C.: IFC, 1995).

9 Ibid Box 4.6, Chapter 4, p. 27.

10 Ibid, Box 4.5, p. 26, which describes the attempt to secure foreign partners for two power equipment producers in the Czech Republic. In one case the transaction was not completed, and the enterprise became insolvent.

11 For a detailed discussion of the privatization processes most attractive to foreign investors see Kathy Megyery and Frank Sader, "Facilitating Foreign Participation in Privatization," FIAS Occasional Paper 8, Washington, D.C., 1996.

12 F. Sader, "Privatizing Public Enterprises and Foreign Investment in Developing Countries, 1988-93," Chapter 6, FIAS Occasional Paper 5, Washington, D.C., 1995, pp. 26-32.

13 S. Guisinger and Associates, Investment Incentives and Performance Requirements (New York, N.Y.:Praeger, 1985). See Table 1-1, p. 2, for a list of the incentives used by governments.

14 For a more detailed discussion of effective tax rates, see J.M. Mintz and T. Tsiopoulos, "Corporate Income Tax and Foreign Direct Investment in Central and Eastern Europe," FIAS Occasional Paper 4, Washington, D.C., 1992.

15 J. Bergsman and W. Edisis, "Debt Equity Swaps and Foreign Direct Investment in Latin America," IFC Discussion Paper 2, Washington, D.C., 1988.

16 Central and East European countries often discriminated against local firms early in their transition to a market economy. They taxed firms with foreign investment at lower rates than state-owned enterprises and extended other benefits such as preferential access to foreign exchange and more flexible labor laws. The understandable reaction of many local firms was to enter into (sometime bogus) joint ventures to get those benefits.

17 For many other developing countries, however, collecting 10 percent to 15 percent of corporate profits would increase corporate tax revenues. These countries would be in a position to establish a low, but collectible tax rate for all firms.

18 J. Battat, I. Frank, and X. Shen, "Suppliers to Multinationals," FIAS Occasional Paper 6, Washington, D.C., 1996.

19 An early study that showed the bureaucratic nature of the search process is Yair Aharoni, The Foreign Investment Decision Process (Boston, Mass.: Harvard Business School, 1966).

20 This tripartite division, and much of the rest of what follows is taken from L. T. Wells, Jr., and A.Wint, "Marketing a Country," FIAS Occasional Paper 1, Washington, D.C., 1990.

POLICY REFORM AND FDI IN INDONESIA

Indonesia has long been an important destination for FDI.[1] However, government policies toward FDI have fluctuated over time, leading to changes in the level and type of FDI flows. FIAS has been advising the government on policies to attract FDI since 1988. Indonesia therefore provides a good case study of the relationship between policy changes and FDI flows.

Indonesia has distinguished foreign companies from domestic companies in several ways: foreign companies have been restricted in which sectors they may enter, in access to domestic capital, in entitlement to government incentives, and are subject to regulations regarding minimum capitalization, minimum foreign ownership, and eventual divestiture to Indonesian ownership. The constitution reserved nine "public interest" sectors under government control, including infrastructure; these were initially reserved for Indonesian public, and then later private investors.

Foreign investment policy in Indonesia has undergone wide swings from liberal to restrictive in the four phases since 1964 (Table 4A.1). These were largely driven by the availability of capital, which was initially closely linked to oil revenues.

1967–73: open door. In the late 1960s, the Suharto Government adopted a favorable stance toward FDI. Nationalized enterprises were returned to their previous owners. An FDI law was passed, which provided, inter alia, a 30-year guarantee against expropriation and incentives in the form of reduced import taxes and income tax holidays. Under the "open door" policy of this period, 100 percent foreign ownership was allowed, divestiture requirements were not mandated, and most sectors were open to foreign companies.

However, FDI was seen as a supplement to domestic investment, and it was expected that foreign participation in the economy would be phased out in time.

1974–1985: growing restrictions with occasional relaxation. Strong nationalist sentiments in the 1970s led to increasing restrictions, culminating in 1974, when government prohibited 100 percent foreign ownership, limited foreign participation in joint ventures to 80 percent, and required divestiture to majority Indonesian ownership in 10 years. An increasing number of sectors were closed to foreign investment. During the rest of the 1970s, there were periods of liberalization when capital flows slowed down such as after the Pertamina crisis in 1975 and before the second oil boom in 1979.

All FDI investments required presidential approval. The Board of Investments was created in 1973 to screen FDI proposals. In 1977, it was made a one stop

Table 4A.1. Changes in Policy and Procedure Toward FDI in Indonesia 1967–94

Year	Administrative procedures	Sectoral access	Incentives	Ownership and finance restrictions
1967		Negative list of closed sectors 30-year license	Income tax holidays Import duty exemptions Exclusion from general incentives	Minimum capital $1m Minimum 20 percent foreign owned; max 100 percent 30 year-expropriation guarantee Limits on domestic capital use
1973	Board of Investment			
1974		Longer negative list		Maximum 80 percent foreign owned Divest locally in 10 years
1977	BOI One Stop Shop	Positive list of open sectors		Greater foreign ownership permitted with local share sales
1984		Shorter positive list	No income tax holidays	
1987			General incentives available if 51 percent local	100 percent FDI in some sectors, with divestiture in 15 years; no divestiture with 10 percent local ownership Fewer restrictions with local sale of equity
1989		Negative list of closed sectors: shortened		100 percent FDI in some sectors/regions
1992				Divestiture after 20 years More 100 percent FDI allowed
1994		Public interest sectors taken off negative list		100 percent FDI in most sectors Limited divestiture requirements

Figure 4A.1. Real FDI to Indonesia, 1970–95

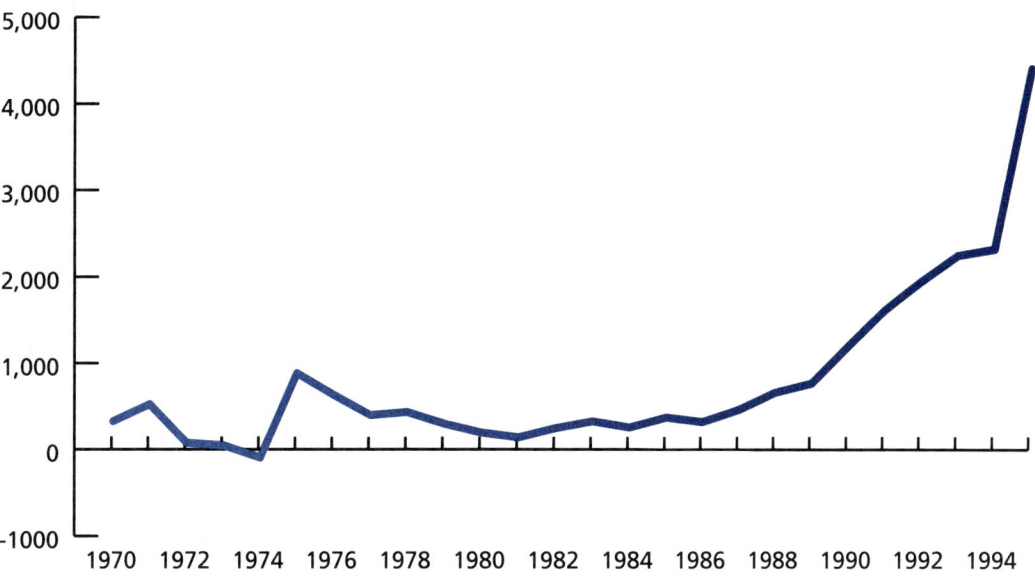

Source: World Bank Debtor Reporting System

service where investment screening and associated license applications could be processed in one place. From 1977, the Board of Investments based recommendations for approval on an annual Priority List of Investments. This was a positive list of permitted investments. It was highly regulatory, as production capacity and the number of licenses in each sector were controlled. The criteria for issuing licenses became increasingly opaque.

Government responded to the fall in oil prices in the early 1980s with an industrialization policy that became increasingly protectionist and nationalistic. The investment climate deteriorated as more sectors were closed to foreign investors. In 1984, tax holidays were eliminated as part of a wider tax reform.

1986–93: renewed liberalization. After 1986, the need to adjust to falling oil prices by restructuring the economy away from oil led to a change in perception by the government on the role of the private sector, including foreign investment. Government came to see FDI as important to bring in capital, technology, managerial capability and access to export markets. A clear direc-

tion of continued liberalization and improvement of foreign investment policy became evident.

In 1986 maximum foreign ownership was raised to 95 percent for export oriented industries in East Indonesia, using high technology, and requiring over $10 million capital. In 1987, the period to achieve divestiture was increased to 15 years. The conditions for treatment of a firm as domestic were progressively widened, to allow domestic treatment for companies with 51 percent local ownership, or 45 percent locally owned plus 20 percent of shares issued locally. On the sensitive issue of 100 percent foreign ownership and divestiture, government moved step by step, not applying liberalization nationwide at first.

In 1986–88, the priority list was made more transparent, by adopting standard ISIC definitions of sectors, and removing limits on capacity and numbers of licenses. From 1987, investors have been able to expand or diversify up to 30 percent of existing capacity without new licensing. The sectors open to foreign investment were greatly expanded to include tourism, garment manufacturing, chemicals and machinery. Imports of used equipment were permitted. In 1987, foreign owned enterprises were allowed to export their own products for the first time and to engage in trading activities. In 1989, a negative list of sectors excluded from FDI was introduced, with a gradual reduction since then from 64 sectors to 35, of which the most important is retail distribution.

1994 onward: extensive liberalization. After experiencing an investment boom in 1989-91, government responded to the slowdown in 1992 with a spate of bold liberalization measures, culminating in a major deregulation package in 1994 removing most restrictions on foreign enterprises. One hundred percent foreign-owned companies are now permitted and the amount to be divested in 15 years is left up to the investors. Joint ventures can be formed with maximum 95 percent foreign ownership and no divestiture requirement. The nine public interest sectors previously closed to foreign investment were opened for joint ventures. The minimum capital requirement, in place since 1967, was removed.

Pattern of FDI flows. The phases of FDI policy are reflected in changes in the levels of FDI (Figure 4A.1), and the types of investment. FDI rose in the late 1960s under the Open Door policy, but was heavily concentrated in extractive industries such as oil and gas, where policies against long-term foreign ownership were less of a deterrent. Following the tightening of controls on FDI in the early 1970s, FDI fell sharply, except for a brief recovery in 1975 following the positive oil price shock.

For the rest of the 1970s, levels of FDI fell in real terms as the investment climate became increasingly restrictive. Following the fall in oil prices in the early 1980s, the protectionist policy followed by government stimulated some FDI to exploit the large, protected Indonesian market; this offset a decline in oil and gas investment. However, FDI only started to grow in real terms after 1986, when the period of renewed liberalization began. Unlike earlier phases, FDI in the 1980s and 1990s has been heavily weighted toward manufacturing for export markets.

As part of the regional integration of production in Southeast Asia, Indonesia has attracted FDI (especially from Japan, Korea and Taiwan, China) to produce a range of industrial and consumer products for export to the region and beyond. As other Southeast Asian countries have seen production costs rise, production shifted to Indonesia as a relatively low cost location. This relative advantage was reduced by improvement in the investment climate elsewhere, notably the liberalization of the FDI regime in China after 1989. Combined with a slowdown in outward investment by Japan due to recession in 1992, this led to a pause in FDI growth, before the upward trend continued and accelerated, as the policy reforms of 1994 enabled Indonesia to share fully in the global surge in FDI to developing countries with attractive policy environments.

Role of FIAS. FIAS has worked with the Government since 1988, when it first reviewed the regulatory framework for FDI in conjunction with the World Bank. In 1989-90, FIAS reviewed policy and regulatory impediments to FDI in the agricultural sector. FIAS then helped reorient the national investment organization BKPM from a regulatory to a promotional role, starting in 1991. In 1995 FIAS advised on policies to promote linkages between domestic and foreign firms. More recently, FIAS has again advised on investment policy issues, particularly those relating to ownership restrictions.

Notes

1 M. Pangestu, "Evolution of Liberalizing Policies Affecting Investment Flows in the Asian Pacific," paper prepared for the FIAS High-Level Roundtable on Competition for FDI—Implications for Asia and the Pacific; 1995; processed.

5 PROMOTING FDI THROUGH PROJECT FINANCING

For over 40 years, IFC has helped to bring foreign direct investment to developing countries by:

■ sharing the risk of projects with private investors. Even the largest multinational corporations have limits on the amount of money they will expose to risks. IFC's ability to provide equity and debt financing enables projects to go forward.

■ helping reduce perceived risk by its presence in a project. As an international organization owned by its member countries, IFC involvement gives investors some reassurance in the face of political risk.

■ providing information on investment opportunities. As an investor itself with strong links to domestic business communities, IFC is a credible source of information about investment opportunities and conditions in the host country.

■ facilitating the steps in the investment process from approval to ground-breaking.

IFC's first investment, in 1958, involved a U.S. direct investment in Mexico. The number of foreign direct investment (FDI) projects has matched IFC's growth: 114 between 1958 and 1979, 149 in the next 10 years to 1989, and 275 in the most recent 8 years through 1997.[1] FDI projects have comprised about 32 percent of IFC's portfolio by number of projects and 36 percent by project cost (Figure 5.1). Overall, IFC has invested in some 538 companies.

IFC invests in projects through a mixture of debt, equity, and quasi-equity. Because it does not take an active role in management, however, its own investment is not classified as FDI. It thus differs from its private partners, who are regarded as foreign direct investors, when they have at least 10 percent equity and an active management role.

CHARACTERISTICS OF IFC'S FDI PROJECTS
As of June 1997, IFC had invested in FDI projects in 100 different countries. IFC's own investments generally correspond to the global pattern of FDI (Chapter 2). Argentina, India, Indonesia, and Mexico have been

Figure 5.1. Share of FDI Projects in IFC Portfolio by Value and Number, 1960–Sept. 96 (percent)

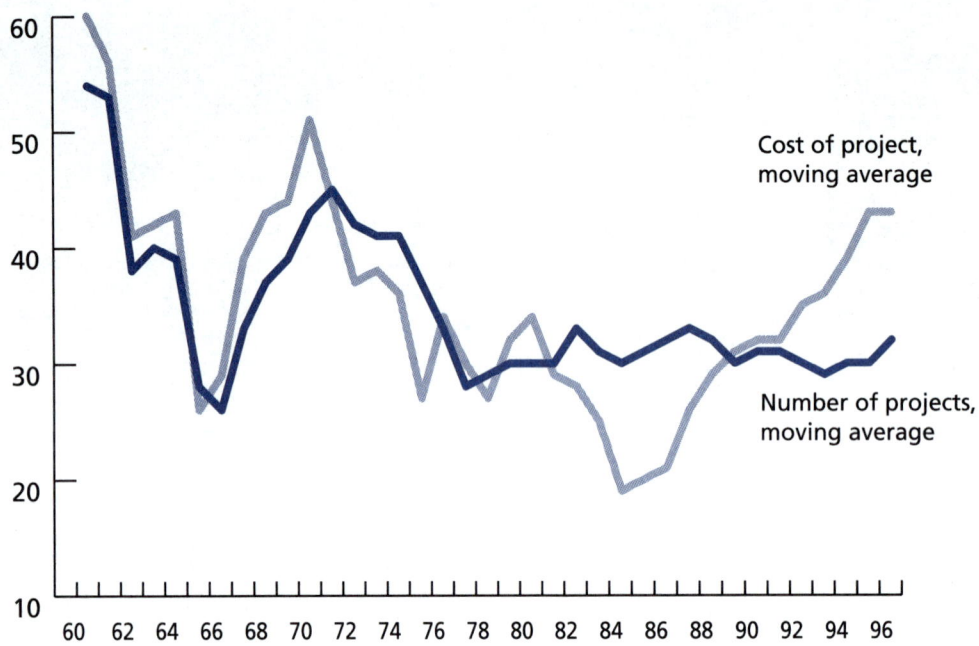

Source: IFC MPD/SIS Database.

Figure 5.2. IFC FDI Project Volume vs Global FDI Volume, by Region 1970–96

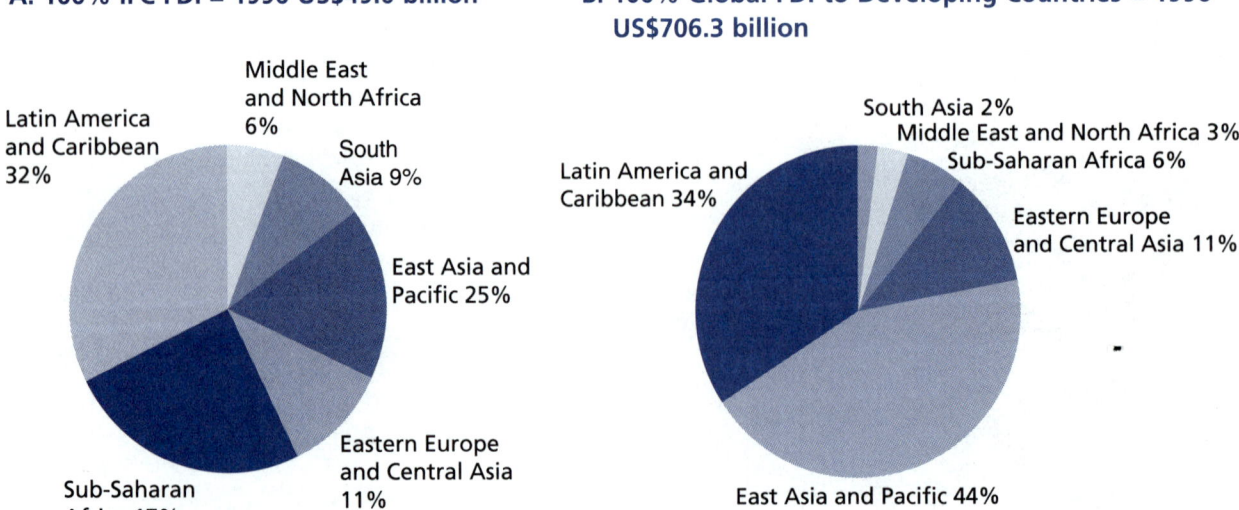

Source: IFC MPD/SIS Database; World Debtor Reporting System.

among the top host countries, reflecting their large size among developing countries. However, IFC's FDI project portfolio does not show the strong bias toward China in recent overall private FDI flows. Compared to all FDI to developing countries, IFC project costs were less concentrated in East Asia and the Pacific and more in the Middle East, South Asia, and Africa (Figure 5.2 and Table 5.1).

Table 5.1. Top 12 IFC FDI Host Countries, by Project Cost

Rank	1958–79	1980–89	1990–97
1	Brazil	Chile	Philippines
2	India	Egypt	Thailand
3	Argentina	Argentina	Indonesia
4	Mexico	Mexico	Pakistan
5	Pakistan	Philippines	Argentina
6	Indonesia	Brazil	Congo, Republic of
7	Philippines	Zambia	Mexico
8	Kenya	Gabon	Chile
9	Chile	Senegal	China
10	Former Yugoslavia	Indonesia	Poland
11	Malaysia	India	India
12	Colombia	Colombia	Russian Federation

Note: excludes states with 1994 population less than 5 million.
Source: IFC MPD/SIS Database.

Of IFC's FDI projects, 37 percent, comprising a fourth of all project costs, have been in low-income countries (excluding China). This compares with only 14 percent of all FDI to developing countries (excluding China).

In keeping with its mandate to develop new markets, IFC has supported FDI projects in countries that had hitherto received little FDI. In 1960, it invested in its first FDI project in newly formed Tanzania; in 1968, it had its first FDI project in Mauritania; in 1977, it began investing in FDI projects in Madagascar: all poor countries largely ignored by FDI until then. The Corporation was also in the forefront of FDI flows to

Box 5.1. Measuring Country Risk

Twice a year Institutional Investor polls 75 to 100 international banks to grade countries from 0 (the least) to 100 (the highest) chance of sovereign default. The analysis gives more weight to responses from banks with greater worldwide exposure and better country analysis systems. A score below 25 (high risk) indicates little access to international financial markets, 40 to reasonably good access. Depending on country conditions and repayment records, Institutional Investor ranks some upper middle-income countries as posing more risk than low-income countries (for example, upper middle-income Venezuela was rated 32.1, while lower income India was rated 46.3 in the September 1996 survey).

previously command economies. In 1987, it had its first FDI project in Hungary. Poland followed in 1991, Romania and the Czech Republic in 1992; Russia, Estonia, and Kazakhstan in 1994; Kyrgyz Republic and Latvia in 1995; Uzbekistan in 1996; and Tajikistan in 1997.

IFC's FDI projects are concentrated in developing countries with medium to high country risk (Box 5.1). This is in contrast to all FDI to developing countries, which is concentrated in the lower risk countries (Figure 5.3).

IFC has cofinanced projects with foreign direct investors from 70 different countries. From the beginning, these have included both developing and devel-

Figure 5.3. Distribution of FDI by Risk Categories, 1982–96 Cumulative

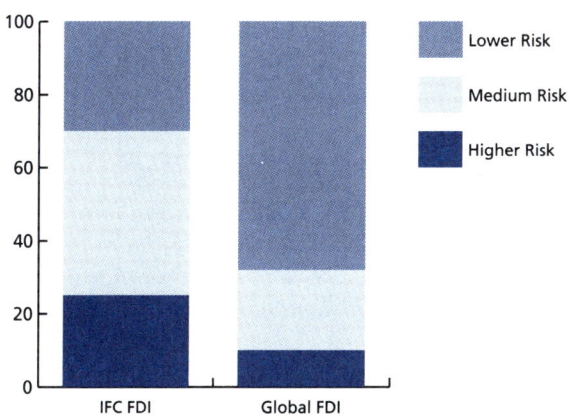

Source: Institutional Investor, *World Bank Debtor Reporting System, and IFC.*

oped countries. IFC has worked with foreign direct investors from nearly 50 developing economies, so helping their integration into the global economy. IFC has done FDI projects in every economic sector, from construction, agriculture, and mining, through manufacturing, processing, and financial and consulting services (Figure 5.4). The largest number of FDI projects have been in agribusiness, mining, and infrastructure. By project cost, the largest sectors of activity have been infrastructure (total project cost of $10.2 billion in 1996 prices), mining ($9.4 billion) and oil and gas ($9.2 billion).

Infrastructure, motor vehicle industry, and construction materials projects have been concentrated in Latin America, agribusiness, mining, and textiles in Sub-Saharan Africa. Other sectors have been more evenly balanced between regions.

Sometimes, even the largest multinationals find benefits in cofinancing with IFC. About 10 percent of IFC's FDI investments have been made with multinationals from the "Top 100," as defined by

the United Nations Conference on Trade and Development (UNCTAD) on the basis of turnover and other criteria. Half of these have been in the petroleum and chemicals extraction and processing industries, where IFC has played an important role in reducing country risk. Partners have included familiar names such as AKZO, Amoco, BP, Chevron, Du Pont, Elf, Exxon, GE, Hoechst, Mitsubishi, Mitsui, Shell and Total.

PROJECT PERFORMANCE

According to IFC's portfolio rating system (Box 5.2), 71 percent of IFC foreign direct investments have been completed successfully or are proceeding without major problems; 21 percent were classified as posing some problems. This performance is slightly below the overall IFC portfolio average of 75 percent with no problem, and 16 percent posing various levels of problems, for reasons discussed below. However, rating a project as problematic does not mean that it will fail or that IFC will lose money on it. Only 1.2 percent of IFC funds invested in FDI projects have had to be written off, the same proportion as for the whole IFC portfolio.

Figure 5.4. Sectoral Distribution of IFC FDI Projects by Value and Number

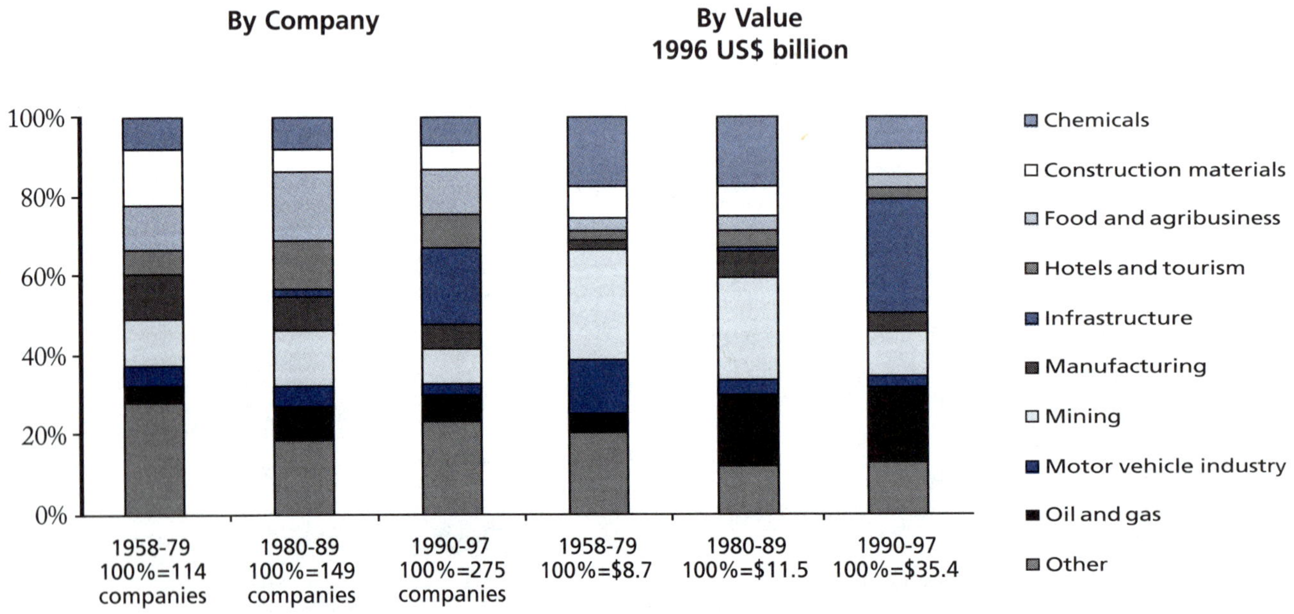

Source: IFC MPD/SIS Database.

Figure 5.5. IFC FDI vs Non-FDI Project Performance (percent)

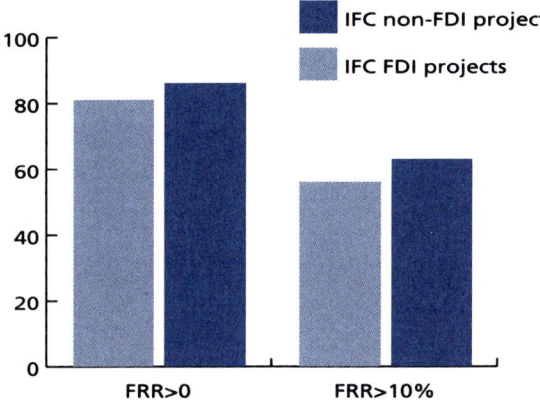

Note: Based on 336 IFC projects for which financial rates of return (FRR) are available.
Source: IFC MPD/SIS Database.

As shown in Figure 5.5, 81 percent of IFC FDI projects with calculated financial rates of return showed positive returns; 56 percent showed rates of return exceeding 10 percent a year. This is slightly below IFC's non-FDI portfolio performance, where 86 percent of projects show a positive return and 63 percent exceed 10 percent a year.

The difference in rate of return may reflect the different roles IFC plays in FDI and non-FDI projects. FDI project sponsors typically have better access to financing from their domestic capital markets than local project sponsors, because most developing countries' local capital markets are less developed. Thus, IFC is less likely to be brought into a project simply to provide financing not otherwise available to the company,

Box 5.2. Assessing IFC Project Performance

IFC has invested in 1,617 companies (referred to "as the overall IFC project portfolio").Of these, 538 projects meet the criterion of FDI (namely that a foreign private sponsor has an equity stake greater than 10 percent). These are listed in Appendix Table B. IFC keeps project structure and performance records on, for example, ownership, financing structures, size of IFC investments, write-offs and loss reserves. These data are updated periodically, but only provide a snapshot of the structure and performance of a project at the time of last updating. They are therefore not wholly reliable but give a good picture of overall portfolio trends.

For all projects in the portfolio, investment staff annually assess a portfolio rating of the current state of performance from IFC's perspective as an investor: satisfactory, potential problem, or problem. When a project exits the portfolio, it is given a final rating of satisfactory or problem. Many projects rated as potential problem or problem at some stage are finally rated satisfactory, since the purpose of the system is to flag emerging problems so that they can be addressed. Nevertheless, the ratings provide a snapshot of the performance of IFC's portfolio at a particular point in time. Portfolio ratings quoted in this chapter refer to the final rating for exited projects or the most recent rating for ongoing projects. Projects less than one year old are excluded from this exercise.

For many projects, an Investment Assessment Report is prepared three to five years after project inception. This reassesses prospects for the project's success, and estimates the ex post financial rate of return. It describes performance to date by the company and identifies lessons learned. Such reports are available for a sample of 99 FDI companies (referred to below as sample projects, or the sample), and provide a rich source of detailed analysis. These projects are identified in Appendix Table B. This sample is broadly representative of the IFC FDI portfolio, but contains some sample biases. For example, larger projects and problem projects are more likely to be assessed, and newer projects have not yet been assessed. Furthermore, the assessment of project performance is undertaken early in the life of the project. At this stage construction risk is behind it, but most market risk still lies ahead. The ex post financial rate of return is thus partly influenced by projections of future market trends.

Ex post financial rates of return have sometimes been calculated for projects apart from an Investment Assessment report. As a result, IFC has a database of ex post financial rates of return for some 334 projects, including 134 projects from the IFC FDI portfolio, that is, a further 35 projects beyond the 99 sample projects (referred to below as IFC (FDI) projects with calculated financial rates of return).

regardless of project risk. Instead, it is usually brought in because the project and country risks make mobilizing finance for the venture difficult and make sponsors seek ways to mitigate the risks. IFC's entire portfolio is weighted toward riskier projects and countries but, because of IFC's developmental role, this weighting is much stronger for FDI projects.

PROJECT STRUCTURE

In two thirds of the sample projects, a foreign investor has been the sponsor, defined as the largest single private shareholder. Of these, 54 percent owned more than 50 percent of the equity, giving them full management control. Foreign sponsors predominated in oil and gas, mining, infrastructure, hotels, textiles, and the motor vehicle industry, and were more common in exporting activities. Of the foreign-sponsored projects in the sample, nearly two thirds were joint ventures with local equity partners. There are a variety of reasons for this. Because many countries restrict entry by foreign investors without local partners, foreign investors may have to find local partners to comply with legal requirements, rather than to meet a business need. One hotel operator, for example, brought local equity partners into its Southeast Asian subsidiary solely to meet government restrictions on foreign ownership; it retained full effective control of the subsidiary (Box 6.5).

Foreign sponsors sometimes select local partners for their local marketing links, access to inputs, and business know-how. For example, when a German manufacturer decided to develop products for south European markets, it formed a joint venture with a local manufacturer in Turkey to handle local marketing. Half of the projects in the sample with foreign sponsors were directed to the local market.

In a third of the joint ventures, the local partner was a public enterprise. In such cases, it is common for their equity contribution to be in kind, for example, use of raw materials and existing fixed assets. For instance, Zambia Hotel Properties, a public holding company owning hotel properties, transferred these properties to a joint venture with Intercontinental as its equity contribution (Box 6.2).

Management skills are part of the value added that FDI can bring. Staff provided by the foreign partner managed 64 percent of foreign-sponsored projects day-to-day, bringing technological and managerial know-how directly into enterprises (Table 5.2). In the other

foreign-sponsored sample projects, day-to-day operational management was undertaken by staff recruited locally, often from the local partner. Hiring local management staff is more common when a company produces for the local market.

Table 5.2. Ownership and Day-to-Day Management in Foreign/Local Joint Ventures

		Sponsor[a]			
		Foreign	Local	Equal	Total
Day-to-day	Foreign	34	3	8	45
management	Local	19	11	5	35
	Total	53	14	13	80

Source: IFC FDI Sample Database. Note that ex post equity structures are available for only 80 projects out of the sample of 99 FDI projects.
a Defined as largest single private shareholder.

In most markets, recruiting staff locally is generally considered more cost-effective than importing expatriate managers. Thus, when the foreign sponsor does not see a clear advantage in providing management, cost considerations lead joint ventures to minimize reliance on expatriate staff (Chapter 4). Sometimes government restricts use of expatriate staff. Sometimes local staff offer management skills that a foreign sponsor does not have. For example, Westel Radiotelefon (a joint venture between US West and Matáv, the Hungarian state telephone company) initially developed its cellular telephone network in Hungary with expatriate staff, but rapidly transferred responsibility to local staff, who knew the local market and could better respond to it. (Box 5.3).

In a quarter of the locally managed sample projects, the foreign partner provided support through a formal technical assistance contract. For example, the Mantos Blancos copper mine in Chile has operated successfully since its establishment in 1958 with day-to-day operations managed by local staff with technical assistance from the foreign sponsor, the Hochschild Group of Bolivia. In Indonesia, PT Viscose produces viscose under local management, with a technical assistance contract with its 42 percent equity holder, Leizing of Austria.

In a fifth of the joint ventures in the sample, a local company was the largest equity partner, a quarter of them holding a majority of the equity. Most of them produced for domestic markets, and were more likely to be in protected than open markets.

Box 5.3. Westel, Hungary: Successful FDI Through Development of Local Management

In 1990, Westel was awarded a concession to build and operate the first analog cellular telephone network in Hungary. Westel is a joint venture between US West and Matáv, the Hungarian state telephone utility. IFC helped finance expansion of the Westel network outside Budapest. By 1993, the national network was complete, and the company was well placed to compete with additional cellular operators from 1994.

Early in the project, US West provided Westel with a great deal of support in every area, including general management, finance, marketing, network design, and training. In the past five years, Westel has gradually turned into a company run almost entirely by Hungarians. Local managers and staff have handled all further technical and marketing development. The strong Hungarian management team, well trained in western managerial and marketing skills, is complemented by a well-trained staff. This team developed by the sponsors has been a key factor in the success of Westel. It has given Westel a good understanding of the local culture and consumer behavior and has made it more responsive to the Hungarian business and operating environment. As a result, Westel's business is growing. Its success is exemplified by the transfer of the former General Manager and a large group of his managers and staff to lead Westel 900, a new business providing digital (GSM) cellular service. Today, Westel Radiotelefon and Westel 900 combined have 1,300 local employees and only one expatriate.

However, not all locally sponsored projects relied on protection: one in five was based on international competitive advantage, rather than protection. In some cases, local sponsors owned natural resources such as mineral deposits or timber and needed foreign partners' help in their exploitation. This was the case with the Rio Norte bauxite deposits in Brazil and the Fluobar minerals mine in Tunisia. However, most natural resource-based projects in the sample were foreign-sponsored.

The large number of joint ventures with minority FDI partners largely reflects policy restrictions on foreign ownership, which means that foreign investment and technology could only come in through minority partnerships with local companies. For example, international dry battery manufacturers did not set up production in Nigeria, despite high protection against imports

of dry batteries. However, in the 1980s a local investor was able to establish a successful battery manufacturing plant with technical support from a foreign battery producer which held a minority equity stake. Similarly, in 1978 Amoco was brought in as a technical partner and 10 percent equity holder in Temex, a PTA project in Mexico; ownership restrictions prevented international petrochemical companies from majority ownership in Mexico at that time.

Whether exploiting a protected market or a natural resource, or entering a competitive market, one of the most important motivations for seeking a foreign partner has been access to technology. Two thirds of locally sponsored projects involved either foreign management or foreign technical assistance contracts. Suppliers of technology may be reluctant to license their use to other companies, for fear of losing control over its use. To mitigate this risk, a technology supplier might become an equity partner in the company, with a seat on the Board, thus gaining access to information about the use of technology and some control over its use. For these reasons, when Pilkington glass supplied new glass production technologies to Viplamex, a Mexican glass producer, it took a 40 percent stake in the company. Such an arrangement is also attractive to the local partner who gains access to proprietary technology. Bringing in the technology partner as an equity partner helps balance incentives and rewards between the technology supplier and the local enterprise. For example, Tunisian pharmaceutical manufacturer Adwya struggled in its manufacture of generic drugs due to lack of support from product licensors. After another pharmaceutical company took an equity stake, the Tunisian company became better able to obtain technologies and market drugs locally (Box 6.1).

This approach is common in the chemicals and pharmaceutical industries. For example, when the Venezuelan state-owned petrochemical company, Pequiven, wanted to develop a plant venture (Pralca) to produce ethylene compounds for the domestic and regional market, it entered into a joint venture with the Olin Corporation of the United States, which provided technical assistance in design, construction, and operation of the plant. Olin was also a customer for the plant's output, as a partner in the adjacent ethoxylates company, Etoxyl.

The long and successful partnership between Akerland and Rausing of Sweden and Packages of Pakistan shows that ventures of this kind can be very successful (Box 6.8). Working together since 1957, they first introduced Tetrapak packaging to Pakistan and have continued to exploit A&R's technology to bring new products to the local market.

A fifth of the locally sponsored joint ventures involved day-to-day management by a foreign partner, often under a formal management contract. This is common in mining and tourism projects, where the local sponsor may possess the physical assets such as real estate or mining rights but not the management capacity to exploit them. Thus, the operation of all the hotels in the sample was under foreign management, even in the three projects where the local sponsor owned a controlling share of the equity. In Thailand, one of the foreign partners in Star Petroleum was contacted by the domestic sponsor to operate the oil refinery. In the Democratic Republic of Congo, the Sotexki textile plant and activities are managed under contract by Maurer Textiles of Switzerland, who holds a 25 percent equity stake in the company.

Local sponsors often seek foreign partners to help with international marketing, and export markets were the target of more than a quarter of the locally sponsored sample projects. Thus, when the China Bicycle Company wanted to expand export production, it invited Schwinn Bicycles Company of the United States to take 30 percent of the equity, with the intention of marketing up to 60 percent of the company's output in the United States through Schwinn (Schwinn's subsequent bankruptcy forced the company to make other arrangements—underlining the importance of careful partner selection). CMPC, a long-established Chilean pulp producer, formed Celpac, a joint venture with Simpson of the United States to help it develop new markets for its products there and in East Asia (Box 6.3).

Foreign and locally sponsored projects have similar success rates, with 75 percent and 70 percent, respectively, achieving financial returns greater than 10 percent a year. However, projects structured as joint ventures where foreign and local partners hold equal shares, have a markedly worse success rate, with only 58 percent of projects exceeding a 10 percent a year financial rate of return. This reflects the difficulties of joint ventures with equal shareholdings (Chapter 6).

IMPACT OF CHANGING POLICY ENVIRONMENT ON FDI PROJECTS

For many years the policy environment in most developing countries posed a number of obstacles to FDI (Chapter 4).

Pre-1980s. Before 1980 almost all IFC FDI projects were subject to policy constraints that affected their design and execution. Later projects began to benefit from more liberal policy frameworks. The defining characteristic of the earlier policy stance was a preference for domestic production over imports. This led to a mixture of import restrictions, quotas, and high tariffs that raised profits in home markets, while leading to overvalued exchange rates that depressed profits from exports. As a result, domestic producers could produce more profitably for domestic markets than for export, and, in fact, 69 percent of sample projects prior to 1980 were targeted mainly at domestic sales (Figure 5.6).

Figure 5.6. Export Orientation of Sample Projects (percent)

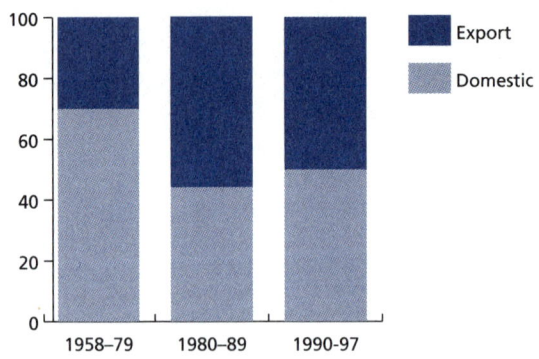

Source: IFC FDI Sample Database.

Businesses that use mainly power, unskilled labor, textile yarn, or other tradable or commonly available inputs and sell on international markets have great flexibility over where they base production. They can set up wherever the economic and regulatory regime provides a competitive advantage, which may be far from the source of some inputs and far from output markets. Unfavorable policy environments strongly influence these projects and can divert the investment to other healthier climates. The effect of this can be seen in the sample from pre-1980: only 19 percent of projects were started on the grounds that the host country was a competitive location to produce for domestic or export markets, in the absence of tariffs, quotas or other government controls (Figure 5.7).

These included food and agribusiness projects such as shrimp farming and tea production, and chemical production.

Figure 5.7. Rationale for Sample IFC FDI Projects (percent)

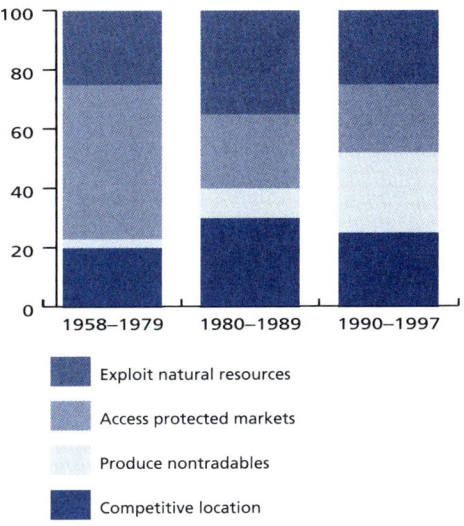

Exploit natural resources

Access protected markets

Produce nontradables

Competitive location

Source: IFC FDI Sample Database.

However, the existence of trade barriers meant that setting up production in the protected markets was the only way to be competitive in selling there. This was the strongest motivation for FDI projects in the IFC sample before 1980, accounting for 56 percent of projects. Examples include SKF Bearings' production of ball bearings in India, Dunlop's production of tires in Nigeria, and Suzuki's car production in Hungary and Pakistan.

A quarter of the sample projects were located in developing countries to exploit their natural resources—oil and gas, minerals, or, in the case of tourism, scenery and climate. These projects include oil exploration and production in Argentina (Hidra Oil), gold mining in Ghana (Ashanti Goldfields), and tourism in the Caribbean (Club St. Lucia).

Such activities are less sensitive to the policy environment, as they have less choice about where to locate. For example, gold can only be mined in a small number of countries. The same applies to many other mineral extraction projects, including oil and gas. It also

applies to some types of natural resource industries such as timber logging and agriculture. It is even true of tourism projects, which must be located where travelers want to go.

Resource extraction projects, especially oil and gas, typically source many of their inputs from abroad and sell in international markets. As a result, their linkages to the domestic economy may be tenuous, and governments often treat them as special cases for taxation and regulation. This sometimes leads to tighter regulation. Equally, it often enables foreign investors to negotiate specific terms for their investments in these sectors, which delink them from the general FDI framework. This has allowed resource extraction FDI to continue, even in countries where the general environment for FDI has been least attractive.

Governments historically gave a large role to the public sector in production, which crowded out private investment, including FDI, particularly in public infrastructure services such as roads, telecommunications, and water. Ownership restrictions also tended to be stricter on the provision of services such as commercial banking than on the production of tradable goods. Until 1980, IFC financed no FDI projects in nontradable sectors such as financial services or infrastructure.

Until recently, developing countries had placed a variety of restrictions on foreign ownership. These had explicitly or implicitly pushed foreign investors into forming joint ventures with local partners, either because it was a condition of investment or because it was the only way to invest while respecting limits on foreign ownership. Furthermore, ownership restrictions prevented foreign sponsors from holding a controlling equity stake in many projects; only 37 percent of pre-1980 IFC FDI projects had majority foreign ownership, and in 69 percent the main sponsor was a local investor. Only 7 percent of projects started prior to 1980 had more than 90 percent foreign ownership.

The proportion of foreign equity in IFC FDI projects has varied over time. In the early 1960s, two thirds of projects had majority foreign ownership. By the late 1960s and 1970s, many governments placed restrictions on FDI shares in equity; as a result, the number of IFC FDI projects with majority foreign ownership fell to a quarter in the late 1970s and early 1980s (Figure 5.8).

Figure 5.8. Proportion of Foreign Equity in IFC FDI Projects, 1962–97

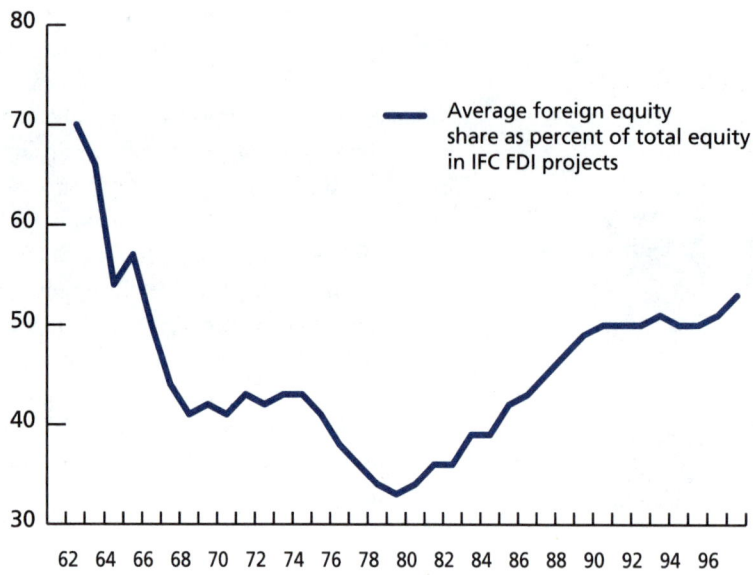

Average foreign equity share as percent of total equity in IFC FDI projects

Note: Based on five-year moving average.
Source: IFC MPD/SIS Database.

FDI projects are financed through a combination of foreign and local equity, foreign and local loans, and cash generation from current activities. Local financing provided 53 percent of the project costs for locally sponsored projects in the IFC sample, reflecting sponsors' limited access to international financing. Unsurprisingly, foreign-sponsored projects had greater foreign financing but still relied on local financing for an average of 32 percent of project costs. Local financing was highest in South Asia (64 percent) and the Middle East and North Africa (57 percent), reflecting both the relative sophistication of domestic capital markets and the relative lack of access to international capital markets. By contrast, the regions where sample FDI projects relied most on foreign financing were Sub-Saharan Africa (65 percent), reflecting very limited domestic capital markets, and Eastern Europe and East Asia, which have had relatively good access to international capital markets.

Foreign-sponsored projects relied on internal cash generation for 12 percent of project financing, compared to 4 percent of locally financed projects. This is partly due to limitations on repatriation of capital, which meant that foreign investors preferred to use funds already in the country instead of transferring in funds that might be hard to transfer out again. It also meant that profitable projects generated funds that could only

be used locally, and hence were an obvious source of financing. Locally sponsored projects relied more on loans, equity, and quasi-equity. Overall, foreign and locally sponsored projects had similar gearing, with debt-equity ratios around 2 to 1.

Figure 5.9. Sectoral Distribution of IFC FDI Projects by Value, pre-1980

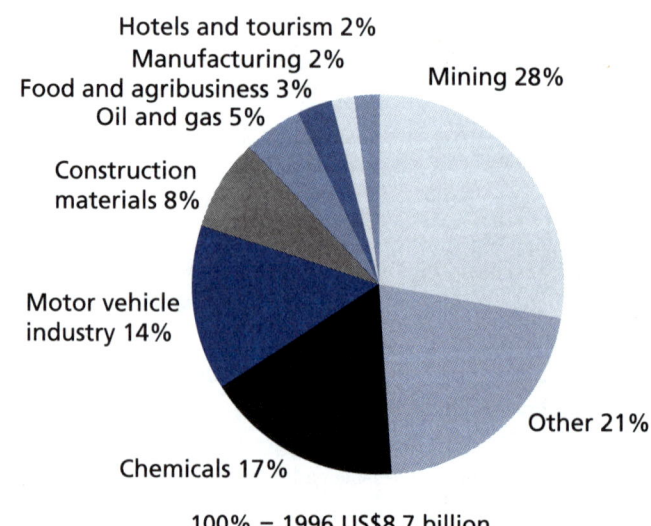

Hotels and tourism 2%
Manufacturing 2%
Food and agribusiness 3%
Oil and gas 5%
Construction materials 8%
Motor vehicle industry 14%
Chemicals 17%
Mining 28%
Other 21%

100% = 1996 US$8.7 billion

Source: IFC MPD/SIS Database.

Before 1980, the main sectors in IFC's FDI portfolio were mining, chemicals, (especially fertilizers and pesticides), and motor vehicles (including parts). Mining was drawn to developing countries despite barriers to FDI, due to the location of unexploited mineral and metal resources. The chemical (especially agricultural chemicals) and the motor vehicle industries were widely and heavily protected, as countries sought to build up what they saw as basic industries for their agricultural and industrial development (Figure 5.9).

Where markets are protected, market size and location of natural resources are the major factors driving FDI. At the same time, some countries placed greater restrictions on FDI than others. Notably, China was virtually closed to FDI before the 1980s. Thus, Latin America dominated IFC's FDI portfolio due to the large size of its markets and the resource extraction opportunities (Figure 5.10).

Figure 5.10. Regional Distribution of IFC FDI Projects by Value, pre-1980

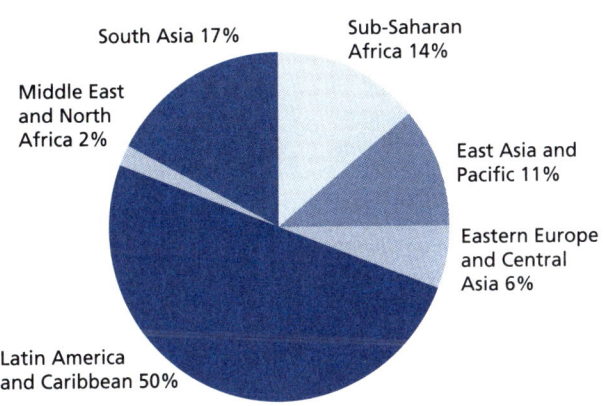

100% = 1996 US$8.7 billion

Source: IFC MPD/SIS Database.

During this period, 22 percent of the projects were classified as posing some problems for IFC's portfolio, compared to 77 percent that were implemented without any problems. Only 41 percent of IFC FDI projects in the pre-1980 period with calculated financial rates of return achieved a 10 percent financial rate of return (Figure 5.11). Moreover, 22 percent showed a negative financial return. This is significantly worse than for IFC's non-FDI projects of the same period, and below the average for all IFC FDI projects.

However, results have improved considerably in later time periods, with 78 percent of both FDI and non-FDI projects since 1990 achieving returns greater than or equal to 10 percent.

Figure 5.11. Performance of IFC FDI vs Non-FDI Projects (percent[a])

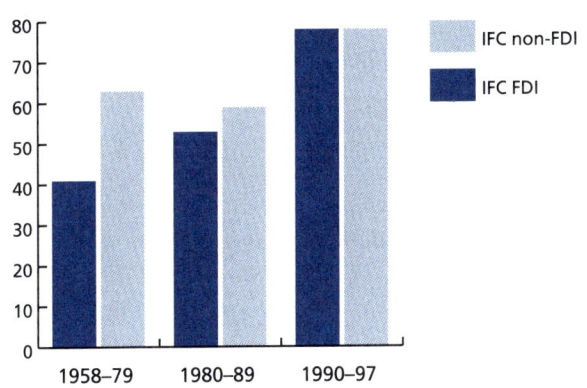

Source: IFC projects with calculated financial rates of return.
a. Percentage of financial rates of return greater than 10 percent a year.

The higher failure rate can be partly explained by the impact of different trade policy environments. Of sample IFC FDI projects selling into protected markets, 29 percent showed negative financial returns, compared with 20 percent of projects selling in open markets. Of sample projects in open markets, 70 percent showed a 10 percent a year or more rate of return, compared with 64 percent for projects in protected markets.

Projects relying on protected markets are vulnerable to changes in levels of protection. Furthermore, they are protected from the competitive forces of global trade which force companies to employ best-practice technologies and management techniques. Projects selling into open markets have to be globally competitive from the beginning and are under constant competitive pressure to maintain high standards. They are also less affected by changes in government policies.

Of these enterprises, 18 percent sold their products under some form of long-term contract or marketing arrangement, for example, under a concessional purchase agreement or to a partner company. Such arrangements provide some insulation from market risks. Market weakness was a factor in nearly half of the poorly performing projects in the portfolio. Thus, projects with some form of contractual marketing arrangement show a better than average performance, with 72 percent of projects exceeding 10 percent a year financial rate of return, compared to 69 percent for the whole sample. Before 1980, only 13 percent of sample projects were of this type.

Post-1980. Since 1980, IFC has seen a marked shift in the composition of its FDI portfolio in response to changes in the policy framework and new opportunities. These changes have become more pronounced in the 1990s, as policy liberalization and globalization of production have together led to a surge of new FDI flows to developing countries.

The greatest change has been in the market for FDI production. Instead of selling into domestic markets protected from international competition, IFC FDI projects are increasingly based on global competitiveness in domestic as well as export markets. This is reflected in the sample. Since 1990, 28 percent of sample IFC FDI projects have been based on international competitive advantage, compared to 22 percent still located in developing countries because of market protection (Figure 5.7). Excluding nontradable infrastructure projects, export orientation rose to 56 percent of sample projects in the 1980s, before falling back to 51 percent in the 1990s reflecting the emergence of investment in other nontradable sectors (Figure 5.6).

Meanwhile, liberalization and privatization have opened up new sectors to FDI, particularly nontradables such as financial services and infrastructure. IFC began investing in nontradable FDI projects in the 1980s, when they comprised 6 percent of the sample FDI portfolio; since 1990, nontradables have accounted for 25 percent of sample IFC FDI projects (Figure 5.7).

As governments have developed policies to attract private investment to new sectors such as infrastructure, they have developed regulatory frameworks that make greater use of contractual marketing arrangements, such as power purchase agreements from power stations, or concessions for telecommunications markets.[2] Under such arrangements, competition occurs in the award of market access for a set period. Such access is not necessarily exclusive; multiple licenses may be issued, and multiple supplier contracts negotiated. Nevertheless, those arrangements attenuate market risk. Although an element of price risk and counterparty risk persist, contractual arrangements can make them more manageable (for example, through use of insurance, guarantees or derivatives).

At the same time, the globalization of production networks has increased the proportion of trade conducted intra-firm or between affiliated firms with contractual relationships. Again, this reduces market risk, in that the commitment between seller and buyer is longer term than in open market sales. Of course, it does not insulate the enterprise from market risks that affect the whole supply chain.

Thus, the proportion of projects whose market risk is mitigated by some form of contractual marketing arrangement rose to 17 percent of the sample in the 1980s, and 22 percent of post-1990 projects (Figure 5.12).

Figure 5.12. Market Access for Sample IFC FDI Projects (percent)

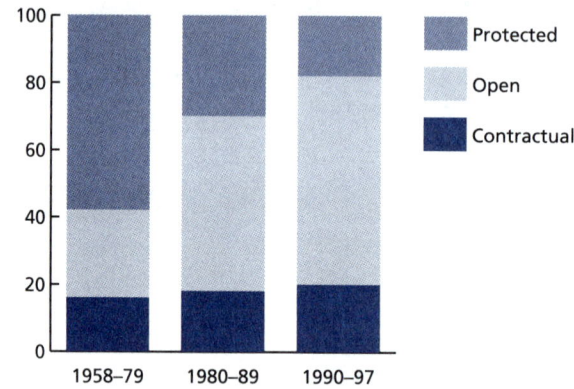

Source: IFC FDI Sample Database.

The evolution of policy framework is reflected in foreign equity shares (Figure 5.13). The average share of foreign equity projects in Eastern Europe and East Asia has increased by more than a third between 1980-89 and 1990-97. The share of foreign equity in IFC FDI projects in Africa rose slowly from 39 percent of equity (average of all IFC FDI projects, 1958-79) to 56 percent (1990-97), as the policy environment became less restrictive. Similarly, the FDI share of equity in the Middle East and North Africa has risen slowly but has not yet reached 50 percent. South Asia, however, averaged only 38 percent over all three periods. The only sector that has consistently averaged over 50 percent foreign equity has been oil and gas ventures, where foreign sponsor equity has averaged 54 percent.

Privatization has brought FDI into many industries that were previously state-owned. Privatization has

Figure 5.13: Average Foreign Equity Share, by Region

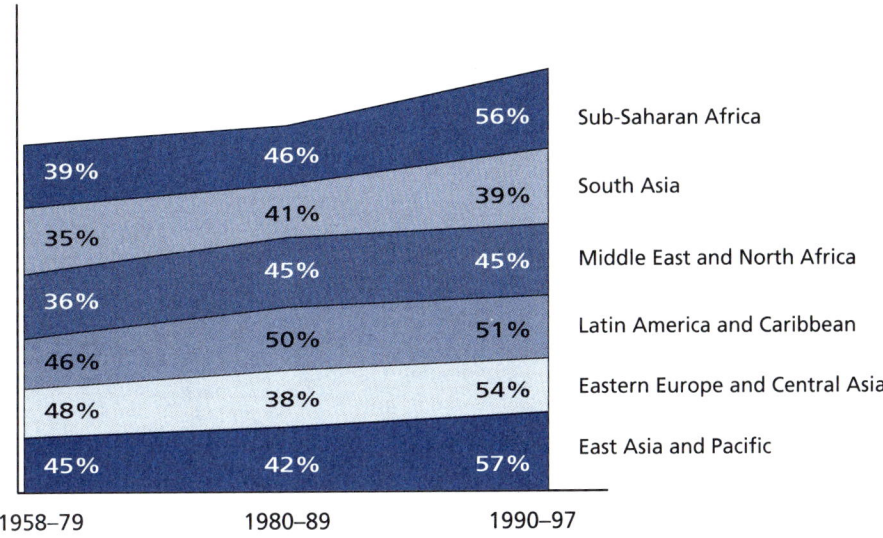

	1958–79	1980–89	1990–97	
Sub-Saharan Africa	39%	46%	56%	
South Asia	35%	41%	39%	
Middle East and North Africa	36%	45%	45%	
Latin America and Caribbean	46%	50%	51%	
Eastern Europe and Central Asia	48%	38%	54%	
East Asia and Pacific	45%	42%	57%	

Source: IFC MPD/SIS Database.

become a popular means to transfer these assets to sponsors with the capacity and the resources to run them more successfully. Twelve of the projects in the sample brought in FDI as a result of privatization. FDI went into infrastructure (gas, water, telecommunications, and transport), manufacturing (Mokra, a cement plant in the Czech Republic), and banks (BNI-Crédit Lyonnais–Madagascar).

These foreign investors not only bought out government equity in the project but also invested in new capacity. For example, the sale of the gas distribution network in Buenos Aires to Transconor, a U.S.-Canadian consortium, led to extension and upgrading of the system; the sale of CTC in Chile to Telefonica of Spain led to a doubling in the number of telephone lines in four years. Philips invested heavily in the lighting factory it purchased in Poland, safeguarding 3,000 jobs, and increasing sales per employee by 93 percent over three years. FDI through privatization also brings in new management and technologies. When Crédit Lyonnais acquired BNI–Crédit Lyonnais–Madagascar from the government of Madagascar, it introduced new working methods and computer systems, and retrained staff (Box 6.6).

Impact on IFC's FDI portfolio. These trends are reflected in IFC's project portfolio. As other regions

have become more open to FDI, IFC has diversified away from Latin America, which accounted for more than one in three projects and over half of project costs up to 1979 (Figure 5.10), to only one in four projects, and 24 percent of project costs since 1990 (Figure 5.14). The other big shift in regional composition has been toward Eastern Europe and Central Asia, where the number of IFC projects rose from 6 percent in the

Figure 5.14. Regional Distribution of Projects by Value, 1990–97

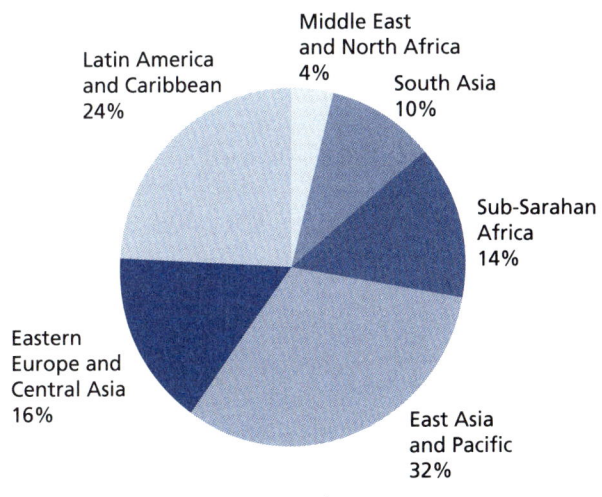

100% = 1996 US$35.4 billion

Source: IFC MPD/SIS Database.

1980s to 25 percent in the 1990s, and project costs from 3 percent to 5 percent. Most East European transition countries joined IFC as part of their process of reengaging with the international financial system. While the number of projects in East Asia rose to 19 percent of all IFC FDI projects, project cost increased markedly in the 1990s, due to the improved policy environment for major infrastructure investments. Between 1990 and 1997, they accounted for one third of the cost of IFC FDI projects.

Liberalization and globalization have led to striking changes in the sectoral composition of the IFC FDI portfolio. For example, chemicals accounted for 17 percent by value of all IFC FDI projects between 1958 and 1979, but only 8 percent since 1990, as countries have moved away from efforts of self-reliance toward free international trade in fertilizer. Similarly, investments in motor vehicles have fallen from 14 percent to 3 percent, as the industry has globalized. Fewer countries restrict imports and thereby provide the basis for separate production in each market. Since 1979, as developing countries have opened more sectors to foreign investment, including infrastructure and financial services, IFC's FDI activity in these areas has expanded, especially since 1990. Infrastructure investments, less than 1 percent of IFC's FDI portfolio before 1990, have been 29 percent since. Within the extractive sectors, mining has fallen in volume from 28 percent of the portfolio before 1980 to 11 percent since 1990, while oil and gas extraction and refining have risen from 5 percent before 1980 to 19 percent since 1990 (Figure 5.15).

As the nature of the portfolio has shifted, its performance has also changed (Figure 5.16). Performance declined in the 1980s, due to economic dislocation in developing countries after the collapse of commodity prices and the onset of the debt crisis. Volatile interest and exchange rates in developing countries and contraction of domestic and export markets affected IFC's entire portfolio to a degree, but FDI projects were affected more due to their greater exposure. Since 1990 the portfolio ratings have been better than ever, with 85 percent classified as posing no problem and only 7 percent regarded as posing some problems, compared to 22 percent before 1980. This means that after a deterioration in the 1980s, the FDI portfolio again compares in quality with the overall IFC project portfolio. [3]

Figure 5.15. Sectoral Distribution of IFC FDI Projects by Value, 1990-97

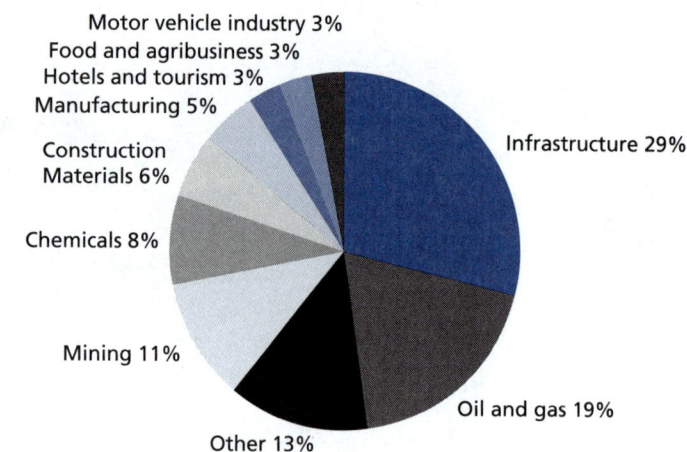

100% = 1996 US$35.4 billion

Source: IFC MPD/SIS Database.

The financial rates of return have also improved since 1980. Since 1990, 93 percent of IFC FDI projects have had positive financial returns, 78 percent exceeding 10 percent. Again, this suggests that FDI projects are no longer inferior to other IFC projects.

Analysis of the sample of projects sheds light on the reasons for the improved performance. The proportion of foreign-sponsored projects exceeding 10 percent a year returns has increased from 71 percent before 1980 to 77 percent since 1990. Thus, foreign-sponsored projects appear to have benefited from the improved investment climate.

Liberalization of trade regimes has enabled IFC to benefit from the higher returns of FDI in open markets. Apart from the 1980s, 80 percent of the projects selling into open markets showed returns above 10 percent, compared to 57 percent of projects selling into protected markets. At the same time, the increase in projects with contractual marketing arrangements (for example, power stations with power purchasing agreements, cellular phone companies with service licenses) has helped returns. Since 1990, 88 percent of such projects have shown returns above 10 percent. Thus, the changing mix of FDI investments has clearly improved project performance.

Figure 5.16. IFC Portfolio Ratings of FDI Projects

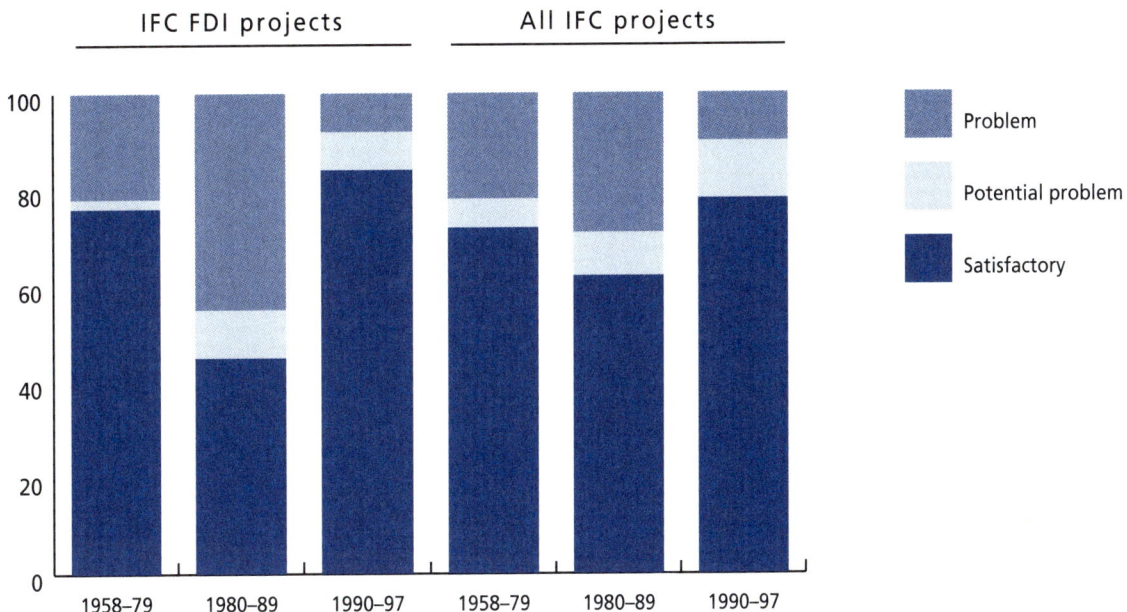

Source: IFC MPD/SIS Database.

LESSONS OF EXPERIENCE

Review of IFC's portfolio of FDI investments across a wide range of countries and sectors, in different periods, shows that:

1. IFC has helped bring FDI to the poorest, riskiest locations.
2. Successful FDI projects may have dominant foreign or local partners, but equal partnerships do relatively poorly.
3. The performance of IFC investments has been affected by the policy environment, which has influenced the market orientation of projects and their ownership and management structures.
4. Economic liberalization since 1980 has led to a reorientation of FDI investments toward production for the global economy, and toward provision of infrastructure, and has improved their performance.

Notes

1 Throughout this chapter projects are dated by the IFC fiscal year (July–June) in which they commenced (first commitment of IFC funds).
2 For a detailed discussion, see Financing Private Infrastructure, Lessons of Experience 4 (Washington, D.C.: IFC, 1996).
3 Portfolio ratings are given either at time of exit from the IFC portfolio, or if still in the portfolio, as of December 1996. Projects less than one year old are excluded from this exercise.

6

GETTING PROJECT STRUCTURES RIGHT

Like all ventures, FDI projects are exposed to a range of project risks.[1] Weak markets, weak management, government controls, and cost overruns are the four most frequently cited causes of poor performance in the sample of IFC FDI projects (Figure 6.1). The very nature of FDI projects increases the risks in several ways. First, cross-border investments pose additional informational challenges. Implementation delays, cost overruns, and misjudgment of market prospects are more likely when investors are less familiar with the business environment. Second, cross-border business has extra hurdles to navigate, caused by trade, capital, and labor restrictions, including policies specifically directed at FDI (Chapter 4).

JOINT VENTURES

Limits on foreign ownership in many countries have left foreign investors with little alternative to joint ventures. Ninety percent of IFC's foreign direct investment (FDI) projects are joint ventures between foreign and local partners. Within these joint ventures, government regulations often prevent the foreign partner from holding a majority stake. As a result, when ownership restrictions are liberalized, foreign investors usually move to increase their ownership and control of joint ventures. This is what happened in India after the liberalization of ownership restrictions in 1991, and more recently in China.

Foreign investors unable or unwilling to invest without local partners are more likely to need IFC participation to reduce risk and help structure and manage the partnership. Foreign investors considering joint ventures in developing countries find that bringing IFC into the partnership can reduce project risk. This is particularly true of joint ventures with government or public enterprises, where IFC's multilateral status puts it in a strong position to negotiate with governments and act as an honest broker between government's and foreign investor's interests. Governments often welcome IFC playing this role, too.

Figure 6.1. Causes of Poor Performance of Projects with Financial Rate of Return < 10 percent

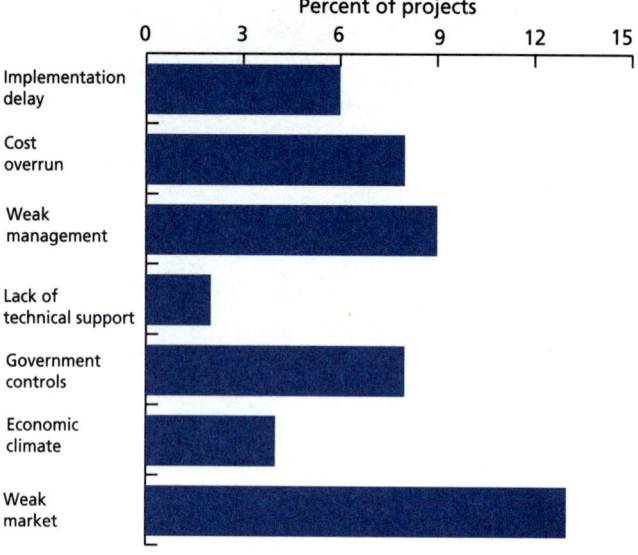

Joint ventures are a common form of corporate structure, both within countries and across borders. Although products and services can usually be purchased through arm's-length agreements, parties sometimes prefer joint venture arrangements. They can increase suppliers' control over the use of their technology, brand names, and other proprietary items and give them a tangible share in the success of the enterprise. For the local sponsor, joint ventures can be a way to ensure the supplier's interest in the success of the enterprise instead of only in selling the service or product. For both parties, a joint venture spreads around the risks and rewards.[2] For example, Adwya, a pharmaceutical producer in Tunisia, struggled under licensing arrangements, but prospered after forming a joint venture with a foreign partner (Box 6.1).

For foreign sponsors, bringing in a local partner in a joint venture can sometimes reduce project risk in several ways. First, it can reduce the financial commitment of the foreign sponsor and cross-border transfers of resources. Second, the local partner can help reduce

Box 6.1. Adwya, Tunisia: Equity Stake Increases Technical Partner Commitment

The government of Tunisia opened the pharmaceuticals market to private producers during the 1980s. A group of Tunisians formed Adwya in 1983 to exploit the opportunity to manufacture brand-name drugs to compete with imports. They initially held 54 percent of Adwya's equity; domestic financial institutions and IFC held the rest.

When IFC invested in the project in 1986, Adwya was negotiating license agreements with six major international pharmaceutical houses to manufacture and sell their products in Tunisia. A new manufacturing facility, constructed at a cost of $10 million, was completed in December 1990, 18 months late. Sales had begun in December 1989 but built up very slowly. By the end of 1990, Adwya was selling only 9 products, instead of the 25 originally planned. The company was pinched for cash, and fell behind on loan service.

During the construction period, two of the intended licenses fell through, and a third was canceled when the licenser decided to set up its own production facility in Tunisia. The sponsors negotiated replacement licenses with two new companies. As a result, the project design had to be repeatedly altered to match the changing product mix. The sponsors' financial and technical management of project implementation was weak, and the licensers did not rush to complete the project because their profit margins were larger from continuing to sell their products as imports. Profitability was further damaged by licensers' increases in input prices.

In 1990, one of the licensers, Rhône-Poulenc, bought 17 percent of the equity, introducing FDI into the project. The company provided a finance director and technical support. By 1991, two thirds of Adwya's products were licensed from Rhône-Poulenc. Production and sales picked up, Adwya became profitable in 1992, and cleared its loan arrears. In 1993 IFC sold its 10 percent equity stake to Synthelabo, bringing in a second FDI investor. By 1995, Adwya was making 71 products and held 13 percent of the Tunisian household drug market, with a 13 percent operating margin. From a shaky start, it has emerged as a successful company. The change in relationship with the technology suppliers from licenser to direct investor was the catalyst for this improvement.

risks to the venture, through greater familiarity with the local business climate, government policies, and economic conditions. Third, a local partner can help mobilize additional local financing and may have better access to land.

More recently, globalization has given companies further reasons for forming closer relationships across borders. International integration of production, supply, and marketing chains makes companies more reliant on their partners' performance. For this reason, joint ventures have increased in popularity as a means of integrating international production and marketing structures, together with other forms of contractual relationships.[3]

As a weak form of business structure, however, joint ventures have a high failure rate. Because joint ventures are dynamic relationships, the basis for the intercorporate marriage can change considerably over time. Both sides need to sustain comparative advantages in the relationship, or their absence, on either side, will cause the venture to be less successful or, at the extreme, to fail.

An IFC study of 70 joint ventures in six developing countries (Argentina, Brazil, India, Mexico, Philippines, and Turkey) found that joint ventures are fragile affairs, difficult to negotiate and to maintain. It saw choice of a complementary partner as the key to success. A well-designed agreement can lay the foundation for a fruitful partnership. Technology transfer was found to be one of the more sensitive and difficult issues.[4]

Half of the joint ventures surveyed in the study resulted from government restrictions on ownership. This may have contributed to the difficulty one third of the potential partners had in negotiating equity structure agreements. The study found difficulties in negotiating management structures for joint ventures and later problems in assuring clear management control, particularly as the interests of the partners evolved. Disputes were common over product line, sourcing of raw materials, and the use and cost of technology.

In view of the scope for disagreement within these partnerships, government regulation to force foreign direct investment into joint ventures impairs the investment quality unless the business reasons for the venture are sound. In the first place, foreign investors often simply decide not to invest under such restrictions. Second, they may seek other ways to obtain control, for example, through diversified local shareholdings, or they may choose local partners who are willing to be passive investors instead of for their ability to contribute to the enterprise.

Such approaches make equity holdings by local investors unattractive, as they may be excluded from key management decisions, and are poorly placed to ensure that they receive a fair share of company profits. They also negate much of the intended benefits of enforcing local participation in FDI projects, for example, transfer of technology or learning by doing.

Alternatively, IFC and other international agencies have sometimes been brought into projects to hold a balance of equity, giving the foreign sponsor effective control, without breaching foreign ownership ceilings. For example, the Capuava carbon black project in Brazil proceeded with 49 percent government and foreign ownership (by CS Cabot), with IFC holding the balance.

Third, limitations on foreign equity holdings shift incentives for the investor away from earning a return on equity, to profiting from the enterprise as a contractor or a customer. Investor commitment to the enterprise is weakened, with adverse effects for the enterprise (below).

Governments sometimes insist that FDI projects include a public enterprise as a partner to ensure that government shares in the profits of the enterprise and has a say in its operation (Chapter 4). This is particularly common in the oil and gas and mining sectors, where governments want to capture economic rents. In Côte d'Ivoire, for example, all mining investments have to be made through joint ventures with the state mining company, SODEMI.

Working under these arrangements is particularly difficult for joint ventures. Public enterprises commonly have other objectives besides profitability, or their commercial decisions come under political pressure. Rarely do they have much freedom to raise capital or to contribute additional funds to the joint venture.

Thus, in Tunisia, the Fluobar mining project had a majority public enterprise partner, with a minority FDI partner. It suffered a 44 percent cost overrun in construction, as the management responded to the public enterprise's concerns for generating employment and pursuing low-priority investments. In Guinea, the

Box 6.2. Zambia Hotels, Zambia: Consequences of a Lack of Agreed Project Management Responsibilities

Zambia Hotel Properties (ZHP) owned two five-star hotels: a business hotel in Lusaka, and a tourist hotel in Livingstone, next to the Victoria Falls. ZHP was a joint venture of a Zambian parastatal, NHDC, and an international hotel operator. NHDC was the dominant partner, with 80 percent of the equity, but contracted with the international partner to operate the hotels.

In the early 1980s, the sponsors decided to refurbish and expand the two hotels to meet strong demand for quality hotel services. Financing was assembled for a $30 million expansion by 1983. However, the sponsors disagreed over project management: the local sponsors wanted to manage the construction work themselves; the foreign sponsor wanted to hire a project manager. After much delay, it was eventually agreed that NHDC would handle the work at Livingstone, and a project management firm was engaged for the Lusaka hotel. Further delays arose because the parastatal partner had to go through the National Tender Board in letting contracts for work.

Project implementation was heavily controlled by NHDC, and the main contractor was another parastatal, ZECCO. Monitoring of the work was poor, and the project was never completed, nor were projects costs fully accounted for. The quality of the work done was of variable quality, and the intended standard of hotel service was never achieved.

In the meantime, a general economic downturn put pressure on hotel revenues, and ZHP became technically insolvent. NHDC was itself wound up, and its holdings transferred to the Directorate of State Enterprises pending privatization, leaving the foreign sponsor without a domestic partner. The operator's equity stake became worthless, but it continued to receive remuneration for its management contract.

Box 6.3. Celpac, Chile: Strengths and Weakness of a Joint Venture Equal Partnership

When CMPC, a long-established Chilean pulp producer, wanted to expand pulp production for export, it looked for a foreign technical partner to share the risk and provide international marketing skills. It linked up with Simpson, a U.S. pulp and paper producer that markets its products internationally, particularly to East Asia. Together, CMPC and Simpson formed a joint venture company, Celpac, in which each sponsor holds equal shares, with IFC holding the remaining 2 percent. This structure was chosen because neither party wanted to give the other management control. Celpac's managers were recruited from both CMPC and Simpson, which also provided limited technical support. The pulp was to be marketed through Simpson in the United States and the Far East, and through CMPC in Europe.

Celpac built a modern pulp mill and related infrastructure, close to budget and schedule. The plant historically has run well, achieving the sponsors' goal of becoming one of the world's lowest cost softwood kraft pulp producers. Celpac quickly established itself in the international market as a producer of high-quality pulp, and its managers have been successful in negotiating difficult market conditions for pulp sales.

Nevertheless the sponsors' differing viewpoints have complicated management decisions about marketing and capital increases, but neither party wants to buy out the other. The even split of ownership between the domestic and foreign partner has resulted in stalemates on some key management decisions. In this case, IFC's balancing equity share enabled it to play a constructive role in brokering agreements between the joint venture partners.

Aurifere gold mining project and the Aredor diamond mining project ran into trouble because the public enterprise joint venture partners were unable to meet additional financing needs. The Zambia Hotel Properties project also illustrates some of the trials and tribulations of working with a public enterprise partner (Box 6.2).

Joint ventures with equal shareholdings can lead to deadlocked decision making. For example, Celpac in Chile was a 50-50 joint venture. As the venture evolved, the views of the two partners diverged. With neither party dominant, or willing to sell to the other partner, strategic choices became difficult to make (Box 6.3). IFC can play a helpful role in such partnerships by holding the balance of equity and acting as honest broker between the parties. For example, the Sariville tourism resort project in Turkey was implemented successfully with the foreign partner (which provided the management) holding 40 percent of the equity, the local partner (which provided the land and buildings) holding 40 percent, and IFC the remaining 20 percent.

LIMITS ON FOREIGN OWNERSHIP

Not surprisingly, the strongest theme that comes through from review of the sample of IFC's FDI projects is the importance of sponsor commitment to the long-term success of an enterprise. Hence, government restrictions on ownership that reduce sponsor commitment are especially damaging to the enterprise. When a sponsor is not fully committed, problems can arise over decisions to devote financial and managerial resources to an enterprise.

Financial resources. Project financing needs frequently change, often requiring additional investments. Without strong commitment, a sponsor may not want to make additional investments, particularly if they conflict with its exposure guidelines. For example, a plantation project in Southeast Asia struggled after a

new owner that did not want to invest in plantations bought out the sponsor (Box 6.4). Once this stake was resold to a sponsor more strongly committed to plantation development, project performance improved. Conversely, the Conrad Hotel in Istanbul needed additional financing to defray construction cost overruns, and received additional financing from its international technical partner, Conrad, because it initially had a 40 percent equity stake in the hotel. Likewise, the Dusa nylon yarn project in Turkey was supported by the foreign partner (du Pont), when construction delays led to cost overruns.

Lack of financial resources to provide this kind of support is one of the main drawbacks of forming joint ventures with governments or public enterprises. Often, their initial equity contribution is in kind and does not provide working capital. If additional financing is needed, public enterprises are often unable to provide it.

For example, when Pancontinental Mining of Australia and Acec-Union Minière of Belgium developed the Koron and Didi gold deposits in Guinea, the government took a 50 percent stake in the joint venture as a means to share revenues from the mine. Development costs turned out to be higher than anticipated, but the government had difficulty funding its share of additional financing despite the project's remaining financially attractive, with a projected financial rate of return of nearly 50 percent. Although the government's inability to fund was not the main reason for the project's ultimate failure, it resulted in serious delays in project implementation and forced a financial restructuring involving rescheduling of debt.

Managerial resources. A sponsor who is not fully committed to a project may refuse to make difficult management decisions, thus jeopardizing project success. For example, in the case of Shenzhen Y.K. Solar Energy in China the priorities of two foreign sponsors diverged: one wanted to concentrate on selling equipment while the other wanted to stay on top of emerging technology. When the foreign technical sponsor ran into financial difficulties and could no longer keep its commitment to the project, the other foreign investor was not in a position to take on the responsibility. As a result, the project ran into technical difficulties and has proved to be a financial drain on its shareholders.

In another example, the Adwya pharmaceuticals project in Tunisia succeeded only after a foreign technical partner took a significant equity stake in the enterprise (Box 6.1). Proteison, a vegetable oil processing project in Mexico, had widespread local shareholding and a foreign partner with only a 25 percent shareholding. When it ran into problems, it was difficult to get shareholder agreement to restructuring.

Restrictions on foreign ownership can prevent the foreign investor from having full control of project management. This can lead to disagreements over management arrangements, which can spell trouble, particularly where major revisions are needed.

When a Japanese engineering company tried to enter the heavy engineering market in a South Asian country in the 1970s, government restrictions on foreign ownership forced it to do so as a minority partner in joint ventures. Its first venture was in shipbuilding in partnership with a local company. Although the Japanese company was the technical partner, it was not able to exercise effective control over the venture. Decisions by the local partner such as negotiating sales contracts at prices below direct costs compromised the viability of the venture. After running continual losses, the joint venture was liquidated.

In Mexico, a joint venture between several local partners and an FDI partner was established in the 1970s to produce chemicals. A local partner, a consumer of the venture's production, opposed increases in product prices sought by other partners. At the same time, the venture's technical partner, a foreign minority equity partner, was unhappy because the venture's products competed with its own products in export markets. This led to management conflicts during the first year after project completion until the partners agreed on marketing and pricing arrangements.

Government policy often reduces the flexibility needed to make a joint venture work, for example, by responding promptly to changes in costs and market developments by adjusting their financing structure or product mix. However, FDI regulations have often required time-consuming government approval for changes in ownership structure, location, or new products.

Box 6.5. A Southeast Asian Resort Hotel: Ownership Restrictions Encourage Foreign Investor to Earn Profits on Side as Contractor

Southeast Asia's natural beauty and rich culture make it a prime tourism destination. To this region, an international hotel operator brought a tried and tested formula for successful beach resorts. It constructed a 700-bed resort hotel through a local subsidiary. IFC was brought in to provide long-term loan finance. To comply with government regulations, the operator also sought local equity investors for the venture, with limited success. It therefore took 75 percent of the equity, with the balance held by the national tourism development corporation and two local financial institutions. Government FDI policy required ventures to become 51 percent locally owned within a set period. The operator therefore envisaged eventual flotation of the venture on the local stock exchange.

The hotel was constructed to a very high standard, and opened on time in 1986. Construction and operating costs were higher than anticipated, due to adverse exchange rate movements and rapid increases in local labor costs. Nevertheless, the resort was a success from the start, with high occupancy rates. Since the hotel offered all-inclusive packages, little revenue was generated at the hotel itself. The operator sold resort packages through its international marketing company. It paid the hotel 50 percent of the revenue, but this was no more than necessary to cover operating costs. Thus, none of the profits reached the local subsidiary. Local shareholders received no dividends, the government little tax revenue, and the subsidiary was only able to stay current on its debt service through advances from the hotel operator.

Partners often have other interests in a project besides their equity stake. To take one common example, an equity partner may also be a contractor to the enterprise. Limits on foreign equity participation can mean that the foreign investor can earn a better return as a contractor to the joint venture than as an equity holder. Thus, when a hotel operator invested in a Southeast Asian country, government regulations forced it into a joint venture with local partners. However, it was able to benefit from its marketing contract with the venture instead of solely from its equity stake in it (Box 6.5).

When a mobile telephone operator established a joint venture with IFC and other partners to provide cellular telephony in an African country, the project partners did not include covenants concerning related businesses. Although the joint venture proved profitable for all shareholders, the operator was able to capture a larger share of returns by establishing an international gateway to the network as a separate wholly owned company.

Even without any contractual relationship, equity partners may have other means to profit from a project besides the return on equity. For example, local investors may have adjacent land holdings, which will benefit from the development of agriculture, tourism, or industry. Foreign partners may be more concerned about the profitability of their global brand than the profitability of any single affiliate. Thus, in the case of Zambia Hotels, the hotel operator maintained its branded product mix (room decor, hotel facilities) even after it proved unprofitable in the Zambian market. This may have been good for the operator globally, but it was not good for Zambia Hotels.

Despite all these problems, IFC experience shows that with careful design, FDI projects can succeed even in less than perfect policy environments (Chapter 5). The key to success lies in taking account of policy-imposed constraints and structuring the project to maximize its effectiveness within these constraints through appropriate management arrangements, clear financing arrangements, and careful handing of each partner's interest as a contractor with the enterprise or as a holder of related assets.

Clear lines of management control are important to ensure adequate involvement in management by the technical partner. Government policy permitting, the simplest way is for the technical partner to take a controlling equity stake in the enterprise. Thus, the privatization of the commercial bank BNI-Crédit Lyonnais-Madagascar gave Crédit Lyonnais 51 percent of the equity. This gave them the management autonomy to upgrade banking practices (Box 6.6).

Where government restrictions mean that the technical partner cannot hold a controlling share of the enterprise, a management contract can allow the controlling shareholder to delegate day-to-day management to the technical partner. Management contracts, clearly defining the technical partner's responsibilities, have governed many of IFC's most successful FDI projects.

Box 6.6. A Commercial Bank in Madagascar: The Value of Management Control by an Experienced Technical Partner

BNI-Crédit Lyonnais-Madagascar was created in 1976 as part of the nationalization of the banking sector. It was the first bank to be privatized in 1991, when Crédit Lyonnais acquired 51 percent of the equity. The privatization has been a success, despite difficult economic conditions. Once a moribund bank, saddled with bad debts and facing grim economic prospects, today BNI-Crédit Lyonnais-Madagascar is a sound bank well placed to take advantage of improvements in Madagascar's economic situation.

When Crédit Lyonnais took over the management of BNI-Crédit Lyonnais-Madagascar, it standardized the bank with the rest of the Crédit Lyonnais International Group, upgrading working methods and computer systems and retraining staff. The presence of a strong sponsor has been a necessary but insufficient condition for the project's success. A strong sponsor is effective only after appointing a seasoned management team, well versed in the sponsor company's methods and able to adapt them to local circumstances. Strong management, totally committed to its strategic plan, has protected BNI-Crédit Lyonnais-Madagascar's commercial viability from potentially damaging outside interference from, for example, the government. BNI-Crédit Lyonnais-Madagascar's management has succeeded where others have failed, by sticking to a tried and tested formula. Its experience in setting up and managing new and existing operations enabled it to take over management of the bank with a minimum of disruption.

For example, a hotel in Southeast Asia was managed by its main sponsor under a management contract. Management achieved an operational cohesiveness that has been partly responsible for the hotel's successful opening and for the fast building up of its occupancy and profits. Although only 8 of the 600-plus staff were brought in from other hotels owned by the sponsor, locally hired staff received thorough company training (Box 6.7). The Philagro coconut mill project in the Philippines was owned equally by Filipino and Indian investors, reflecting government restrictions on foreign ownership, but a minority (21 percent) partner, Tungabhadra Industries of India, managed the mill under contract.

Box 6.7. A Southeast Asian Hotel: Strengths and Weaknesses of a Foreign Management Contract

In 1991, an Asian hotel operator decided to build a 260-room, international standard resort hotel on a beach in a newly developing tourism region of a Southeast Asian country. It would be the country's first luxury resort hotel. The project equity was 80 percent owned by the foreign sponsor, and 20 percent by local portfolio investors. Managers from the sponsor company were responsible for project management.

Unexpected difficulties with land titling, site preparation, lack of water, and poor contractor performance delayed the hotel's opening. Escalations in payments to contractors and project managers increased construction costs by 50 percent. Preopening expenses were excessive, since staff were hired and marketing launched before the hotel was ready to open. These failings partly reflected the expatriate project managers' limited knowledge of, and adaptability to, local conditions for construction.

Nevertheless, the finished hotel met very high standards of esthetics, comfort, and style. Soon after opening in 1993, it achieved high occupancy rates and above average operating margins. The hotel's opening coincided with a spurt of visitor arrivals in the country. Led by the success of the hotel, six more resort hotels have opened or are planned.

The success of the project rested principally on the foreign sponsor's experience, widely known international brand, and marketing expertise.

Box 6.8. Packages, Pakistan: Success Through Effective Technical Partner Support

Packages began producing paper board and packaging in 1957. It was originally majority owned by a Pakistani family who brought in a Swedish company, Akerland and Rausing (A&R), as a minority equity partner. Subsequently, much of the equity has been offered to the public, but the family retains control; A&R's minority stake has been taken on by Stora, a Swedish holding company, which until recently owned A&R.

In addition to its equity stake, A&R provided technical assistance and training in return for a royalty on sales. Financial and operational management has been the responsibility of the Wazir Ali family. This arrangement proved itself over many years, as Packages has expanded its line of paper products and built a very successful business. The advances in technology provided by A&R have kept the company at the high end of the domestic market, maintaining profitability despite increasing competition. For example, it introduced "Tetrapak" paper cartons for milk and other perishable liquids, capturing much of the Pakistani market from glass containers. A&R still has a technical services contract with Packages, but now based on an annual retainer plus fee for service.

The success of this business can be attributed to the local sponsors' integrity and good business sense. Their financial resources, allowing problems to be handled as they arise, their good managerial ability, their forward looking attitude, and good technical support from the FDI partner have kept the company on the leading edge of its market.

Alternatively, a clear technical assistance contract can ensure adequate support from the foreign technical partner. Thus, Packages, a Pakistani paper products company, has prospered under local management with strong technical support from a foreign minority partner under a technical assistance contract (Box 6.8).

RESTRICTIONS ON CAPITAL TRANSFERS

Like limitations on foreign ownership, limitations on repatriation of equity earnings reduced the incentive to ensure that the joint venture generates a return on equity. Many countries have limited transfers of equity earnings, either as a permanent measure or in response to balance of payments problems. These have had the effect of reducing the value of enterprise profits to the foreign investor.

Investors often respond by not investing, out of concern that they could not subsequently repatriate the returns from the investment (Chapter 4). Sometimes investors respond by rearranging the company's affairs to transfer value through other means such as contractual arrangements with the parent company. In this way, parent companies can treat subsidiary companies as "cost centers" instead of "profit centers." This means that they do not try to earn profits on their investment in the subsidiary but benefit from the services or products the subsidiary provides.

For example, a hotel operator transferred the profits from a subsidiary operating a Southeast Asian hotel to its international marketing company by means of a revenue-sharing formula that allocated only enough sales revenue to the subsidiary to cover hotel operating costs (Box 6.5). It is also a common approach with processing facilities such as aluminum smelters.

Each partner brings different contributions and interests to a joint venture partnership, but the agreement has to be structured at the outset to allow for the inevitable adjustments in the balance of interests over time. Since sponsors finance many joint ventures as separate projects, off balance sheet, after the initial capitalization there may be no automatic provision for meeting further financing needs. That is why enough financing should be provided at the beginning to cover contingencies. Because off-balance sheet status also means that surplus funds are not automatically available to the sponsors, the sponsors may prefer not to overcapitalize the venture initially, but provide further injections of capital if needed. This makes it vital that sponsors agree in advance on provisions for injecting and withdrawing capital.

Shareholder agreements for capital withdrawal can allow orderly replacement of a foreign investor, if investor or project objectives and constraints change. Because IFC's objective is to turn over its holdings to maximize its development impact, it usually negotiates exit arrangements before taking equity. Such agreements can include put options or agreement to a public offering. Alternatively, investors may take forms of quasi-equity. Since such agreements depend on the ability of the parties involved to meet their commitments, their financial strength should be carefully assessed.

IFC's project experience suggests that cost overruns, often closely related to delays in project implementation, are the most common divergence from joint venture plans in a developing country. Of the sample of projects, 27 percent suffered serious delays and 22 percent, major cost overruns. That is why the joint venture agreement must define responsibility for meeting cost escalation during the implementation phase. Otherwise, projects can slip into a vicious cycle of delay leading to cost overruns, as the sponsors negotiate how to meet the additional costs.

The most straightforward way of dealing with cost overruns is through a Project Funds Agreement (PFA), signed when the joint venture is established (Box 6.9). This defines responsibility among partners for meeting project cost increases in a timely manner until the pro-

Box 6.9. Project Funds Agreements

For investors in a joint venture, the risk of "non-completion," of a project's not becoming fully operational, is increased by the possibility that completion costs may exceed the funds invested in the venture. Additional funds would then be needed promptly to ensure completion without undue delay. One way of managing this risk is for joint venture partners to agree beforehand on a Project Funds Agreement. This predefines the responsibilities of investors for providing additional funds (including working capital) needed to complete the project. Completion is usually defined in three dimensions: physical completion, operating verification, and financial completion.

Physical completion means finishing the physical structures of the project, including acquiring all equipment, suppliers, and consumables needed for operation.

Operational completion means that the project can do what it was meant to do: that all permits, licenses and other government permissions have been obtained and that the project has actually operated at a specified capacity for a given period, predicting a satisfactory output. This is more difficult to define than physical completion. Usually, operational completion tests are defined in terms of units of output of commercial quality.

Financial completion ascertains that there is sufficient working capital in the project. This requires a financial audit at project completion.

Project Funds Agreements should not only allow parties to call for additional funds once it becomes evident that the project will not be able to meet the completion tests. Additional funds can be provided in the forms of equity, quasi-equity such as deeply subordinated and perhaps convertible loans, or by shareholder advances. The choice will depend upon existing debt-equity ratios, the ability of partners to provide different forms of financing, and the importance of preserving the existing distribution of equity between the partners.

ject is up and running. Alternatively, the sponsors may provide full or partial guarantees, or other forms of completion agreement. The risk of cost escalation can also be reduced by contracting out construction under a fixed-price contract.

Box 6.10. UCAL Fuel Systems, India: Arms-Length Transactions Confer Competitive Advantage

In 1989, Mikuni of Japan formed a joint venture with Carburetors Limited (CL) of India to manufacture carburetors and fuel pumps, based on Mikuni technology. The main customer for these products was Maruti, an Indian car maker, which was a 60-40 joint venture with Suzuki of Japan (now 50 percent owned by Suzuki).

The sponsors hold equal stakes in UCAL. Two thirds of CL's equity contribution was in the form of a transfer of land, buildings, and machinery to UCAL. The land and buildings were transferred at market value, as determined by independent valuations, and the machinery, which was all unused, was transferred at book value. Under the Heads of Agreement, UCAL committed to undertake all transactions on an arms-length basis and to obtain its indigenous capital equipment and machinery from the cheapest and most reliable sources. Most of the imported machinery was to come from Mikuni, which agreed to lock in price quotations.

The effectiveness of these procurement arrangements is evident from the flexibility that UCAL was able to show during the implementation phase in substituting domestic equipment for imported equipment and manual equipment for automatic equipment, and to adapt to changed market circumstances. It sourced a significant quantity of machinery from India, instead of from Mikuni, without sacrificing performance parameters. It was also able to substitute manual or semi-automatic systems for fully automatic systems in a number of instances, thus saving capital costs without jeopardizing operational requirement. UCAL estimates that its capital costs were about half those of an equivalent-sized Japanese plant as a result of capital and import substitutions, while its labor productivity is about 80 percent of the Japanese level.

The management team was drawn from CL, assisted by two Mikuni executives. Mikuni felt that this enhanced the value of its stake in UCAL. The company has been well managed throughout, and no problems or disputes have arisen between the sponsors. The relationship between Mikuni and UCAL's in-house R&D capabilities has not only encouraged a constant transfer of technology from Mikuni to UCAL but has also enabled UCAL to adapt it efficiently to Indian conditions. For example, UCAL's R&D department developed an all-aluminum two-wheeler carburetor based on Mikuni's zinc and aluminum design, which was lighter and hence more fuel efficient, and which also avoided the need to import zinc. The two companies coordinate closely, and Mikuni tests all critical components in Japan.

The project has enabled Maruti to improve the efficiency of domestic component sourcing and lower its exposure to yen-rupee parity changes. UCAL's carburetor costs Maruti about 30 percent less than the Mikuni import and about 15 percent less than European substitutes. Since the relationship between the partners was well defined and balanced in the Heads of Agreement that each party signed at the outset, management was able to adjust the project configuration to keep up with rapidly changing conditions and brought the project in very close to the budget and target dates.

PFAs have played an important role in keeping many IFC projects on track. For example, the Mexinox steel project in Mexico built a facility for cold-rolled stainless steel products. Unexpected site problems and delays in procuring equipment delayed construction. Thanks to a Project Funds Agreement, the six local and two foreign shareholders provided timely additional equity financing, which covered the additional pre-production costs and allowed successful implementation of the project. Similarly, lengthy start-up problems at the Cosigua steel project in Brazil led to a 100 percent cost overrun, but a Project Funds Agreement between the Brazilian and German partners promptly made additional financing available.

Where an equity partner is also a contractor to or customer of the venture, or holds related assets, conflicts of interest are hard to avoid. However, other equity holders should be aware of related interests and adopt appropriate decision-making procedures to ensure that enterprise decisions are not unduly influenced by them. IFC frequently includes covenants in project agreements requiring arm's-length treatment of transactions between affiliated companies and sometimes requires the project company to handle all related business so as to avoid "creaming off" profitable aspects of the business to affiliate companies. This eliminates the possibility of transferring value to partner companies at the expense of joint venture profits but at the expense of weakening links to partner companies. Since much FDI is explicitly intended to develop and exploit synergies between partner companies, this approach is clearly not always appropriate.

In India, UCAL Fuel Systems gained considerable competitive advantage from a joint venture agreement that allowed the company to source capital equipment and machinery from the cheapest and most reliable source, not necessarily from the sponsors (Box 6.10).

Contracts related to the profitability of the enterprise can help align the interests of the contracting partner and other joint venture partners. In Poland, Chemagev is a joint venture between U.S. real estate and engineering companies and a Polish state-owned construction company. It owns an office and retail complex in the heart of Warsaw. One of the minority U.S. partners is the leasing agent, who is compensated by a fee based on the lease revenue over the life of the leases. This has proved to be a strong motivator to get the best lease terms, and the building is very profitable. Similarly, Akerland and Rausing's technical assistance contract with Packages was originally remunerated by a royalty on sales (Box 6.8).

Cross shareholdings in partner parent companies can provide another means of ensuring that all partners share project returns. IFC sometimes takes equity or some other form of profit participation in the parent company, if it is to be heavily engaged in transactions with the project company. If this is not possible, partners may negotiate exit values for their investment by means of put options to sell the equity to the other partners. This provides a guaranteed floor to future equity values, while allowing the partner to share in gains in equity value from the project.

Other forms of quasi-equity such as redeemable preference shares, subordinated loans, and income notes can also be used to assure partners of dividend streams, while maintaining participation in risks and rewards. IFC uses put options and a range of quasi-equity instruments to secure an appropriate share in the returns on its investments.

Even with limited equity stakes, sponsor commitment is possible when the project is important to a sponsor's broader interests. A foreign investor's global business interests will be more important to its bottom line than any particular investment, however large its stake in it,

Box 6.11. Magyar Suzuki, Hungary: A Strong, Committed Foreign Sponsor Can Reorient a Project to Achieve Success

In 1991, Suzuki launched a joint venture with a consortium of Hungarian state-owned automotive component producers to build Hungary's first car assembly plant. Low-cost, small cars were to be assembled, at first mainly for domestic sale. In the next five years, European component content would be raised to exceed the 60 percent threshold at which the cars would gain quota-free access to the European Union (EU). At this stage, EU sales of this model would be sourced from Hungary rather than Japan. Hungary would then replace Japan as the source for Suzuki's EU sales of this model.

A greenfield plant was built near Budapest with a capacity of 60,000 cars per year. Suzuki provided a small number of expatriate managers to train local staff. Staff were also sent to Japan for varying periods of time. Car production was launched successfully in 1993 and soon met Japanese quality and productivity standards. However, domestic sales were disappointing due to slower than expected economic growth and strong competition from imported second-hand cars. At the same time, appreciation of the yen increased the cost of Japanese components and yen-denominated debt. Consequently, sales and profit margins were low, and the company rapidly accumulated losses.

Confronted by these problems, the foreign sponsor injected more equity to repay most of the company's long-term debt, particularly yen-denominated debt, and accelerated domestic component sourcing. By mid-1994, production met the local content threshold for unrestricted sales to the EU. In 1995, Suzuki transferred sourcing for EU sales of this car to Hungary. The restructuring plan has led to increased sales volumes and increased profitability.

This experience underlines the importance of strong sponsor support and commitment to a project's ability to survive adverse circumstances. The foreign sponsor's commitment to the project was substantial both in terms of equity contribution and in terms of operational support, reflecting its strategic commitment to the project's success.

as in the case of Zambia Hotel Properties (Box 6.2). Equally, a local investor may have other business interests that are more important than the success of an individual enterprise.

Conversely, a partner may invest time and money to turn around a project that is initially unsuccessful if it meets its wider business goals. Thus, Suzuki weathered adverse market developments in Hungary to establish profitable car manufacturing plants (Box 6.11). Likewise, Volvo do Brazil became profitable after initially difficult trading conditions, with strong support from its Swedish parent. In both cases, the FDI investment was important for the parent company's broader strategy of globalizing production. A sponsor is also more likely to stay committed to a project if it needs the enterprise to succeed as a supplier of inputs or as a market for outputs.

CONCLUSIONS

IFC's project experience reveals the impact of the policy conditions under which the projects were implemented. Restrictions on foreign shareholding and capital transfers, for example, created obstacles that, while not insurmountable, weaken project structure and reduce competitive efficiency. Together, they reduce the flows of foreign direct investment and its benefits.

Review of a sample of IFC FDI investments shows that:

1. Restrictive policies have forced FDI investments into relatively weak joint venture structures.
2. Limits on foreign ownership and capital transfers have been counterproductive, reducing the contribution of foreign investment and weakening project performance.
3. Careful attention to project structuring and implementation arrangements is key to sustained good performance.

Notes

1 The project examples used in this chapter are drawn from IFC's FDI portfolio.
2 J.H. Dunning, Multinational Enterprises and the Global Economy (Wokingham, U.K.: Addison-Wesley, 1993).
3 For an earlier description of cross-border corporate relationships, see C. Oman, New Forms of International Investment in Developing Countries (Paris: OECD, Development Center, 1984).
4 R. R. Miller, "International Joint Ventures in Developing Countries," IFC Discussion Paper 29, Washington, D.C., 1996.

7

GETTING MORE
FROM FDI

Eager to increase investment and economic growth, a growing number of developing countries welcome foreign direct investment (FDI) as one way to do it. In the past, however, some developing countries have been skeptical of FDI's benefits, based on some of its supposedly negative characteristics. These concerns focused on:

- adverse balance of payments impact if dividend and royalty repatriation exceed inflows of capital
- loss of tax revenue through use of transfer pricing to reduce declared profits
- creation of enclaves with few ties to the domestic economy
- impaired development of domestic firms through direct competition, abuse of market power, and political influence
- loss of economic sovereignty through dependence on the actions of foreign investors.

RESTRICTIVE ECONOMIC POLICIES CAN BOOMERANG

Though intended to address these concerns and capture greater benefits from FDI, restrictive policies often deterred it instead (Chapter 4). When FDI did occur, restrictive economic regimes reduced its benefits to the domestic economy through deadweight costs of regulation, economic costs of protection, inefficient project structures, encouragement of transfer pricing to repatriate profits, and fiscal losses from unnecessary tax incentives.

Costs of regulation. Government regulations and policies that impair efficient business operations reduce the return to both investors and the economy. This is a "deadweight loss"—everybody loses. Complex regulations for establishing and running foreign enterprises are of this type (Chapter 4). If an economically beneficial investment is delayed or diverted to another country as a result, the country loses out.

Costs of protection. The overall economic framework influences the economic efficiency of financially viable enterprises. If government intervention distorts prices and markets, the foreign enterprise may make profits but at a cost to the economy. Protection of the domestic market is the most common cause of this. Though often intended to promote domestic industry by raising the profits from domestic production of protected goods, it encourages FDI, even where the scale of production means that producing locally costs more than importing. Domestic consumers pay higher prices which become increased profits for foreign investors. Unlike high profits for domestic enterprises, which are a transfer between citizens, foreign profits are a direct cost to the country. Liberalization of markets and trade policies reduces the potential for such projects to harm the domestic economy.

When FDI enterprises were established behind tariff barriers, they were often designed to produce for an uncompetitive local market instead of serving as a base for internationally competitive production. This allowed industries to develop with obsolete technologies and with limited linkages to international markets, instead of bringing the host country the new technological and marketing links that governments wanted to encourage. Often, lower import tariffs on intermediate than on final goods encouraged foreign enterprises to import inputs at a lower tariff for final assembly in the host country to avoid the higher tariff on finished goods. In many countries, domestic car assembly began using imported kits containing all the necessary parts.

Costs of restrictions on project structures. Regulations that affected the structure of foreign ventures often resulted in less viable ventures and inefficient forms of business organization, reducing their benefits to the economy (Chapter 6). Joint ventures with local firms formed simply to satisfy government requirements for local partners often led to weakly structured projects and ineffective management. Such restrictions also weakened sponsor commitment to a long-term presence in the economy. They encouraged foreign enterprises to enter markets more to make money selling or buying from the local company instead of benefiting from the success of the enterprise. Foreign investors of that mindset were less likely to promote linkages to the

domestic economy than an investor who was in the country to stay.

Costs of restrictions on profit transfers. Policy frameworks restricting the open transfer of profits out of a country that limited a foreign investor's equity holdings in an enterprise, or which placed heavy tax and regulatory burdens on enterprises that declared profits, served to encourage alternative means to extract profits. In particular, transfer pricing was sometimes manipulated to enable repatriation of profits and reduce the foreign investor's tax payments to the host government. Accounting standards and tax enforcement were often too lax to prevent these practices.

Restrictions on transfer of profits and equity shares sometimes stemmed from a mistaken concern that profits transferred out of the country cost the country a net loss. If successful investment did not transfer more back to the investor than was originally invested, however, there would be no motive to invest. The host country still benefits from the surplus above the profit that the investor needs to earn as a reward for investing. These benefits can come as returns to any domestic equity holders or as profits earned by any related domestic enterprises. Moreover, investors often choose to reinvest profits in the host country. Studies of individual countries suggest that on average a third of FDI flows consist of reinvested profits.[1]

Costs of tax incentives. Even without channels for sharing benefits, the host country can gain on taxes collected from the enterprise. That is why policymakers should not negotiate away too much tax revenue through incentives and should ensure tax compliance.

Governments often try to compensate for unattractive economic and regulatory policies by providing fiscal incentives to FDI. Here, governments sometimes forgo revenue without getting the consequent benefits from FDI. For example, in countries with high import taxes, investors that import equipment often seek waivers of import duties. If an enterprise does not generate enough taxable profits, waivers are not recouped.

Partly as a result of these inefficiencies, developing countries sometimes thought they had to intervene to promote linkages to domestic firms (Chapter 4). But these policies have generally been counterproductive, either deterring FDI altogether or reducing its efficiency.

Recent economic liberalization has led not only to rapid increases in FDI flows to developing countries but has also provided the framework for improved investment quality. FDI projects in liberal environments are more likely to be oriented to global markets and based on international competitiveness (Chapter 5). In this way, FDI draws developing countries into the global economy, raises standards across the host country's economy, and leads to transfers of technology and management techniques, according to one study. FDI boosted growth in eight Pacific basin economies where distortions were low but had a negative effect in other countries with less favorable economic environments.[2]

When enterprises can freely choose their ownership structures, sponsors will be more strongly committed to enterprise success and more oriented to maximize profits instead of profiting through contractual links (Chapter 6). With secure access to domestic and export markets, property, local labor, and capital markets, foreign investors become more committed to a long-term presence in a country. Investors who plan to stay in a country will be more willing to make long-term investments such as upgrading infrastructure and training staff. They will also take pains to develop connections with local suppliers and purchasers. Without bothersome taxation and transfer restrictions, enterprises have less incentive to distort their operations to reduce their taxes or repatriate their profits.

THE UNFINISHED AGENDA

The obstacles to foreign direct investment take time to remove (Chapter 4). Although many countries have taken some measures to encourage FDI, few have completed the whole agenda of policy reform. Developing countries are in three stages of the reform process: some are leading FDI hosts, others are emerging FDI hosts, and some countries have not started to promote FDI.

Leading FDI hosts. Having removed the major impediments to FDI, Chile, Indonesia, Malaysia, and other liberalized countries receive large amounts. Even within this group of countries, however, some sectors or industries remain effectively closed to FDI. These exceptions include industries still dominated by state enterprises or heavily regulated by government, for example, infrastructure and financial services. The case study of Indonesia (Annex 4A) shows that sometimes successive rounds of reform may be needed to move toward an open environment for FDI. Often, only after one constraint is removed does another become apparent.

Emerging FDI hosts. Countries such as Brazil, Ghana, and India have taken a number of important steps toward creating an enabling environment for FDI, but significant obstacles persist. These obstacles keep the FDI flows below their potential, although, as in Brazil, they are already substantial. For this group, further efforts to identify and alleviate remaining obstacles are the key to achieving increased FDI (Chapter 4).

Pre-emergent FDI hosts. Still other countries have yet to take the first steps to reorient their policies to attract FDI under a liberal economic framework. Some of them receive some FDI because of their abundant natural resources or large, protected markets and may therefore not see the need to change. Others have not yet made the policy decision to attract FDI. These countries face the most challenging programs of reform, since action may be needed on a number of fronts before a significant pick up in FDI can be expected (Chapter 4).

Thus, across most developing countries, a large unfinished agenda of reform remains. These later reformers can learn from the experience of early reformers which policies most need attention.

The pace of integration into the global economy is related to progress on creating an enabling policy environment for FDI (Chapter 1). Further progress on this unfinished agenda can therefore be expected to lead to increases in FDI to reforming countries. Although the pace of reform will continue to vary from country to country, the overall direction of change is expected to remain strongly oriented toward more liberal frameworks. This process is self-reinforcing, as initial reforms lead to expanded FDI flows that encourage further reforms. Moreover, later reformers seeing the benefits of strong FDI flows already accruing to early reformers, receive encouragement to persist.

Progress on the broad agenda of structural reform and liberalization is beginning to pay off in improved economic growth prospects in developing countries. As a result, developing countries should grow twice as fast as developed countries over the next decade.[3] This, too, will encourage additional FDI flows.

Unlike earlier FDI flows, which often exploited inefficiencies in developing countries, these new FDI flows are more likely to be oriented toward efficient production for global markets (Chapter 1). This generates momentum for further investment, both domestic and foreign, to maintain competitiveness. As leading producers increase their efficiency through global production patterns, their competitors will be driven to follow suit to maintain their competitiveness. In this way, whole industries will go global, in much in the same way as the motor vehicle industry already has.

Globalization of production will increase pressure on governments to address policy impediments to investment in order to avoid losing share in world production. This is already prompting heightened international discussions on multilateral policy regimes toward investment. For example, policymakers are negotiating a Multilateral Agreement on Investment within the Organization for Economic Cooperation and Development. Other nonmember countries could accede to such an agreement, too.

The prevalence of two-way flows of inputs, products, and finance between affiliated companies in different countries is one aspect of global integration. The broad international composition of enterprise financing is another. For example, FDI is frequently combined with financing from domestic markets. As barriers to international capital flows fall, and capital markets in developing countries improve, foreign and domestic finance increasingly convene in global enterprise financing. Companies raise money where the terms are best and invest where the returns are highest.

These developments are eroding the distinction between foreign and domestic enterprises. Attempts to provide differential policies for domestic enterprises become increasingly difficult to sustain. For this reason, Indonesia and a growing number of other countries offer domestic and foreign enterprises a single standard of treatment (Annex 4A). This will further improve the environment for FDI.

The rise of outward investment by developing countries is another characteristic of recent FDI patterns (Chapter 2). For example, the Chile Telecom Corporation (CTC) is investing in cellular telephony in other Latin American countries (Box 2.5). Beginning with flows to other developing countries, particularly within regions, FDI is starting to flow toward developed countries, too. This reflects the delinkage between the location of an enterprise and its financing. Developing-country companies that meet

global standards can increasingly access finance on international capital markets. This means that scarcity of capital in home countries is less and less a constraint on expansion.

In the future, FDI is likely to become less a vehicle for capital transfer, which capital markets will achieve much more easily, and more a vehicle for transfer of global knowledge, systems, and technologies. Multinational enterprises will continue to develop as a means for generating economies of scale in core services, including technology and knowledge that can be shared throughout the enterprise. But this sharing is becoming a two-way street, too. Technology is not simply transferred from developed to developing economies. What developing-country subsidiaries learn will increasingly be transferred back to parent companies, too.

Even after taking relative size into account, differences in the policy framework perpetuate wide disparities in the distribution of FDI flows (Chapter 2). This leaves enormous scope for FDI to flow to countries, sectors, and regions as yet untouched by globalization, with attention to policy reform. This does not imply a diversion, but rather an augmentation, of FDI flows. Extension of the reach of FDI in developing countries will expose a greater proportion of their economic activity to the potential for integration into global production and service standards. This will both benefit consumers in developing countries and enable developing countries to compete effectively in global export markets.

LESSONS OF EXPERIENCE
Four main lessons emerge from IFC's experience with FDI in developing countries:

1. Appropriate policies are the key to capturing foreign investor interest. Government policies and regulations toward FDI should be enabling, not restricting. Wider economic policies and regulations also matter, especially a liberal trade and payments regime. Across the developing world stretches a large unfinished agenda of policy reform, to create a more welcoming environment for FDI.
2. Paradoxically, attempts to regulate FDI to increase benefits to the host country and to reduce the costs tend to have the opposite effect. Countries gain most from FDI in a liberal policy framework.
3. Careful structuring is the key to project success.

This is more difficult in restrictive policy environments. Joint ventures are inherently fragile but can be successful with appropriate structuring. Limits on foreign ownership impede effective project structuring: forced partnerships, particularly with public enterprises, are hard to make work.

4. With better policies, even countries currently considered risky by the market can succeed in attracting FDI flows. Global integration will continue to drive FDI flows—wherever the economic environment is open to it.

Notes

1   *United Nations,* World Investment Report 1996: Investment, Trade and International Policy Arrangements, *New York, N.Y., 1996.*

2   *M. Fry, "Foreign Direct Investment in a Macroeconomic Framework: Finance, Efficiency, Incentives and Distortions," World Bank Policy Research Working Paper 1141, Washington, D.C., 1993.*

3   *World Bank, Global Development Finance, Washington, D.C., 1997.*

BIBLIOGRAPHY

Aharoni, Y. 1966. *The Foreign Investment Decision Process.* Boston, Mass.: Harvard Business School.

Battat, J.; I. Frank; and X. Shen. 1996 "Suppliers to Multinationals." *FIAS Occasional Paper 6*, Washington, D.C.

Beamish, P.W. 1988. *Multinational Joint Ventures in Developing Countries.* London: Routledge.

Belot, T., and D. R. Weigel. 1992. "Progress in Industrial Countries to Promote Foreign Direct Investment in Developing Countries." *FIAS Occasional Paper* 3, IFC and MIGA, Washington, D.C.

Bergsman, J., and W. Edisis. 1988. "Debt Equity Swaps and Foreign Direct Investment in Latin America." *IFC Discussion Paper* 2, Washington, D.C.

Borenzstein, E.; J. de Gregorio; and J. Lee. 1995. "How Does Foreign Direct Investment Affect Growth?" *NBER Working Paper* 5057, Cambridge, Mass.

de Soto, H. 1989. *The Other Path.* New York, N.Y.: Harper & Row.

Dunning, J.H. 1993. *Multinational Enterprises and the Global Economy.* Wokingham, U.K.: Addison-Wesley.

Frank, I. 1980. *Foreign Enterprise in Developing Countries.* Baltimore, Md.: Johns Hopkins.

Fry, M. 1993. "Foreign Direct Investment in a Macroeconomic Framework: Finance, Efficiency, Incentives and Distortions." *World Bank Policy Research Working, Paper* 114, Washington, D.C.: World Bank.

Guisinger, S., and Associates. 1985. *Investment Incentives and Performance Requirements.* New York, N.Y.: Praeger.

ICSID. 1997. *Bilateral Investment Treaties.* Washington, D.C.: ICSID.

IFC. 1996. *Financing Private Infrastructure.* IFC Lessons of Experience 4, Washington, D.C.

——. 1996. *Leasing in Emerging Markets.* IFC Lessons of Experience 3, Washington, D.C.

——. 1995. *Privatization: Principles and Practice.* IFC Lessons of Experience 1, Washington, D.C.

Megyery, K., and F. Sader. 1996. "Facilitating Foreign Participation in Privatization." *FIAS Occasional Paper* 8, Washington, D.C.

Michalet, C.A. "Investment Strategies of Multinational Corporations and the Attractiveness of Host Countries." *FIAS Occasional Paper*, Washington, D.C. Forthcoming.

Miller, R.R. 1996. "International Joint Ventures in Developing Countries." *IFC Discussion Paper* 29, Washington, D.C.

Mintz, J.M., and T. Tsiopoulos. 1992. "Corporate Income Tax and Foreign Direct Investment in Central and Eastern Europe." *FIAS Occasional Paper* 4, Washington, D.C.

Oman, C. 1984. *New Forms of Investment in Developing Countries.* Paris: OECD.

Pangestu, M. 1995. "Evolution of Liberalizing Policies Affecting Investment Flows in the Asian Pacific." Paper prepared for the FIAS High-Level Roundtable on Competition for FDI—Implications for Asia and the Pacific. Processed.

Sader, F. 1995. "Privatizing Public Enterprises and Foreign Investment in Developing Countries 1988–93" *FIAS Occasional Paper* 5, Washington, D.C.

United Nations Conference on Trade and Development. Annual. *World Investment Report*, Geneva.

——. 1996. *Companies Without Borders: Transnational Corporations in the 1990s.* London: International Thomson Business Press.

Weigel, D.R. 1970. "Restrictions on Dividend Repatriation and the Flow of Direct Investment to Brazil." *Journal of International Business Studies* (Fall), pp 35–50.

Wells, L.T., and A. Wint. 1991. "Facilitating Foreign Investment." *FIAS Occasional Paper* 2, Washington, D.C.

——. 1990. "Marketing a Country." *FIAS Occasional Paper* 1, Washington, D.C.

World Bank. Annual. *Global Development Finance.* Washington, D.C.

——. 1992. *Legal Framework for Treatment of Foreign Investment.* Washington, D.C.: World Bank.

APPENDIXES

Appendix A. Net Foreign Direct Investment Flows to Developing Countries, 1970–95 (1996 US$ million)

Region/Country	1970	1971	1972	1973	1974	1975	1976	1977	1978	1979	1980	1981	1982	1983	1984	1985	1986	1987	1988	1989	1990	1991	1992	1993	1994	1995
East Asia and the Pacific																										
Cambodia																							36	60	76	153
China													471	707	1,436	1,976	2,300	2,752	3,631	3,778	3,796	4,733	12,159	30,746	37,056	36,279
Fiji	25	24	30	44	29	26	0	0	0	13	39	38	40	36	27	26	10	14	36	9	87	16	54	32	71	68
Indonesia	325	521	726	44	-100	879	630	396	431	297	194	139	246	324	253	369	317	458	655	759	1,190	1,607	1,937	2,239	2,313	4,400
Kiribati														-1												
Korea, Democratic People's Republic of																										1
Lao People's Democratic Republic																				2	7	8	9	134	65	89
Malaysia	368	375	399	483	1,153	648	698	683	773	753	1,007	1,325	1,530	1,400	911	827	600	503	818	1,857	2,540	4,334	5,649	5,594	4,769	5,870
Mongolia																					2	9	9	11	10	
Myanmar															1	0	0	-2	0	9	5	0	3	4	4	10
Papua New Guinea							38	33	60	58	81	90	94	154	132	99	111	111	175	226	169	220	320	-2	-5	458
Philippines	-98	-4	-42	154	7	182	241	355	156	9	-114	180	18	117	10	14	156	365	1,064	627	577	590	248	1,383	1,745	1,496
Samoa																	1	1	0	0	8	3	5	6	3	3
Solomon Islands						15	9	7	7	5	3	0	1	0	2	1	4	12	2	13	11	16	15	17	19	17
Thailand	169	146	239	218	381	41	145	179	86	73	205	304	209	388	458	194	322	418	1,257	1,977	2,661	2,183	2,303	2,016	1,498	2,093
Tonga																	0	0	0	0	0	0	1	2	2	2
Vanuatu													8	7	8	5	2	15	12	10	14	27	28	29	33	31
Vietnam												19	14						9	4	17	35	26	28	110	152
Subtotal	789	1,063	1,353	943	1,470	1,790	1,760	1,654	1,513	1,207	1,415	2,096	2,631	3,133	3,239	3,513	3,822	4,647	7,661	9,275	11,081	13,773	22,804	42,298	47,770	51,132
Europe and Central Asia																										
Albania																							22	65	58	71
Armenia																										8
Azerbaijan																										111
Belarus																							8	11	16	20
Bulgaria																					4	61	46	61	115	137
Croatia																								83	107	82
Czech Republic																					225	434	654	731	963	2,599
Estonia																							89	181	235	203
Former Yugoslavia												14	0	20	-9	18	-34	8	25	10	73	129	101	89		
Greece	196	157	194	174	136	45	558	652	661	804	725	545	478	488	554	532	578	812	1,031	837	1,094	1,230	1,247	1,092	1,076	1,066
Hungary																						1,585	1,612	2,626	1,255	4,573
Kazakhstan																							109	168	203	287
Kyrgyz Republic																									11	15
Latvia																							32	50	235	182
Lithuania																							11	13	34	74
Macedonia, Former Yugoslav Republic of																										
Malta	45	43	16	15	21	29	26	31	33	21	29	41	23	27	30	23	27	23	46	58	50	83	44	63	132	99

Appendix A (continued)

Region/ Country	1970	1971	1972	1973	1974	1975	1976	1977	1978	1979	1980	1981	1982	1983	1984	1985	1986	1987	1988	1989	1990	1991	1992	1993	1994	1995
Moldova																							19	16	13	65
Poland							11	8	39	39	11	19	15	18	32	18	20	14	17	12	97	315	739	1,916	2,056	3,703
Romania																						43	84	105	374	424
Russian Federation																							763	782	699	2,041
Slovak Republic																								222	223	185
Slovenia																								126	140	178
Tajikistan																									11	15
Turkey	227	169	152	221	129	211	18	45	53	98	19	100	60	51	129	118	153	137	402	738	745	878	920	711	667	896
Ukraine																							218	223	174	270
Uzbekistan																							44	50	55	116
Subtotal	469	369	362	410	287	285	613	737	786	963	784	717	576	604	736	709	743	995	1,522	1,942	2,288	4,759	6,760	9,385	8,852	17,422

Latin America

Region/ Country	1970	1971	1972	1973	1974	1975	1976	1977	1978	1979	1980	1981	1982	1983	1984	1985	1986	1987	1988	1989	1990	1991	1992	1993	1994	1995
Antigua and Barbuda	43	41	34	27	19			4	-11	11	21	23	25	6	5	19	28	46	35	46	66	60	22	17	27	25
Argentina								242	386	270	731	877	249	206	306	1,095	704	-23	1,304	1,145	1,999	2,644	2,785	3,891	661	1,335
Barbados	34	60	61	16	5	42	13	8	14	7	3	9	5	4	0	6	9	8	13	9	12	8	15	10	11	12
Belize															-4	4	6	8	16	21	19	15	17	10	16	21
Bolivia	-297	7	-37	13	52	99	-15	-2	18	46	51	79	34	8	8	12	12	45	-11	-27	12	27	38	28	22	152
Brazil	1,650	2,006	2,090	3,876	2,678	2,406	2,845	3,086	3,099	3,174	2,061	2,639	3,187	1,733	1,824	1,606	393	1,457	3,375	1,411	1,077	1,196	2,246	1,444	3,369	4,917
Chile	-310	-247	-4	-13	-1,124	92	-2	35	280	320	230	401	439	150	89	136	142	274	160	1,435	642	567	762	904	1,945	1,715
Colombia	169	161	65	67	83	69	46	109	165	167	169	278	401	687	667	1,219	827	379	231	641	544	495	795	1,072	1,828	2,531
Costa Rica	103	83	90	106	93	128	113	105	75	57	57	73	32	67	64	83	75	95	139	113	177	193	246	276	327	401
Cuba																					1	11	5	4	5	7
Dominica													0	0	3	4	3	12	8	9	14	16	23	15	24	12
Dominican Republic	281	243	152	97	108	118	110	120	98	22	100	83	-2	54	78	43	61	106	121	122	145	157	196	213	145	274
Ecuador	347	606	283	147	155	176	-36	58	75	83	76	63	44	56	57	74	86	89	91	89	137	173	194	524	582	476
El Salvador	15	26	23	17	41	24	24	31	36	-13	6	-6	-1	31	14	15	30	22	19	14	2	27	16	18	22	38
Grenada								0	2	0	0	0	2	3	3	5	6	17	17	12	14	16	25	22	21	24
Guatemala	115	107	56	98	96	148	23	164	197	154	119	133	84	50	43	74	84	179	375	85	52	99	102	160	71	76
Guyana	35	-209	9	23	3	1	-48	-3	0	1	1	-2	5	5	5	2									3	3
Haiti	11	13	14	20	16	5	14	13	15	20	14	9	8	9	5	6	6	6	11	10	9	15	9	9	2	2
Honduras	33	27	11	19	-2	13	10	15	20	37	6	-4	15	23	23	33	37	46	55	57	48	56	52	30	38	51
Jamaica	635	655	341	206	62	-3	-1	-16	-41	-35	-30	-12	-17	-21	14	-11	-6	64	-14	64	150	144	155	87	128	169
Mexico	1,266	1,147	1,053	1,284	1,370	1,125	1,149	937	1,273	1,748	2,326	2,969	1,813	512	445	585	1,869	3,860	2,949	3,382	2,775	5,140	4,788	4,904	12,034	7,047
Nicaragua	59	50	35	37	28	20	24	17	11	4													16	44	44	71
Panama	131	82	47	100	70	14	-19	18	-4	65	-50	6	3	80	11	71	-76	68	-59	41	144	44	151	174	219	223
Paraguay	15	27	10	26	42	45	40	37	38	66	34	33	40	5	6	1	-18	6	10	14	83	91	149	124	197	202
Peru	-274	-218	84	198	117	583	311	91	39	93	29	131	53	42	-102	1	27	38	30	66	45	-8	148	749	3,137	1,918
St. Kitts and Nevis													1	2	15	7	10	20	11	45	53	23	14	16	16	20
St. Lucia							5	22	32	34	33	40	29	11	14	20	18	18	19	30	49	63	45	38	35	64
St. Vincent and the Grenadines										-1			1	2	2	2	1	5	7	12	9	10	21	35	56	31
Suriname	-20	-25	-6	40	-1	0	0	-21	-12	-20	11	36	-7	51	-45	14	-41	-86	-109	-187	-47	11	-33	-53	-33	15
Trinidad and Tobago	326	386	301	184	242	172	242	141	199	123	199	270	223	131	129	1	-18	39	72	166	119	183	194	424	566	303
Uruguay							111	199	199	283	312	51					45	60	53	0	0	0	1	114	170	125

Appendix A (continued)

Region/ Country	1970	1971	1972	1973	1974	1975	1976	1977	1978	1979	1980	1981	1982	1983	1984	1985	1986	1987	1988	1989	1990	1991	1992	1993	1994	1995
Venezuela	-90	789	-1,316	-236	-868	772	-1,627	-5	104	115	59	193	281	96	21	81	20	25	101	237	491	2,077	686	416	892	911
Subtotal	4,276	5,816	3,396	6,350	3,283	6,050	3,221	5,317	6,307	6,829	6,632	8,375	6,949	4,016	3,692	5,208	4,363	6,884	9,036	9,062	8,841	13,554	13,885	15,718	26,583	23,172
Middle East and North Africa																										
Algeria	184	-562	68	144	724	220	342	300	209	34	376	14	-59	0	1	0	7	4	15	13	0	13	13	17	20	5
Bahrain									36	191	-451	0	31	71	161	121	-39	-43	252	201	-4	-8	-10	-6	-34	-27
Egypt						15	112	176	492	1,596	591	788	322	544	832	1,403	1,494	1,127	1,353	1,392	799	274	500	551	1,378	605
Iran, Islamic Republic of	110	244	319	1,579	653	260							-149	-88	49	-45	-137	-366	69	-21	-394	25	-185	-56	2	17
Iraq	94	-465	-2,702	835	-432	20							2	1	-6	0	2	15	0	3	0	-3	-1	1	0	0
Jordan			2	6	14	47	-14	19	87	35	36	147	65	39	88	30	28	47	27	-1	41	-13	45	-38	3	44
Lebanon													-1	1	6	8	13	1	0	2	7	2	4	7	8	35
Libya	545	525	-8	-412	-483	-1,135	-950	-760	-1,070	-771	-1,175	-779	-429	-363	-19	142	-231	-126	111	139	173	173	163	179	88	91
Morocco	78	86	46	-3	-41	0	70	96	73	51	96	61	87	51	54	24	1	71	96	186	180	344	460	549	604	293
Oman					-123	196	149	81	133	154	106	65	199	172	181	192	172	42	104	125	154	162	95	111	143	152
Saudi Arabia	78	-416	118	-1,760	-7,536	3,446	-726	1,318	859	-1,667	-3,444	36	68	32	112	298	51	489	-94	-22	2,029	173	-86	1,531	384	-1,900
Syrian Arab Republic																44	80	8	138	82	77	67	73	197	157	66
Tunisia	63	86	114	164	56	83	201	157	141	65	253	307	373	205	129	129	77	109	69	88	83	137	573	628	474	267
Yemen, Republic of										30	37	42	33	9	8	4	7	1	0	0	-143	632	784	1,009	19	0
Subtotal	1,152	-502	-2,042	552	-7,170	3,152	-817	1,388	960	-284	-3,573	682	543	675	1,596	2,349	1,523	1,380	2,140	2,189	3,001	1,978	2,428	4,679	3,244	-351
South Asia																										
Bangladesh	180	179	64	107	115	158	95	-61	28	64	85	96	79	0	-1	0	3	6	1	0	3	1	4	16	12	2
India														7	22	126	145	252	103	281	176	153	165	305	680	1,316
Maldives														-1	1	1	7	6	1	5	7	8	8	8	9	9
Nepal																	1	1	2	1	7	2	4	7	8	8
Pakistan	90	4	61	-10	7	47	15	26	50	76	68	113	70	33	63	156	129	153	211	233	266	279	365	387	460	414
Sri Lanka	-1	1	1	1	3	0	0	-2	2	62	46	52	70	42	37	31	36	71	52	22	47	52	134	218	182	64
Subtotal	269	184	126	99	125	205	110	-37	80	202	200	261	218	81	122	314	321	487	371	542	505	494	680	940	1,350	1,812
Sub-Saharan Africa																										
Angola																331	287	142	149	233	-365	721	314	337	384	405
Benin	26	10	17	10	-5	4	5	5	1	5	5	2					1	0	0	1	1	14	8	11	5	1
Botswana						-71	21	21	63	168	120	93	23	26	71	64	86	135	45	47	103	-9	-2	-321	-15	71
Burkina Faso	2	4	-2	12	5	1	4	8	2	2	3	2	2	2	2	-2	4	6	1	7	7	2	4	1	0	8
Burundi											12	1	2	3	1	1	2	2	1	1	1	1	1	0	0	2
Cameroon	63	6	12	9	44	50	30	15	63	81	140	142	122	238	20	377	23	14	77	-97	-123	-16	32	6	115	103
Cape Verde																	3	3	0	0	0	1	-1	3	2	10
Central African Republic	5	3	5	-1	12	10	7	-5	9	30	6	6	10	5	6	4	10	14	-4	1	1	-5	-12	-11	4	3
Chad	2	1	0	17	28	38	49	36	53			6	10	5	11	64	35	10	1	21	0	4	2	17	8	7
Comoros																		9	4	4	-1	3	1	1	2	2
Congo, Democratic Republic of						30	146	100	178	79	0	73	-2	-214	-37	82	7	-65	-5	-7	-13	16	1	1	1	1

Appendix A *(continued)*

Region/ Country	1970	1971	1972	1973	1974	1975	1976	1977	1978	1979	1980	1981	1982	1983	1984	1985	1986	1987	1988	1989	1990	1991	1992	1993	1994	1995
Congo, Republic of	182	232	192	93	28	3	3	3	6	22	43	32	39	62	40	15	27	52	10	21	52	17	-252	98	19	19
Côte d'Ivoire	120	59	65	143	66	128	82	25	129	98	102	34	52	42	25	35	87	104	59	52	11	2	3	3	4	1
Djibouti																				0	11	46	22	26	29	1
Equatorial Guinea																										
Ethiopia	15	21	34	87	58	36	8	10					2	-3	6	0	-1	-4	2	0	13	1	7	7	8	7
Gabon	-3	59	61	45	161	308	71	59	87	72	34	57	144	124	9	18	135	107	151	-34	81	-60	138	-127	-113	-51
Gambia, The	0	6	6	4	2	0	2	0	3	15	0	2	18				5	2	1	16	0	11	7	12	11	10
Ghana	266	114	40	40	21	131	-33	32	15	-4	17	17	18	3	2	7	5	6	6	17	16	22	25	140	256	233
Guinea											36	-1	0	0	1	1	10	15	18	14	20	42	22	33	33	35
Guinea-Bissau													0	0	2	1	1	0	1	1	2	0	0	0	1	1
Kenya	54	46	0	0	0	32	85	95	53	110	85	15	14	26	12	22	40	51	0	69	62	21	7	2	4	32
Lesotho											5	5	3	5	3	6	3	7	24	15	19	9	3	17	21	23
Liberia	39	-7	42	30	28	149	72	75	-6	-9	-1		38	55	41	-19	-20	46								
Madagascar						9	3	-5	14	-2	10	1	0	4	10	0	17	4	3	14	24	15	23	17	7	10
Malawi	34	36	35	22	46	16	18	9	14	-2	10	1	0	3	0	1	-10	0	1	17	-8	4	-9	-22	49	1
Mali	-2	12	2	0	5	5	5	-1	0	3	3	4	2	3	12	3	-7	1	2	17	8	2	9	18	2	3
Mauritania	3	0	0	28	4	-227	3	7	4	83	29	13	16	3	10	8	6	2	2	4	8	21	16	17	21	15
Mauritius	6	5	-1	-4	5	7	6	4	7	2	1	1	2	2	5	10	9	21	27	40	45	25	27	34	36	36
Mozambique													2	3	-3	0	2	7	5	4	10	25	27	34	36	36
Namibia																					32	131	113	44	56	48
Niger	2	-20	3	3	14	42	18	22	66	61	53	-6	31	1	2	-11	-2	74	-1	0	-1	0	0	1	0	1
Nigeria	803	1,068	1,068	1,049	520	772	621	739	327	407	-798	572	474	383	228	570	205	717	428	2,096	640	772	978	1,503	2,149	658
Rwanda	-1	6	2	6	4	6	11	8	7	17	18	19	23	12	17	17	22	21	24	17	9	5	2	3	1	1
Senegal	20	37	53	14	21	42	66	47	-8	12	16	36	31	-39	33	-19	-10	-5	16	0	62	-9	23	-1	73	1
Seychelles							12	12	10	10	10	11	11	10	11	14	17	23	26	26	22	22	32	21	55	40
Sierra Leone	32	19	13	12	21	19	16	9	38	21	-20	0	5	2	7	-37	-172	47	-26	25	35	9	-7	-8	-4	1
Somalia	18	6	16	2	1	12	4	13	0	0	0	0	-1	-9	-17	-1	6	76	-49	-46	7	0	3	2	1	1
South Africa	1,313	971	411	77	1,399	341	34	-205	-169	-640	-21	127	370	77	496	-535	-66	-90	132	9	-5	-233	-821	-318	-157	3
Sudan			1												10	-4			0	4	4					
Swaziland					7	27	14	34	34	73	29	39	-15	-6	6	14	31	72	62	84	42	86	88	67	89	59
Tanzania												20	19	2	-10	17	-10	-1	5	7	0	0	13	22	55	152
Togo	3	17	4	9	-79	10	10	20	144	69	46	11	18	2	-11	20	8	9	15	8	0	1	3	61	97	122
Uganda	16	-4	-42	15	3	4	2	1	2							-5				-13						
Zambia	-1,164	0	103	91	78	69	57	29	60	46	67	-40	43	29	20	61	35	89	106	182	221	37	54	61	66	67
Zimbabwe														-2	-3	3		-36	-21	-11	-13	3	16	31	38	40
Subtotal	1,675	2,641	2,189	1,912	2,557	2,026	1,446	1,222	1,194	832	36	1,310	1,498	853	1,038	1,132	838	1,670	1,303	2,788	1,008	1,731	889	1,780	3,414	2,183
Total	8,631	9,571	5,383	10,266	552	13,509	6,332	10,281	10,840	9,748	5,493	13,441	12,415	9,360	10,423	13,225	11,612	16,063	22,033	25,799	26,725	36,290	47,446	74,799	91,214	95,370

Source: World Bank Debtor Reporting System.

Appendix B. IFC FDI Projects

Company[a]	Country	Sector	Commitment FY[b]	Estimated project cost (US$m)	IFC loan (US$m)	IFC equity (US$m)	Country of largest foreign investor	Largest foreign direct investor equity (%[c])	Total foreign investor equity (%[d])
Bristol	Mexico	Transportation equipment	1958	1.4	0.5		Canada	83	83
Mantos Blancos*	Chile	Nonferrous metals - copper	1958	18.6	3.1		Brazil	94	94
Olinkraft	Brazil	Market pulp	1958	3.8	1.2		United States	100	100
Perfect Circle	Mexico	Electrical machinery	1958	1.4	0.6		United States	17	17
Willys Brasil	Brazil	Auto manufacturing	1958	22.0	2.5		United States	45	45
Mineira Cement	Brazil	Cement manufacturing	1959	7.0	1.2		Romania	80	100
BIO-BIO	Chile	Cement manufacturing	1960	5.0	1.2		United States	13	25
Durisol	Peru	Cement manufacturing	1960	0.8	0.3		Switzerland	25	25
Fertilizantes	Peru	Fertilizers	1960	12.9	1.8		Italy	26	26
Kilombero	Tanzania	Processing of edible crops - sugar	1960	8.0	4.7		Netherlands	20	20
Diablitos	Venezuela	Processing of edible crops - sugar	1961	1.0	0.5		United States	100	100
Engranajes	Argentina	Auto components	1961	72.0	1.2		Switzerland	100	100
Envases	Colombia	Industrial metal products	1961	2.8	0.5		NA	43	43
Jamaica Pre-Mix	Jamaica	Cement manufacturing	1961	0.3	0.2		United States	72	72
KSB Pumps	India	Electrical machinery	1961	0.6	0.2		Germany	58	58
Morfeo	Colombia	Furniture, other wood products	1961	0.5	0.2	0.0	United States	25	50
Aevol	Greece	Fertilizers	1962	1.3	0.6		NA	77	77
FEMSA	Spain	Auto components	1962	3.7	0.9	0.5	Italy	80	80
Pasa	Argentina	Oil refining - carbon black	1962	72.0	3.1		United States	24	100
NPK-Engrais	Tunisia	Fertilizers	1963	14.0	1.2	1.2	Sweden	58	75
Precision India	India	Electrical machinery	1963	4.8	0.3	0.4	United States	28	28
Arewa Textiles	Nigeria	Primary textile operations	1964	4.5	0.1	0.3	Japan	60	60
MUSCO	India	Integrated steel works	1964	13.7	2.2	1.0	France	17	17
Dire Dawa	Ethiopia	Primary textile operations	1965	5.4	0.7	1.0	Japan	15	30
Packages	Pakistan	Paper manufacturing	1965	12.7	1.2	0.8	Sweden	20	20
Ethiopian Pulp	Ethiopia	Market pulp	1966	5.4		1.9	United States	24	24
Tasek	Malaysia	Cement manufacturing	1966	4.0	0.8	0.3	Singapore	32	53
Titan Cement	Greece	Cement manufacturing	1966	7.5		0.0	NA	45	45
Enka*	Colombia	Primary textile operations	1967	15.1		1.0	Netherlands	48	48
India Explosive	India	Fertilizers	1967	82.5	7.4	2.9	United Kingdom	51	51
KHP	Kenya	City and business hotel	1967	6.7	1.6	0.6	United States	44	44
SIES	Senegal	Fertilizers	1967	12.4	1.7	1.0	Germany	11	11
Fabritex	Nicaragua	Primary textile operations	1968	9.2	0.5	0.6	Colombia	25	25
Malayawata	Malaysia	Integrated steel works	1968	26.9	1.0	1.0	Japan	40	40
SOMIMA	Mauritania	Nonferrous metals - copper	1968	59.8	9.7	0.7	NA	34	45
COPINO	Honduras	Paper manufacturing	1969	0.1		0.0	Canada	51	51
Dalmine	Argentina	Steel, pipe and tube manu.	1969	6.0	0.8		NA	56	78
Dawood	Pakistan	Fertilizers	1969	78.2	1.0	2.9	United States	40	40
Hoteles	El Salvador	City and business hotel	1969	3.7	0.6	0.2	United States	16	16
Pegasus	Jamaica	City and business hotel	1969	8.6	1.3	0.7	United Kingdom	36	53
Zuari Agro	India	Fertilizers	1969	70.0	11.0	3.7	United States	36	36
ADG	Greece	Nonferrous metals - aluminum	1970	29.4	1.5	3.4	France	35	35
India-Malaysia	Malaysia	Primary textile operations	1970	5.9	1.3	0.2	India	40	40
Panafrican	Kenya	Paper manufacturing	1970	35.0	7.9	3.6	India	33	33
PICOP	Philippines	Paper manufacturing	1970	68.6		0.8	United States	13	13
Pro-Hoteles	Colombia	City and business hotel	1970	4.2	0.8	0.2	United States	23	23
Sagasca	Chile	Nonferrous metals - copper	1970	32.5	10.3	0.5	United States	59	59
Viking	Turkey	Paper manufacturing	1970	9.2	2.5	0.6	Denmark	27	27
CELMEX	Mexico	Primary textile operations	1971	61.3	8.0		United States	40	40
Cibinong	Indonesia	Cement manufacturing	1971	26.6	7.6	2.0	NA	51	51

Appendix B (continued)

Company[a]	Country	Sector	Commitment FY[b]	Estimated project cost (US$m)	IFC loan (US$m)	IFC equity (US$m)	Country of largest foreign investor	Largest foreign direct investor equity (%[c])	Total foreign investor equity (%[d])
Kabelin	Indonesia	Electrical machinery	1971	5.9	1.8	0.4	Netherlands	61	61
Primatexco	Indonesia	Primary textile operations	1971	7.0	1.4	0.5	Japan	33	60
Rio Grande	Brazil	Market pulp	1971	76.1	4.9	0.8	Norway	31	31
Unitex	Indonesia	Primary textile operations	1971	11.0	0.8	0.8	Japan	35	71
Bata Shoe ZA	Zambia	Shoes/leather	1972	2.0	0.5	0.2	Canada	70	100
Bud Senegal	Senegal	Inedible crops - horticultural products	1972	0.3		0.1	Canada	20	20
CIMINAS	Brazil	Cement manufacturing	1972	46.8	4.4	3.2	Switzerland	31	62
Daralon	Indonesia	Primary textile operations	1972	16.7	3.4	1.1	NA	50	50
Fap-Famos	Form. Yugoslavia	Auto manufacturing	1972	81.4	13.2	2.6	Germany	12	12
Promotora Papel	Mexico	Paper manufacturing	1972	0.2		0.0	Canada	33	33
Akdeniz	Turkey	City and business hotel	1973	4.1	0.3	0.3	Italy	67	67
COSIGUA*	Brazil	Integrated steel works	1973	43.1	2.0	2.0	Germany	38	38
Cyprus Cement*	Cyprus	Cement manufacturing	1973	11.7	1.7	0.5	Switzerland	28	28
Funtua	Nigeria	Edible crops - veg oil	1973	3.3	1.1		United Kingdom	19	19
Iran Carbon	Iran	Oil refining - carbon black	1973	10.6	2.3	0.4	United States	50	50
Jakarta Hotel	Indonesia	City and business hotel	1973	27.6	4.0	0.4	United States	11	11
Rym Hotel	Tunisia	City and business hotel	1973	11.5	1.6	0.3	Thailand	40	40
Veracruz	Mexico	Cement manufacturing	1973	23.9	6.0		Switzerland	20	20
Cementos Boyaca	Colombia	Cement manufacturing	1974	7.1	1.5		Switzerland	19	19
Cementos Nacion	Dom. Rep.	Cement manufacturing	1974	34.5	6.0	1.5	United States	25	25
FILSYN	Philippines	Primary textile operations	1974	7.5	1.5		Japan	35	35
Jordan Ceramic*	Jordan	Glazed ceramic tiles	1974	7.6	1.4	0.2	Germany	14	14
Kamaltex	Indonesia	Primary textile operations	1974	7.5	1.9	0.6	India	53	53
Monsanto Pan	Indonesia	Appliances/utensils	1974	3.3	0.9		NA	80	80
Nigalex	Nigeria	Nonferrous metals - aluminum	1974	4.0	1.0	0.3	Switzerland	25	51
Rhodia-Ster	Brazil	Nonferrous metals - nickel	1974	100.0	15.0		Canada	100	100
Bata Cameroon	Cameroon	Shoes/leather	1975	5.2		0.4	France	15	15
BNE	Lebanon	Housing/mortgage bank	1975	6.6		1.3	NA	25	25
Capuava*	Brazil	Oil refining - carbon black	1975	11.0	2.5	1.1	United States	49	49
Finap	Paraguay	Tree farming	1975	19.5	4.4	1.0	Argentina	13	13
Hellenic Food	Greece	Processing of edible crops	1975	4.1	1.0	0.1	United States	50	50
Mexinox*	Mexico	Integrated steel works	1975	83.6	12.0	2.8	France	40	40
PPIC	Philippines	Primary textile operations	1975	21.3	7.0		Japan	20	35
Valinvenca	Venezuela	Investment bank	1975	2.3		0.4	United States	25	25
Arab Ceramic	Egypt	Glazed ceramic tiles	1976	18.7	3.2	0.9	Lebanon	15	15
CTM	Sudan	Primary textile operations	1976	30.0	8.7	1.3	Pakistan	12	12
David Whitehead	Malawi	Primary textile operations	1976	12.4	6.0		United Kingdom	51	51
Philagro*	Philippines	Edible crops - veg oil	1976	6.6	2.7	0.2	India	21	42
SORWATHE	Rwanda	Edible crops - coffee cocoa tea	1976	1.6	0.5		United States	40	40
Cyprus Pipes	Cyprus	Cement manufacturing	1977	3.4	0.5	0.2	Switzerland	15	15
Dwangwa Sugar	Malawi	Processing of edible crops - sugar	1977	64.9	11.3		United Kingdom	31	31
FMB Productos*	Brazil	Auto parts foundry	1977	205.4	20.0		Italy	59	59
Rio Norte*	Brazil	Nonferrous metals - aluminum	1977	330.0	15.0		Canada	19	19
SAFACAM	Cameroon	Edible crops - palm	1977	5.6		0.8	France	67	67
SOTEMA	Madagascar	Primary textile operations	1977	38.2	11.0	0.3	Germany	42	42
La Cemento*	Ecuador	Cement manufacturing	1978	55.0	12.0	0.8	Switzerland	44	44
MOLANDINO	Bolivia	Processing of edible crops - grain	1978	7.9	1.3		Uruguay	15	15
Nile Clothing	Egypt	Primary textile operations	1978	2.7	0.4	0.2	United Kingdom	28	28
Scott Paper*	Costa Rica	Paper manufacturing	1978	12.0	2.5		United States	50	50
TEMEX*	Mexico	Organic chemicals	1978	99.1	19.0		United States	10	10
Alpesca*	Argentina	Livestock - aquaculture	1979	42.7	5.2	0.5	Spain	41	41

Appendix B (continued)

Company[a]	Country	Sector	Commitment FY[b]	Estimated project cost (US$m)	IFC loan (US$m)	IFC equity (US$m)	Country of largest foreign investor	Largest foreign direct investor equity (%[c])	Total foreign investor equity (%[d])
Alucam*	Cameroon	Nonferrous metals - aluminum	1979	120.0	7.0	0.9	France	23	23
Astra Fish	Uruguay	Processing of livestock - fish	1979	21.6	7.1	0.9	Canada	20	20
Attock Refinery	Pakistan	Oil refining processes	1979	31.6	7.5	0.9	United Kingdom	53	53
Bangkok Glass*	Thailand	Industrial glass	1979	26.5	4.9	0.2	United Kingdom	15	15
CONDUMONT	Mexico	Electronic, telecom, precision equip.	1979	36.4	5.0		Germany	41	41
Highspeed*	Bangladesh	Transportation equipment	1979	6.3	1.2	0.4	Canada	20	20
JSC	Jordan	Securities market institution	1979	6.6		0.7	Japan	38	38
Maricultura	Costa Rica	Livestock - aquaculture	1979	10.0	1.4	0.7	Kuwait	11	11
Metal Products*	Tanzania	Appliances/utensils	1979	5.9	1.3	0.2	United States	50	50
Pak Oilfields	Pakistan	Oil/gas exploration	1979	52.9	7.0	0.8	United Kingdom	54	54
SOVOLPLAS	Burkina Faso	Organic chemicals	1979	2.3	0.4	0.1	United Kingdom	37	37
Volvo do Brasil	Brazil	Auto manufacturing	1979	124.0	10.0	4.1	NA	62	62
Zaire Gulf	Congo, Dem. Rep. of	Engineering service	1979	33.0	4.1		Sweden	50	50
Bata Malgache	Madagascar	Shoes/leather	1980	5.2	1.3		United States	65	65
Indo-American	Indonesia	Appliances/utensils	1980	26.0	5.1	0.9	Canada	28	43
Ipiranga (Polisul)	Brazil	Organic chemicals	1980	110.0	15.0	5.3	Netherlands	33	33
Ismailia Fish	Egypt	Livestock - aquaculture	1980	9.7	1.9	0.6	Germany	19	19
Minera Real	Mexico	Nonferrous metals - zinc	1980	146.9	30.0		Saudi Arabia	34	34
MSO	Côte d'Ivoire	Processing of edible crops - grain	1980	14.0	2.9	0.4	Canada	22	22
Novotel SE	Senegal	City and business hotel	1980	18.8	3.0		France	20	20
NTM	Nigeria	Primary textile operations	1980	27.7	8.1	0.7	France	34	34
Papan	Indonesia	Housing/mortgage bank	1980	16.0	4.0	1.2	NA	15	15
PASAR*	Philippines	Nonferrous metals - copper	1980	402.0		5.0	Netherlands	16	16
Resistol	Mexico	Integrated chem./petro. operations	1980	45.0	8.0		Japan	39	39
Semen Andalas	Indonesia	Cement manufacturing	1980	200.0	28.0	5.0	United Kingdom	26	40
SERACEM	Sierra Leone	Cement manufacturing	1980	8.2	2.1		France	40	40
Siveng*	Côte d'Ivoire	Fertilizers	1980	28.1	5.1	1.3	Germany	14	14
Sudan Cement	Sudan	Cement manufacturing	1980	1.0		0.2	Spain	33	33
Surinvest	Uruguay	Merchant bank	1980	13.3	10.0	0.6	United Kingdom	20	20
VIPLAMEX*	Mexico	Industrial glass	1980	160.1	15.0		United Kingdom	35	35
ZCCM	Zambia	Nonferrous metals - copper	1980	163.8	20.0		South Africa	40	40
Coromandel	India	Cement manufacturing	1981	98.8	15.9		United States	25	47
EHESA	Paraguay	City and business hotel	1981	4.8	0.9	0.3	Brazil	34	34
Habib Arkady	Pakistan	Processing of edible crops - sugar	1981	13.4	3.2	0.2	United States	20	40
Lanka Hotels	Sri Lanka	Resort hotel	1981	35.5	8.2	0.7	India	37	37
Somali Molasses	Somalia	Agribusiness services	1981	1.5	0.4		Côte d'Ivoire	14	14
Taihan Bulk	Korea, Rep. of	Transport infrastructure	1981	27.6	3.5	2.5	United Kingdom	53	53
Toachi	Ecuador	Nonferrous metals - copper	1981	5.2	1.0	0.3	United States	28	77
Asbestos Cement	Pakistan	Cement manufacturing	1982	15.8	4.0		Venezuela	40	40
Bamburi Cement	Kenya	Cement manufacturing	1982	24.7	4.4		Luxembourg	40	40
ICS*	Senegal	Fertilizers	1982	330.1	25.0		United Kingdom	37	73
ITW Signode	India	Integrated steel works	1982	8.8	2.4		Côte d'Ivoire	14	14
Luxor Hotel	Egypt	Resort hotel	1982	25.4	4.4	0.7	United States	39	67
Moulins Sahel	Niger	Processing of edible crops - grain	1982	8.1	2.0	0.2	Switzerland	11	11
NDC-Guthrie*	Philippines	Edible crops - palm	1982	42.6	11.0		Benin	33	49
Nile Petroleum	Sudan	Oil/gas transport	1982	1.5			United Kingdom	40	40
SIKA	Mali	Edible crops - veg oil	1982	9.2	1.8	0.3	United States	40	40
Aredor*	Guinea	Precious metals/minerals - diamonds	1983	95.7	13.6	0.5	NA	16	27
Dome	Cyprus	Resort hotel	1983	9.2	1.8	1.2	Australia	50	50
Matas	Costa Rica	Inedible crops - horticultural products	1983	10.2	1.5	0.3	United States	100	100
Nepal Magnesite	Nepal	Industrial minerals/ores	1983	24.9	5.0		India	25	25

Appendix B (continued)

Company[a]	Country	Sector	Commitment FY[b]	Estimated project cost (US$m)	IFC loan (US$m)	IFC equity (US$m)	Country of largest foreign investor	Largest foreign direct investor equity (%)[c]	Total foreign investor equity (%)[d]
Nord-Sud	Congo, Dem. Rep. of	Nonferrous metals - aluminum	1983	3.5	0.2		Switzerland	20	20
Sea Minerals	Thailand	Nonferrous metals - tin	1983	3.8	2.2	0.6	Malaysia	16	33
Tetra Pak Converters*	Kenya	Paper manufacturing	1983	10.6		0.4	Thailand	63	63
Carbones	Colombia	Coal mining	1984	51.6	10.2	1.6	United Kingdom	31	31
CFSC	Barbados	Securities market institution	1984	25.0		0.3	Canada	16	52
Jamaica Flour	Jamaica	Processing of edible crops - grain	1984	20.6	5.0		United States	31	42
Kombo Beach	Gambia, The	Resort hotel	1984	11.7	2.8		Sweden	17	34
Metalsa*	Mexico	Auto components	1984	35.2	3.0	1.4	United States	40	40
Nossi-Be*	Madagascar	Livestock - aquaculture	1984	10.8	2.6	0.1	Canada	26	26
TAMTECO	Uganda	Edible crops - coffee cocoa tea	1984	8.8	1.1		United Kingdom	49	49
ZHP*	Zambia	City and business hotel	1984	30.1	7.5		United States	20	20
Acoje	Philippines	Industrial minerals/ores	1985	10.0	0.1		Austria	20	20
Amboni	Tanzania	Inedible crops - natural fibers	1985	12.7	4.4		NA	88	88
Ashanti Gold*	Ghana	Precious metals/minerals - gold	1985	161.4	27.5		United Kingdom	45	45
Bata Shoe BD	Bangladesh	Shoes/leather	1985	13.0	3.0	0.5	Canada	70	70
Bihar Sponge*	India	Iron manufacturing	1985	62.7	15.2	0.6	Germany	11	11
CIB	Congo, Rep. of	Tree farming	1985	11.0	1.3		Germany	75	100
Ferme Suisse	Cameroon	Processing of edible crops - palm oil	1985	9.7	2.0	0.6	France	51	51
Fluobar*	Tunisia	Industrial minerals/ores	1985	6.3		0.2	Jordan	39	39
Grands Hotels	Congo, Dem. Rep. of	City and business hotel	1985	37.9	15.0		United States	50	50
Guangzhou Auto	China	Auto manufacturing	1985	79.5	15.0	3.2	France	22	22
Proteison*	Mexico	Edible crops - veg oil	1985	11.2	2.0	0.8	Israel	25	25
SOTEXKI*	Congo, Dem. Rep. of	Primary textile operations	1985	17.4	8.5	0.6	Switzerland	16	29
Tiger Battery*	Nigeria	Appliances/utensils	1985	12.0	2.8		Denmark	28	28
Uganda Tea*	Uganda	Processing of edible crops - coffee, tea	1985	9.4	2.8		United Kingdom	49	49
African Seafood	Senegal	Processing of livestock - fish	1986	12.0	3.3		Denmark	17	17
Alum Sulphate*	Egypt	Inorganic chemicals	1986	16.5		0.8	Sweden	25	25
Bajaj Tempo	India	Auto manufacturing	1986	52.6	15.1	0.6	Germany	26	26
Cape Horn	Chile	Organic chemicals	1986	298.0	50.0	5.0	United States	76	76
Capos Limited*	Fiji	Resort hotel	1986	27.6	8.8		United States	29	100
Chucuri Oil	Colombia	Oil/gas exploration	1986	33.0		5.0	Canada	25	50
CICAM	Cameroon	Primary textile operations	1986	6.8	6.5		France	35	35
COTONA*	Madagascar	Primary textile operations	1986	17.2	9.3	0.2	Luxembourg	28	28
EBP	Kenya	City and business hotel	1986	13.8	3.7		NA	40	40
Issa Nicholas	Grenada	Resort hotel	1986	16.7	6.0		Trinidad and Tobago	80	100
Masbhurni	Thailand	Precious metals/minerals - gold	1986	3.7		0.0	Canada	30	30
Pure Foods*	Philippines	Processing of livestock - abattoir, meat	1986	4.7		1.4	United States	14	14
Silkar Turizm	Turkey	Resort hotel	1986	16.1	5.8		Switzerland	48	48
SITEX	Tunisia	Primary textile operations	1986	20.2	5.0	3.2	United Kingdom	44	44
Western Agri	Paraguay	Edible crops - diversified edible crops	1986	2.5	0.8		United States	25	50
Yemen Hunt Oil*	Yemen, Rep. of	Oil/gas production	1986	50.3	9.0		United States	37	62
Ailee	Seychelles	Resort hotel	1987	40.8	10.5		India	36	77
BICI-GUI*	Guinea	Commercial bank	1987	16.1		1.0	France	15	15
CBI*	Congo, Rep. of	Tree farming	1987	6.4	1.9	0.3	United States	41	41
Comete	Tunisia	Engineering service	1987	0.3		0.0	Canada	45	45
Fiji Bank	Fiji	Merchant bank	1987	17.7	2.0	0.3	Australia	30	30
Fiji Forest	Fiji	Tree farming	1987	13.3	2.0	1.6	Australia	49	49
Gonfreville	Côte d'Ivoire	Primary textile operations	1987	21.3	12.0		France	10	10
Granjas Marinas*	Honduras	Livestock - aquaculture	1987	8.1		0.6	United States	35	35
Hero Honda	India	Motor bicycles	1987	21.9	7.7		Japan	26	26
Hidra Oil*	Argentina	Oil/gas production	1987	470.0	22.5		France	38	38

Appendix B (continued)

Company[a]	Country	Sector	Commitment FY[b]	Estimated project cost (US$m)	IFC loan (US$m)	IFC equity (US$m)	Country of largest foreign investor	Largest foreign direct investor equity (%[c])	Total foreign investor equity (%[c,d])
Keta Oil	Ghana	Oil/gas exploration	1987	30.1		4.5	United States	85	85
LOMACO	Mozambique	Edible crops - diversified edible crops	1987	15.5	2.7		United Kingdom	51	51
NEW	Nigeria	Auto components	1987	20.0	11.1		India	40	40
Pan Atlantic	Togo	Primary textile operations	1987	29.7	7.0	1.1	United States	91	91
REIT	Tunisia	Non-wood housing products	1987	6.5	1.5	0.4	Italy	51	51
Sigmar	Guinea	Quarried construction materials	1987	34.7	0.1		France	60	95
SILAC	Cameroon	Processing of livestock - dairy	1987	9.6	2.3	0.6	Belgium	19	44
Socota Textile	Mauritius	Primary textile operations	1987	22.1	5.0	1.0	Luxembourg	71	71
T&C Properties	Barbados	Resort hotel	1987	5.0	1.3		NA	20	20
Thatta	Pakistan	Oil/gas exploration	1987	16.9		4.3	Netherlands	50	50
Transamerican*	Dom. Rep.	Resort hotel	1987	24.0	6.0		United States	33	100
TRINGEN	Trin. & Tobago	Fertilizers	1987	265.0	40.0		United States	49	49
Unicbank	Hungary	Commercial bank	1987	20.0		3.2	Austria	30	30
Viphya Plywoods*	Malawi	Industrial wood products	1987	30.4	3.9	0.5	NA	37	37
Anam	Korea, Rep. of	Electronic, telecom, precision equip.	1988	88.3		15.7	United States	27	27
Aurifere*	Guinea	Precious metals/minerals - gold	1988	27.9	8.3		United Kingdom	51	51
Bechtel Egypt	Egypt	Engineering service	1988	500.0		0.1	United States	51	51
CALICA	Mexico	Quarried construction materials	1988	149.5	37.0		United States	50	50
China Bicycles*	China	Bicycles	1988	17.7	5.0		Hong Kong, China	33	67
Chirete	Argentina	Oil/gas exploration	1988	33.0		5.2	Australia	45	45
Comarit*	Morocco	Industrial glass	1988	179.5	40.0	5.0	Brazil	50	98
Ducros	Togo	Diversified food manufacturing	1988	4.3	1.4		France	65	65
Dunlop*	Nigeria	Auto tires	1988	39.1	12.5		United Kingdom	37	37
GKN Invel	India	Auto components	1988	14.2		1.1	Germany	40	40
Glass Wool*	Hungary	Non-wood housing products	1988	20.4	3.4	1.4	Japan	13	26
Gwembe	Zambia	Inedible crops - natural fibers	1988	13.5	3.7	0.8	United Kingdom	53	53
HMC Polymers	Thailand	Organic chemicals	1988	82.8	15.0	1.5	United States	45	45
LTPO*	Liberia	Industrial wood products	1988	25.9	8.5		United Kingdom	100	100
Manulife	Indonesia	Insurance company	1988	4.0		0.3	Canada	51	51
MBR	Brazil	Iron ore mining	1988	82.0	20.0		Japan	25	25
Meleiha Oil*	Egypt	Oil/gas production	1988	250.9		9.2	NA	55	55
Monterado	Indonesia	Precious metals/minerals - gold	1988	17.0	3.5	2.0	United Kingdom	65	65
Phoenix Resource*	Egypt	Oil/gas exploration	1988	97.5	20.0		Spain	50	90
Prestige	Cameroon	Beverage manufacturing	1988	7.8	2.7	0.3	France	12	12
PT Bali*	Indonesia	Resort hotel	1988	28.1	9.3		France	75	75
SITER	Tunisia	Primary textile operations	1988	13.8	2.9	2.1	France	25	25
SORWAL	Rwanda	Furniture, other wood products	1988	8.5	0.6	0.2	Sweden	14	14
SPNP	Cameroon	Edible crops - fruits	1988	11.6	1.9	0.4	France	45	45
STS	Togo	Bar, rod & flat steel plants	1988	2.0	0.8		NA	47	47
Utexafrica	Congo, Dem. Rep. of	Primary textile operations	1988	46.5	13.5		Belgium	92	92
Xai Xai	Mozambique	Oil/gas operations	1988	31.0		7.8	United Kingdom	75	75
AG&P	Philippines	Industrial equipment	1989	75.0			Japan	20	20
Chihuidos	Argentina	Oil/gas exploration	1989	32.4		5.0	United States	39	56
Coats Iplik*	Turkey	Primary textile operations	1989	15.1	7.7		United Kingdom	75	75
Comilog*	Gabon	Transport infrastructure	1989	80.4	32.0		United States	36	36
Crown Elec*	China	Appliances/utensils	1989	62.0	15.0		Japan	90	90
Dunastyr*	Hungary	Organic chemicals	1989	72.2	14.2	3.8	Italy	35	35
Dusa*	Turkey	Organic chemicals	1989	75.6	17.0		Canada	50	50
ELUMA	Brazil	Nonferrous semi-finished products	1989	83.2	16.4		Canada	19	19
Escondida	Chile	Nonferrous metals - copper	1989	996.1	71.3	15.0	Australia	58	88
Kiris	Turkey	Resort hotel	1989	34.3	12.2		Switzerland	35	55

Appendix B (continued)

Company[a]	Country	Sector	Commitment FY[b]	Estimated project cost (US$m)	IFC loan (US$m)	IFC equity (US$m)	Country of largest foreign investor	Largest foreign direct investor equity (%)	Total foreign investor equity (%)[d]
Masstock	Zambia	Edible crops - wheat	1989	44.2	8.7		Ireland	47	47
OPCO*	Venezuela	Iron ore mining	1989	115.0	37.4		Japan	55	86
Peroxythai	Thailand	Inorganic chemicals	1989	46.2	10.7		United Kingdom	25	49
Polimar	Mexico	Fine chemicals and derivatives	1989	52.5	14.5		United Kingdom	50	50
Red Sea	Ethiopia	Oil/gas exploration	1989	31.0		7.8	United Kingdom	75	75
Sariville*	Turkey	Resort hotel	1989	20.1	2.7	2.2	Luxembourg	33	33
Shell Gabon	Gabon	Oil/gas production	1989	395.0	50.0		United Kingdom/ Netherlands	65	65
Shenzhen Solar*	China	Electrical machinery	1989	10.2	2.0	1.0	United States	40	40
WTI	India	Computer applications/software	1989	3.6		0.2	United States	40	51
Afcott*	Nigeria	Processing of edible crops - veg oil	1990	17.3	4.5		NA	40	40
Bogosu	Ghana	Precious metals/minerals - gold	1990	86.0	18.5	0.5	Netherlands	63	63
CELPAC*	Chile	Market pulp	1990	586.6	40.0	10.0	United States	47	47
COMSUR	Bolivia	Nonferrous metals - zinc	1990	26.1	7.0	3.0	Bolivia	100	100
Condumex	Mexico	Diversified goods	1990	128.0	35.0		Italy	28	28
Conrad*	Turkey	City and business hotel	1990	93.0	21.0	4.0	United States	40	40
Elf Gabon	Gabon	Oil/gas production	1990	352.0	10.0		France	54	54
F S P (Kamelya)	Turkey	Resort hotel	1990	43.0	12.2		Spain	20	20
Iduapriem*	Ghana	Precious metals/minerals - gold	1990	11.0		3.0	Australia	63	63
Indelpro	Mexico	Organic chemicals	1990	110.0	27.0		United States	49	49
Mersin	Turkey	City and business hotel	1990	25.0	8.5		NA	40	40
Pak Suzuki Motor*	Pakistan	Auto manufacturing	1990	87.5	18.6		Japan	25	25
PT Indo-Rama	Indonesia	Primary textile operations	1990	74.0	12.0		United Kingdom	58	58
Siam Asahi	Thailand	Appliances/utensils	1990	334.5		8.3	Japan	63	63
Simplot	Turkey	Processing of edible crops	1990	47.3	9.4		United States	40	40
Tetra Pak HUN	Hungary	Paper manufacturing	1990	48.4	7.4	3.2	Sweden	60	60
TIL*	Mauritius	Garment manufacturing	1990	7.6	3.1		Hong Kong, China	100	100
Togotex*	Togo	Primary textile operations	1990	22.7		1.7	Hong Kong, China	26	26
UCAL*	India	Auto components	1990	7.5		0.6	Japan	26	26
Wahome Steel	Ghana	Bar, rod & flat steel plants	1990	8.3	3.2		Taiwan, China	57	95
Adwya*	Tunisia	Pharmaceuticals	1991	0.6		0.1	Canada	17	17
Al Bardi	Egypt	Paper manufacturing	1991	27.5	6.2		Jordan	45	90
Al-Hikma (Por)	Portugal	Pharmaceuticals	1991	8.6	2.0		Jordan	73	73
Apasco*	Mexico	Cement manufacturing	1991	166.0	20.0		Switzerland	60	60
Avantex Mill*	Philippines	Primary textile operations	1991	51.0	11.3	2.3	Taiwan, China	55	55
Bermejo	Bolivia	Oil/gas production	1991	39.0	4.0	5.9	Argentina	75	75
Best Chemicals*	Philippines	Organic chemicals	1991	33.0	6.5	2.3	Korea, Republic of	90	90
Bristol Hotel	Poland	City and business hotel	1991	36.2	10.7		United Kingdom	55	55
Club St. Lucia*	Saint Lucia	Resort hotel	1991	10.0	3.7		United Kingdom	100	100
CTC*	Chile	Telecoms	1991	248.0	80.0		Spain	44	44
ENGEPOL	Brazil	Industrial rubber/plastic	1991	11.5	3.5		Chile	40	40
ENV	Venezuela	Inorganic chemicals	1991	52.3	14.3		United States	20	40
Finantia	Portugal	Merchant bank	1991	23.5		2.8	France	16	16
Intl Bank Poland	Poland	Commercial bank	1991	20.0		3.2	Netherlands	18	54
Journeys End	Belize	Resort hotel	1991	3.0	1.0		NA	29	47
Magyar Suzuki*	Hungary	Auto manufacturing	1991	234.9	32.2	6.5	Japan	40	51
Makati Hotel*	Philippines	City and business hotel	1991	118.0	29.5		Hong Kong, China	25	35
MORAK*	Mauritania	Precious metals/minerals - gold	1991	17.5	3.4	0.8	United States	43	43
Navotas*	Philippines	Power generation and transmission	1991	41.0	10.0	1.1	Hong Kong, China	60	60
NMBB	Hungary	Investment bank	1991	16.0		1.5	Japan	51	51
ODC*	Colombia	Oil/gas trans. pipeline	1991	321.0	35.0		United Kingdom/ Netherlands	34	34
Pelican	Gambia, The	Processing of livestock - fish	1991	2.6	1.1		Sweden	70	70

Appendix B (continued)

Company[a]	Country	Sector	Commitment FY[b]	Estimated project cost (US$m)	IFC loan (US$m)	IFC equity (US$m)	Country of largest foreign investor	Largest foreign direct investor equity (%[c])	Total foreign investor equity (%[d])
Petrocel	Mexico	Organic chemicals	1991	101.6	32.0		United States	33	33
Pralca*	Venezuela	Organic chemicals	1991	142.6	30.8	8.6	United States	25	25
PT Agro Muko	Indonesia	Processing of edible crops - palm oil	1991	54.2	10.5	2.2	Belgium	55	55
SDC	Ghana	Securities market institution	1991	1.7		0.2	United Kingdom	20	20
SOMOTEX	Tunisia	Primary textile operations	1991	17.4	4.4	1.2	Italy	46	46
Alcatel	Romania	Telecoms	1992	18.0	5.8	0.7	France	51	51
Bissau Pesca	Guinea-Bissau	Livestock - aquaculture	1992	1.2		0.2	Canada	58	58
Block KG-OS-IV	India	Oil/gas exploration	1992	32.7		8.2	United Kingdom	42	75
BNI*	Madagascar	Commercial bank	1992	26.0		2.6	France	51	51
CHEMAGEV*	Poland	Construction/real estate	1992	14.9	3.0		United States	25	25
Ciments du Maroc	Morocco	Cement manufacturing	1992	97.8	17.7		France	60	60
CINOUCA*	Morocco	Cement manufacturing	1992	88.9	13.2		France	27	27
DTC	Dom. Rep.	Resort hotel	1992	40.3	10.0		Spain	85	85
Dynamic Textile	Bangladesh	Primary textile operations	1992	11.5	2.5		Canada	31	31
ELBO*	Turkey	Appliances/utensils	1992	77.6	19.3		Germany	50	50
FIB	Pakistan	Merchant bank	1992	6.0		0.9	United States	30	30
GHANAL	Ghana	Nonferrous metals - aluminum	1992	1.5		0.4	NA	80	80
Miniere Bougrine	Tunisia	Nonferrous metals - zinc	1992	74.2	14.0	2.3	Canada	45	45
Minproc Bolivia	Bolivia	Nonferrous metals - zinc	1992	3.6	0.3	0.7	United States	79	79
Mokra	Czech Rep.	Cement manufacturing	1992	142.3		17.2	Belgium	61	61
Pecten Cameroon	Cameroon	Oil/gas production	1992	123.0	30.0		United States	80	80
PETROZIM	Zimbabwe	Oil/gas transport	1992	66.7	16.7		United Kingdom	50	50
Philips Poland*	Poland	Appliances/utensils	1992	60.0	15.0		Netherlands	85	85
Pioneer Egypt	Egypt	Processing of edible crops - veg oil	1992	17.0		1.2	United States	51	51
PT Bakrie Kasei	Indonesia	Organic chemicals	1992	335.1	30.0	9.6	Japan	56	56
PT Indaci	Indonesia	Primary textile operations	1992	23.0	4.0	1.8	Japan	51	51
PT Swadharma	Indonesia	City and business hotel	1992	177.0	35.0		Hong Kong, China	25	25
Serena Beach	Egypt	Resort hotel	1992	23.5	7.5	1.2	Poland	33	57
Shin Ho Paper	Thailand	Paper manufacturing	1992	120.0	22.0	6.0	Korea, Republic of	29	29
Sierra Rutile	Sierra Leone	Industrial minerals/ores	1992	95.5	15.0		United States	100	100
SKF Bearings*	India	Electrical machinery	1992	80.6	11.5		Sweden	51	51
TELECEL*	Congo, Dem. Rep. of	Telecoms	1992	21.4	6.0		United States	45	45
Westel	Hungary	Telecoms	1992	82.0	15.0		United States	49	49
APEX	Colombia	Securities market institution	1993	5.5		0.9	Mexico	21	21
AQUALMA	Madagascar	Processing of livestock - shrimp	1993	19.0	1.9		Luxembourg	15	15
BECOL	Belize	Power generation and transmission	1993	59.4	15.0		United States	95	95
Block CI-11	Côte d'Ivoire	Oil/gas production	1993	45.5		11.4	United States	15	15
BSJS	Pakistan	Securities market institution	1993	2.0		0.9	United States	30	30
C.S. Cabot Spol.*	Czech Rep.	Oil refining - carbon black	1993	87.1	20.3		United States	52	52
Carbon Black-EGT*	Egypt	Oil refining - carbon black	1993	40.0	7.0	1.5	Indonesia	36	51
Cayeli Bakir*	Turkey	Nonferrous metals - copper	1993	154.5	30.0		Canada	48	48
CDCPL	Pakistan	Securities market institution	1993	2.5		0.3	United States	20	20
GENEX	Bolivia	Inorganic chemicals	1993	8.5	2.9		Argentina	92	92
Ghim Li Fashion	Fiji	Garment manufacturing	1993	7.0	1.7		Singapore	70	100
Helios	Algeria	Inorganic chemicals	1993	96.2	10.0		France	49	49
Hotel Flamenco	Dom. Rep.	Resort hotel	1993	26.5	6.8		Spain	100	100
Huta Warszawa	Poland	Integrated steel works	1993	299.0	38.7	4.8	Italy	42	42
Jose Methanol	Venezuela	Organic chemicals	1993	340.0	37.5	6.8	Japan	24	47
Jubilee	Uganda	Insurance company	1993	0.4		0.1	Kenya	35	35
Mactan Hotel*	Philippines	Resort hotel	1993	48.0	12.0		Hong Kong, China	22	36
Malteria Pampa	Argentina	Processing of edible crops - grain	1993	42.0	12.0		Brazil	54	54

Appendix B (continued)

Company[a]	Country	Sector	Commitment FY[b]	Estimated project cost (US$m)	IFC loan (US$m)	IFC equity (US$m)	Country of largest foreign investor	Largest foreign direct investor equity (%)	Total foreign investor equity (%)[d]
Millicom	Costa Rica	Telecoms	1993	11.0	2.5	1.0	Luxembourg	75	75
Mindanao Power	Philippines	Power generation and transmission	1993	103.0	12.5	4.5	Japan	15	29
Pagbilao	Philippines	Power generation and transmission	1993	888.0	60.0	10.0	Hong Kong, China	87	87
Pilipinas Shell	Philippines	Oil refining - other	1993	667.0	50.0		United Kingdom/ Netherlands	68	68
Polana Hotel	Mozambique	City and business hotel	1993	16.5	3.5		South Africa	33	33
PT Viscose*	Indonesia	Primary textile operations	1993	92.0	20.0		Austria	42	81
PTD Limited	Seychelles	Tourism services	1993	9.6	3.8		South Africa	70	70
Puerto Quetzal*	Guatemala	Power generation and transmission	1993	92.0	20.0		United States	65	65
Quellaveco	Peru	Nonferrous metals - copper	1993	31.0		6.2	Chile	80	80
Sandoglass	Poland	Industrial glass	1993	171.5	36.4	8.3	United Kingdom	40	40
Shenzhen PCCP	China	Cement manufacturing	1993	20.0	4.0	1.0	Hong Kong, China	40	40
Triangle	Zimbabwe	Processing of edible crops - sugar	1993	28.4	7.0		South Africa	100	100
Vigua	Guatemala	Industrial glass	1993	23.5	11.0		Mexico	49	75
Yanacocha	Peru	Precious metals/minerals - gold	1993	45.0	12.3	0.3	United States	38	38
Yantai Cement	China	Cement manufacturing	1993	122.7	28.7	2.0	Japan	39	59
ABN AMRO Kazakstan	Kazakhstan	Commercial bank	1994	10.0		2.0	Netherlands	51	51
Albadomu Malata	Hungary	Processing of edible crops - sugar	1994	19.9	5.4	2.0	Germany	51	51
Autokola	Czech Rep.	Auto components	1994	63.0	16.4		United States	45	45
AYTAC	Turkey	Processing of livestock - abattoir, meat	1994	75.3	8.0	2.0	Belgium	84	84
BACELL	Brazil	Market pulp	1994	200.9	14.0	10.7	Austria	37	37
Basic Petroleum	Guatemala	Oil/gas production	1994	33.0	10.0	4.0	NA	33	33
BGN	Argentina	Commercial bank	1994	15.0	15.0		Switzerland	12	12
BONA	Poland	Processing of livestock - dairy	1994	5.1	2.0		United States	75	75
Bumrungrad	Thailand	Hospital/clinic	1994	111.0	25.0	2.2	United States	40	40
Ciments Guinee	Guinea	Cement manufacturing	1994	7.0	1.5		Belgium	51	51
Cmrcl Intl Bank	Egypt	Commercial bank	1994	100.0		15.6	Kenya	44	44
Crescent Greenwd	Pakistan	Garment manufacturing	1994	77.0	16.1	3.1	United States	32	32
EDENOR	Argentina	Power generation and transmission	1994	402.4	45.0		France	25	50
FILTISAC	Côte d'Ivoire	Industrial packaging	1994	10.8	1.1		Switzerland	46	46
GAVEA	Brazil	City and business hotel	1994	55.7	16.8		United States	31	31
GHACEM	Ghana	Cement manufacturing	1994	7.0	3.0		Norway	60	60
GIDESA	Mexico	Organic chemicals	1994	107.2	15.0	8.0	United States	22	22
GOTM	Mexico	Transport infrastructure	1994	14.5	4.0	2.0	Japan	37	37
Hanoi Metropole	Vietnam	City and business hotel	1994	34.7	8.5		France	29	42
Indo Rama	India	Primary textile operations	1994	205.4	35.0	9.8	Indonesia	32	32
Kunda Tsement	Estonia	Cement manufacturing	1994	43.5	6.0	4.0	Norway	46	46
Lanka Cellular	Sri Lanka	Telecoms	1994	13.6		1.4	Singapore	76	76
MaFra	Czech Rep.	Printing/publishing	1994	39.2	14.2		France	96	96
MASISA	Argentina	Industrial wood products	1994	56.2	11.0		Chile	100	100
PACRA	Pakistan	Credit rating agency	1994	1.0		0.2	United Kingdom	40	40
PapaTel	Hungary	Telecoms	1994	14.4		0.5	United States	27	27
Polar Lights	Russian Fed.	Oil/gas production	1994	340.0	60.0		United States	50	50
PPMs Opole	Poland	Processing of livestock - abattoir, meat	1994	18.0	5.2	1.0	Austria	83	83
PT Saripuri	Indonesia	City and business hotel	1994	68.0	8.0		Hong Kong, China	11	11
Quilmes	Argentina	Processing of edible crops - sugar	1994	45.0	15.0	3.6	Netherlands	15	15
SIEROMCO	Sierra Leone	Nonferrous metals - aluminum	1994	26.8	8.0		Switzerland	100	100
SOMISY	Mali	Precious metals/minerals - gold	1994	122.6	25.5	1.4	United States	70	70
Star Petroleum	Thailand	Oil refining - other	1994	1,850.0	100.0		United States	64	64
TELEMOVIL	El Salvador	Telecoms	1994	7.1	1.7	0.2	Luxembourg	55	55
TUNTEX	Thailand	Organic chemicals	1994	355.0	20.0	4.9	China	17	17
Vetropack	Czech Rep.	Industrial glass	1994	48.0	18.7		Austria	51	51

Appendix B (continued)

Company[a]	Country	Sector	Commitment FY[b]	Estimated project cost (US$m)	IFC loan (US$m)	IFC equity (US$m)	Country of largest foreign investor	Largest foreign direct investor equity (%[c])	Total foreign investor equity (%[d])
Yacylec	Argentina	Power generation and transmission	1994	134.7	20.0	0.0	Canada	25	38
ZZZ PNG Cannery	Pap. New Guin.	Processing of livestock - fish	1994	55.0	12.0	1.0	United States	66	66
A.O. Volga	Russian Fed.	Paper manufacturing	1995	371.0	30.0	11.0	Germany	36	36
AES Lal Pir	Pakistan	Power generation and transmission	1995	361.0	40.0	9.5	United States	90	90
Aguas	Argentina	Water and waste utilities	1995	381.0	38.0	7.0	France	25	36
Banco Roberts	Argentina	Commercial bank	1995	120.0	20.0		United Kingdom	30	30
Baria Serece Prt	Vietnam	Transport infrastructure	1995	10.0	3.0		France	27	60
Beronit	Czech Rep.	Steel re-rolling mills	1995	14.9	5.0		Denmark	41	41
Borcelik	Turkey	Quarried construction materials	1995	196.3	25.0	7.0	France	24	40
Centurion Bank	India	Commercial bank	1995	44.0		3.9	Singapore	20	20
CIPREL	Côte d'Ivoire	Power generation and transmission	1995	70.0	18.2	1.0	France	90	90
Clovergem Celtel	Uganda	Telecoms	1995	16.0	5.0	0.6	United Kingdom	37	79
CTAPV	Mexico	Water and waste utilities	1995	33.2	7.3		United Kingdom	44	44
Dalian Glass	China	Industrial glass	1995	134.0	30.5	2.4	Hong Kong, China	60	60
Elf Congo	Congo, Rep. of	Oil/gas production	1995	1,635.8	50.0		France	75	75
Globi Retailing	Poland	Wholesale/retail trade	1995	56.7		10.0	Belgium	64	64
Indo-Jordan	Jordan	Fertilizers	1995	170.0	30.0		India	52	52
Intercell	Poland	Paper manufacturing	1995	55.0	11.0	7.0	Sweden	15	26
Intl Hotels-Ken	Kenya	City and business hotel	1995	12.0	6.0		United Kingdom	24	43
ISIC	India	Securities market institution	1995	3.2		0.3	Hong Kong, China	40	40
Kohinoor	Pakistan	Power generation and transmission	1995	138.0	25.0	6.3	Japan	20	20
Kumtor Gold	Kyrgyz Rep.	Precious metals/minerals - gold	1995	355.0	40.0		Canada	33	33
Kwidzyn	Poland	Paper manufacturing	1995	164.8	24.0		France	64	64
Laborex	Côte d'Ivoire	Wholesale/retail trade	1995	6.6	3.1		France	35	35
Lattelekom SIA	Latvia	Telecoms	1995	220.1	5.4	13.7	Denmark	30	30
Maghreb IM Bank	Tunisia	Merchant bank	1995	3.2		0.3	France	40	40
Nahuelsat	Argentina	Telecoms	1995	240.0	30.0	5.0	Germany	11	11
Nantong Wanfu	China	Livestock - aquaculture	1995	30.0	6.5	2.8	Japan	80	80
Nesky	Poland	Auto components	1995	13.3	1.6	0.5	United States	77	77
Para Pigmentos	Brazil	Industrial minerals/ores	1995	183.0	30.0	9.0	Japan	18	18
Pescanova	Namibia	Processing of livestock - fish	1995	13.5	6.5		Spain	100	100
PPL*	Pakistan	Oil/gas production	1995	72.5	25.0		United Kingdom	64	64
PT Bakrie Kasei	Indonesia	Organic chemicals	1995	210.0	30.0	3.0	Japan	64	51
PT Bakrie Pet	Indonesia	Organic chemicals	1995	68.9	12.0	2.0	Japan	51	65
PT Citimas Captl	Indonesia	Asset securitization institution	1995	9.1		2.6	Singapore	23	53
RTDC	Russian Fed.	Telecoms	1995	40.0		7.5	United States	71	71
Rudus Oy	Estonia	Cement manufacturing	1995	7.3		1.5	Finland	60	60
Russia Registry	Russian Fed.	Securities market institution	1995	10.0		1.5	United States	30	30
SEMOS	Mali	Precious metals/minerals - gold	1995	246.2	35.0	4.8	Germany	38	76
SGHI	Guinea	City and business hotel	1995	16.0	3.7	0.6	France	33	33
Smith-Enron	Dom. Rep.	Power generation and transmission	1995	200.0	32.3		United States	50	100
Sprint Polska	Poland	Telecoms	1995	165.0	25.0	7.0	United States	25	25
Sumperk	Czech Rep.	Quarried construction materials	1995	18.2	5.6		Denmark	75	75
Tanzania Brewery	Tanzania	Beverage manufacturing	1995	87.2	11.0	6.0	Netherlands	72	72
United Power Crp	Oman	Power generation and transmission	1995	235.7	15.0	4.0	Belgium	30	30
Vasyugan	Russian Fed	Oil/gas production	1995	37.1	9.0		Canada	50	50
Vinythai	Thailand	Organic chemicals	1995	406.0	45.0		Belgium	50	49
Westel 900*	Hungary	Telecoms	1995	185.0	35.0	4.0	United States	49	42
ABN AMRO Uzbek	Uzbekistan	Commercial bank	1996	10.0		1.0	Netherlands	50	50
AES Pak Gen	Pakistan	Power generation and transmission	1996	340.0	20.0	9.5	United States	99	99
Alpha Cement	Russian Fed.	Cement manufacturing	1996	191.9		13.3	Switzerland	27	27

Appendix B (continued)

Company[a]	Country	Sector	Commitment FY[b]	Estimated project cost (US$m)	IFC loan (US$m)	IFC equity (US$m)	Country of largest foreign investor	Largest foreign direct investor equity (%[c])	Total foreign investor equity (%[d])
Amantaytau Gold	Uzbekistan	Precious metals/minerals - gold	1996	6.4		0.9	United Kingdom	35	35
Anse Chastanet	Saint Lucia	Resort hotel	1996	15.4	6.2		Canada	100	100
APIB	W. Bank & Gaza	Multipurpose bank	1996	45.0		3.8	Jordan	51	51
Bereby Finances	Côte d'Ivoire	Inedible crops - natural fibers	1996	22.0		3.0	Belgium	64	64
Brahma - ARG	Argentina	Beverage manufacturing	1996	119.2	18.5		Brazil	51	100
Caribbean Ispat	Trin. & Tobago	Integrated steel works	1996	142.4	27.4		Brazil	100	100
Consorcio Aerop.	Uruguay	Transport infrastructure	1996	31.0	8.0		India	41	41
Crescent Chem	Pakistan	Primary textile operations	1996	106.4	15.0	5.0	United Kingdom	12	12
Depsona Z.A.O.	Russian Fed.	Processing of edible crops	1996	19.4	6.8	1.5	Japan	29	41
Dupont Suzhou	China	Primary textile operations	1996	124.4	24.9	3.8	Italy	17	30
Engen Congo	Congo, Rep. of	Oil/gas production	1996	99.8	41.2	2.9	Japan	56	56
Eurafrican Bank	Tanzania	Commercial bank	1996	9.0	3.0	0.7	South Africa	30	30
FTG	Côte d'Ivoire	Primary textile operations	1996	1.9			Belgium	11	11
Gaspol	Poland	Transport infrastructure	1996	60.0	20.0	5.0	France	62	62
Gul Ahmed	Pakistan	Power generation and transmission	1996	138.0	27.0	4.1	Netherlands	20	20
GVK	India	Power generation and transmission	1996	290.7	40.0	8.3	Japan	19	19
Himal Power	Nepal	Power generation and transmission	1996	125.7	31.0		United States	58	58
Jordan Telephone	Jordan	Telecoms	1996	85.0	15.0	3.0	Norway	25	25
Le Meridien Port	Vanuatu	Resort hotel	1996	13.7	5.5		United States	100	100
Liteksas	Lithuania	Primary textile operations	1996	27.2	10.0	1.0	Singapore	66	66
Mallory	Brazil	Appliances/utensils	1996	32.1	8.0	4.0	Germany	38	38
Morn.Star Cement	Vietnam	Cement manufacturing	1996	309.0	30.0		United States	65	65
Nanjing Kumho	China	Auto tires	1996	119.2	16.0	3.8	Switzerland	20	51
NEMAK	Mexico	Auto components	1996	90.2	30.0		Korea, Republic of	20	40
Orix Finance	Pakistan	Investment bank	1996	6.4		0.6	United States	20	20
Rain Calcining	India	Oil refining - petroleum coke	1996	94.2	19.3	5.4	Japan	20	20
Savvinskaya	Russian Fed.	Construction/real estate	1996	30.4	7.7		United States	70	70
SET	Venezuela	Securities market institution	1996	5.5		0.5	Japan	11	11
Sual Power	Philippines	Power generation and transmission	1996	1,402.4	30.0		United States	92	92
Terminal 6	Argentina	Transport infrastructure	1996	19.8	10.5		Hong Kong, China	22	22
Terminales Port.	Argentina	Transport infrastructure	1996	50.3	10.0	2.0	Brazil	17	17
Tosac Hotel	Vietnam	City and business hotel	1996	11.9	3.4		United States	68	68
Tourane Hotel	Vietnam	City and business hotel	1996	23.7	8.3		Singapore	70	70
Uch Power	Pakistan	Power generation and transmission	1996	630.0			Australia	40	89
Weihai Weidongri	China	Diversified food manufacturing	1996	20.0	5.0		United Kingdom	25	75
Agrocapital	Ecuador	Inedible crops - horticultural products	1996	14.0	3.5		Korea, Republic of	50	50
Aminex TUN	Tunisia	Oil/gas production	1997	7.2		0.6	United States	22	22
Asia Power	Sri Lanka	Power generation and transmission	1997	62.5	10.0		Russian Federation	32	50
Baltic Malt	Poland	Processing of edible crops - grain	1997	27.5	6.9	2.3	United Kingdom	50	50
Beijing Hormel	China	Diversified food manufacturing	1997	17.5	5.0	2.0	Germany	49	49
Caju Mocita	Mozambique	Diversified food manufacturing	1997	10.6	3.0	0.5	United States	75	87
COMSIGUA	Venezuela	Iron manufacturing	1997	262.3	35.0		South Africa	39	54
DATEL	Tanzania	Telecoms	1997	10.0	2.3	10.0	France	36	36
Demirbank Kyrgyz	Kyrgyz Republic	Commercial bank	1997	6.0		0.5	Turkey	60	60
ECHMB	LAC Region	Housing/mortgage bank	1997	14.8		0.3	Trinidad and Tobago	20	20
Elcoteq Tallinn	Estonia	Electronic, telecom, precision equip.	1997	40.6	7.7	0.4	Finland	67	67
Eldor	Turkey	Electronic, telecom, precision equip.	1997	15.4	6.0		Italy	100	100
Engro Paktank	Pakistan	Fertilizers	1997	65.0	12.0		Netherlands	50	50
ERU Hungaria	Hungary	Processing of livestock - dairy	1997	7.4	2.5		Netherlands	100	100
Fairyoung Ports	China	Transport infrastructure	1997	5.0		5.0	Hong Kong, China	44	44
Foremost Dairy	Vietnam	Processing of livestock - dairy	1997	30.0	8.0		Netherlands	70	70

Appendix B (continued)

Company[a]	Country	Sector	Commitment FY[b]	Estimated project cost (US$m)	IFC loan (US$m)	IFC equity (US$m)	Country of largest foreign investor	Largest foreign direct investor equity (%[c])	Total foreign investor equity (%[d])
Guipeba	Argentina	Processing of edible crops - veg oil	1997	5.0	1.5		Brazil	100	100
IHP	Tanzania	Construction/real estate	1997	9.0	1.7	0.6	Japan	34	54
Jam Energy Prtnr	Jamaica	Power generation and transmission	1997	98.0	22.0	1.9	United States	38	58
Jingyang	China	Cement manufacturing	1997	265.0	40.0		Singapore	95	95
Kladno	Czech Rep.	Power generation and transmission	1997	375.0	57.2		United States	43	85
MGDK	Egypt	Inorganic chemicals	1997	24.9		1.5	Germany	45	45
Norgips	Poland	Quarried construction materials	1997	52.0	11.1		Norway	67	67
Owens Corning	India	Industrial glass	1997	102.2	25.0		United States	40	40
Packages Lanka	Sri Lanka	Paper products	1997	9.3		1.1	Pakistan	30	30
Pam Bank	Poland	Housing/mortgage bank	1997	35.0	15.0		United States	50	50
Promigas	Colombia	Oil/gas transport	1997	57.5	10.0		United States	39	39
Proyectos	Colombia	Transport infrastructure	1997	100.0	10.0	5.0	Spain	20	20
PT Gleneagles	Indonesia	Hospital/clinic	1997	47.9	11.9		Singapore	30	30
PT Pramindo Ikat	Indonesia	Telecoms	1997	624.2	50.0	7.4	France	35	35
Refimet	Chile	Nonferrous metals - copper	1997	97.0	15.0		Canada	33	33
SEF ABN AMRO	Kazakhstan	Securities market institution	1997	0.1		0.0	Netherlands	51	51
SEM Hotel	Vietnam, Socialist Rep.	City and business hotel	1997	81.5	13.1		France	58	75
SMH Glass Co.	Vietnam, Socialist Rep.	Industrial glass	1997	32.0	10.0		Philippines	65	65
Sucre de Bourbon	Vietnam, Socialist Rep.	Processing of edible crops - sugar	1997	95.0	22.0		France	70	70
Suzhou PVC	China	Organic chemicals	1997	64.7	22.0	2.5	Norway	32	75
Telecel Bolivia	Bolivia	Telecoms	1997	64.7	15.0		Luxembourg	90	90
Tianjin Kumho	China	Auto tires	1997	93.2	11.2		Korea, Republic of	95	95
TOFTAN	Estonia	Tree farming	1997	12.0	2.0		Finland	42	42
Transconor	Argentina	Oil/gas transport	1997	402.1	42.5		United States	25	39
UA-IARD	Côte d'Ivoire	Insurance company	1997	3.0		0.3	France	63	63
Vereinsbank Riga	Latvia	Commercial bank	1997	6.8		1.8	Germany	55	75
Vika Wood	Latvia	Tree farming	1997	19.0	4.0		Sweden	61	80
Vimaflour	Vietnam	Processing of edible crops - grain	1997	26.0	8.0		Malaysia	70	70
Zeravshan Gold	Tajikistan	Precious metals/minerals - gold	1997	127.0	6.3	1.2	United Kingdom	44	44

NA Not on record.

Notes:

• *Projects examined in detail (see Box 5.2 in Chapter 5).*

a *Non-bank financial institutions (NBFIs) such as development finance companies, trade finance companies, factoring/discount houses, NBFI credit lines as well as portfolio, venture capital, and pension funds have not been included in this study.*

b *Year of first IFC commitment alongside of FDI (fiscal year July 1 – June 30).*

c *For this study, a project is classified as FDI when there is at least one foreign private investor (other than vehicles for portfolio investment) with an equity stake greater than 10 percent at the time of initial IFC investment.*

d *Foreign direct investor equity as a percent of total equity.*

Appendix B (continued)

Summary

Region	Number of companies				Total project cost (1996 US$ billion)[a]			
	1958–79	1980–89	1990–97	Total	1958–79	1980–89	1990–97	Total
East Asia and Pacific	16	24	52	92	943	1,484	11,248	13,675
Eastern Europe and Central Asia	10	9	68	87	545	313	5,635	6,493
Latin America and Caribbean	47	30	63	140	4,380	4,954	8,623	17,956
Middle East and North Africa	8	13	18	39	171	1,367	1,312	2,850
South Asia	10	13	29	52	1,505	561	3,613	5,679
Sub-Saharan Africa	23	60	45	128	1,198	2,866	4,976	9,040
Total	114	149	275	538	8,742	11,545	35,407	55,694

Sector	Number of companies				Total project cost (1996 US$ billion)[a]			
	1958–79	1980–89	1990–97	Total	1958–79	1980–89	1990–97	Total
Construction materials	16	8	16	40	734	906	2,206	3,846
Chemicals	2	9	18	29	133	1,238	2,699	4,070
Fertilizers and agricultral chemicals	7	3	2	12	1,370	764	235	2,370
Financial services	3	7	31	41	23	139	604	767
Food and agribusiness	13	26	31	70	292	392	1,139	1,823
Hotels and tourism	7	18	24	49	190	461	1,141	1,793
Industrial and consumer services	1	3	7	11	36	561	280	876
Infrastructure	0	3	52	55	0	133	10,062	10,195
Manufacturing	13	13	17	43	179	762	1,607	2,548
Mining and extraction of fuel minerals	1	13	13	27	57	2,095	3,816	5,968
Mining and extraction of metals/ores	13	21	24	58	2,414	3,048	3,937	9,400
Motor vehicles and components	6	7	8	21	1,177	361	1,043	2,581
Oil refining	4	0	5	9	375	0	2,879	3,254
Textiles	16	11	15	42	813	454	1,685	2,952
Timber, pulp, and paper	12	7	12	31	949	229	2,072	3,251
Total	114	149	275	538	8,742	11,545	35,407	55,694

a Real values were used in summary tables to provide a more accurate picture of trends over time.

FIAS Advisory Projects

Country	Fiscal year	Type of project	Description
ASIA AND THE PACIFIC			
ASEAN	1990	Investment policy, incentives	FIAS prepared a study of investment incentives and destructive competition for FDI in ASEAN and the implications for harmonization and cooperation.
ASEAN	1988	Investment policy	FIAS provided suggestions on incentive harmonization for the ASEAN member states at the Secretariat's request.
Bangladesh	1993	Diagnostic	FIAS examined the policy, regulatory and incentive regime affecting private investment and made recommendations for improvements.
Bangladesh	1993	Institutions	FIAS provided assistance to the Board of Investment on organizational structure and functions, operating procedures, personnel policy and establishing a framework for investment promotion through the production of promotional materials.
Bangladesh	1990	Institutions	FIAS assisted in strengthening the institutional capacity of the Board of Investment.
Bangladesh	1990	Diagnostic update	FIAS updated its 1988 diagnostic review at the Government's request.
Bangladesh	1988	Diagnostic	FIAS conducted a diagnostic review of the obstacles to increased flows of foreign direct investment.
Cambodia	1997	Institutions	FIAS assisted in developing a system for monitoring investment incentives granted to foreign investors.
Cambodia	1994	Investment policy, laws	FIAS helped in the preparation of a new foreign investment law.
China	1997	Institutions	FIAS reviewed the existing foreign direct investment data sources, definition and classification, and made recommendations to strengthen the foreign direct investment data statistical system.
China	1997	Investment policy	FIAS assisted in the preparation of new regulations on the treatment of branches of foreign firms.
China	1996	Promotion strategy, Sichuan province	FIAS drafted a report on the relationship between investment environment and investment promotion in the Sichuan Province, and helped organize a Roundtable in Chengdu on the same subject for the benefit of Provincial authorities.
China	1996	Implementation, BOT	FIAS assisted in finalizing new regulations governing the BOT approval procedures, bidding documents, and model contracts.
China	1995	Sector, infrastructure	FIAS reviewed the policy implications of promoting foreign direct investment in the infrastructure sector.
China	1994	Investment policy, screening/approval	FIAS conducted a review of screening and approval procedures.
China	1992	Investment policy, survey	FIAS conducted a review of the foreign investment environment.

Country	Fiscal year	Type of project	Description
China	1989	Investment policy	FIAS provided advice on reconciling the conflicting objectives of the joint-ventures foreign exchange balance requirements and the desire to increase flows of FDI.
China	1987	Diagnostic (with World Bank)	FIAS, with the World Bank, prepared a diagnostic review of the foreign investment climate.
China	1987	Investment policy	FIAS assisted in the preparation of a new contractual joint venture law.
China	1986	Seminar	FIAS conducted a seminar in Beijing for senior Chinese officials involved in the planning, approval and monitoring of FDI.
Fiji	1994	Investment policy, institutions	FIAS reviewed the institutional arrangements for foreign direct investment and assisted in the preparation of a new investment act.
Fiji	1994	Investment policy, incentives	FIAS conducted an examination of the incentives framework.
Greater Mekong Subregion	1996	Institutions, promotion strategy	FIAS assisted in the first meeting of promotion agencies and helped them in conceptualizing the nature and the scope of their regional cooperation.
India	1993	Diagnostic, promotion	FIAS conducted a comparative assessment of foreign investment policies and assisted in the formulation of a foreign investment promotional strategy.
Indonesia	1996	Investment policy, backward linkages II	FIAS reviewed the policy aspects of developing backward linkages between foreign and domestic firms.
Indonesia	1996	Institutions, FDI database	FIAS reviewed the existing FDI data sources, definition and classification, and the inter-agency collaboration, making recommendations to improve data collection, quality, coverage, and consistency.
Indonesia	1995	Investment policy	FIAS conducted an extensive survey on further liberalization of ownership and control restrictions.
Indonesia	1995	Investment policy, backward linkages	FIAS reviewed the policy aspects of developing backward linkages between foreign and domestic firms.
Indonesia	1991	Institutions	FIAS assisted in the formulation of an investment promotion strategy and, more specifically, the roles of the national and regional investment institutions in that strategy.
Indonesia	1990	Promotion	FIAS reviewed policy and regulatory impediments to foreign investment in the agricultural sector with the intent of increasing such investment.
Indonesia	1989	Sector, agriculture	FIAS conducted a review of impediments to foreign direct investment in the agricultural sector.
Indonesia	1988	Diagnostic (with World Bank)	FIAS reviewed the regulatory framework for foreign investment.
Kiribati	1997	Diagnostic	FIAS conducted a diagnostic review of the investment climate.
Lao, PDR	1992	Investment policy, EPZ	FIAS reviewed the feasibility of an Export Processing Zone to promote foreign direct investment.
Malaysia	1994	Institutions	FIAS helped the Industrial Development Authority to strengthen its promotional and facilitation functions.
Malaysia	1992	Investment monitoring	FIAS helped the Industrial Development Authority design a system to monitor foreign direct investment.
Malaysia	1992	Investment policy, incentives	FIAS conducted a comparative assessment of the investment incentive system.
Malaysia	1988	Institutions	FIAS assisted the Ministry of Trade and Industry officials to improve techniques for the economic evaluation of foreign investment proposals.
Maldives	1994	Diagnostic	FIAS conducted a diagnostic study of the investment climate.
Marshall Islands	1996	Diagnostic	FIAS conducted a diagnostic review of the investment climate.
Micronesia, Federated States of	1997	Implementation	FIAS assisted in the implementation of earlier recommendations for a revised legal framework to attract foreign investment.

Country	Fiscal year	Type of project	Description
Micronesia	1995	Investment policy	FIAS focused on the appropriate legislative framework to attract foreign direct investment.
Mongolia	1997	Promotion strategy	FIAS drafted a report and organized a Roundtable on the relationship between investment environment and investment promotion.
Mongolia	1997	Investment policy, law	FIAS helped in the revision of the investment law.
Mongolia	1993	Diagnostic	FIAS conducted a diagnostic review of the investment climate.
Nepal	1997	Investment policy, incentives	FIAS reviewed the incentives regime and the legal framework for foreign investment.
Nepal	1993	Diagnostic	FIAS conducted a diagnostic review of the investment climate.
Papua-New Guinea	1989	Investment policy, law	FIAS prepared a revision of the investment law.
Philippines	1997	Sector, infrastructure	FIAS reviewed the policy implications of promoting foreign direct investment in the infrastructure sector.
Philippines	1996	Institutions	FIAS helped define an institutional framework and strategy for investment promotion.
Philippines	1995	Investment policy, backward linkages II	FIAS reviewed the policy aspects of developing backward linkages between foreign and domestic firms.
Philippines	1992	Institutions	FIAS assisted in the reorientation of the Board of Investments from regulation to promotion of investment.
Philippines	1992	Investment policy, backward linkages	FIAS conducted a study designed to identify opportunities for, and impediments to, backward linkages between foreign and local firms.
Philippines	1991	Promotion strategy	FIAS assisted in the preparation of a new investment promotion strategy.
Philippines	1990	Institutions, FDI database	FIAS provided recommendations for improvements to the FDI database.
Philippines	1989	Investment policy, swaps	FIAS helped the Central Bank assess whether the country should resume its debt-equity swaps program.
Philippines	1988	Sector, agriculture	FIAS helped the Department of Agriculture and Food determine how policy and institutional changes could stimulate domestic and foreign private investment to help reduce post-harvest losses of grains.
Solomon Islands	1997	Investment policy, law	FIAS conducted a review of the investment law.
Sri Lanka	1993	Promotion strategy	FIAS assisted in the development of an investment promotion strategy.
Sri Lanka	1991	Institutions	FIAS assisted in the development of a new institutional and procedural framework to attract foreign direct investment.
Sri Lanka	1991	Diagnostic	FIAS assisted in the preparation of an investment policy and institutional framework for foreign direct investment.
Thailand	1995	Promotion strategy	FIAS prepared a framework for a promotion strategy for the Eastern Seaboard region.
Thailand	1992	Investment policy, backward linkages	FIAS conducted a study designed to identify opportunities for, and impediments to, backward linkages between foreign and local firms.
Thailand	1990	Investment policy	FIAS reviewed backward linkage experience of selected countries and their relevance in Thailand.
Thailand	1988	Investment policy, incentives	FIAS reviewed Thailand's investment policy and incentives strategy in light of the objectives in the Sixth National Economic and Social Plan.
Tonga	1996	Diagnostic	FIAS conducted a diagnostic review of the investment climate.
Vanuatu	1996	Investment policy	FIAS assisted in the preparation of a documented foreign investment policy.
Vietnam	1996	Sector, infrastructure	FIAS reviewed the country's experience in attracting and implementing FDI into infrastructure projects and evaluated obstacles to increasing such FDI in Vietnam.

Country	Fiscal year	Type of project	Description
Vietnam	1995	Investment policy	FIAS reviewed the policy implications of promoting foreign direct investment in the infrastructure sector.
Vietnam	1994	Investment policy, approval/ promotion	FIAS assisted in improving coordination of approval procedures and promotional activities.
Vietnam	1993	Investment policy, laws	FIAS conducted a study on the role of bilateral, regional and multi-lateral legal instruments to encourage foreign direct investment.
Vietnam	1991	Investment policy	FIAS was requested to establish priorities for legal reforms to encourage and accelerate the flow of foreign direct investment.
Western Samoa	1995	Investment policy, incentives	FIAS reviewed the investment incentives regime.
Western Samoa	1992	Diagnostic	FIAS conducted a diagnostic review of the investment climate.

CENTRAL ASIA, MIDDLE EAST AND NORTH AFRICA

Country	Fiscal year	Type of project	Description
Algeria	1992	Diagnostic	FIAS conducted a diagnostic review of the investment climate.
Egypt	1994	Investment policy, backward linkages	FIAS, in conjunction with IFC's Economics Department, completed a study on ways to facilitate linkages between foreign and local firms.
Egypt	1991	Diagnostic	FIAS conducted a diagnostic review of the investment climate.
Jordan	1995	Implementation	FIAS provided assistance in implementing earlier advice on the investment law and structure of the promotion agency.
Jordan	1993	Diagnostic	FIAS conducted a diagnostic review of the investment climate.
Kazakhstan	1995	Diagnostic	FIAS conducted a survey of multinational companies on the foreign investment environment in the country and assisted the government in revising the foreign investment law.
Kyrgyz Republic	1997	Diagnostic II	FIAS conducted a second review of the environment for foreign direct investment, with emphasis on administrative and legal barriers, and the way to structure a promotion agency.
Kyrgyz Republic	1995	Diagnostic	FIAS conducted a diagnostic study of the investment climate.
Lebanon	1994	Diagnostic	FIAS conducted a diagnostic study of the investment climate.
Morocco	1995	Institutions, promotion strategy	FIAS conducted a competitiveness study of selected manufacturing sectors and assisted in the design of an investment promotion strategy.
Morocco	1991	Investment policy, promotion	FIAS reviewed administrative procedures and developed a foreign investment promotion strategy.
Oman	1994	Institutions	FIAS assisted in the establishment of an investment promotion unit in the Ministry of Industry and Commerce.
Pakistan	1994	Institutions	FIAS completed a comprehensive technical assistance program by advising the newly established Pakistan Investment Board on investment facilitation.
Pakistan	1994	Promotion strategy	FIAS assisted in the development of a promotion strategy.
Pakistan	1993	Institutions	FIAS developed a strategy to strengthen the Pakistan Investment Board.
Pakistan	1992	Diagnostic	FIAS conducted a diagnostic study of the investment climate.
Pakistan	1990	Diagnostic (with World Bank)	FIAS reviewed the role of government in attracting foreign direct investment.
Saudi Arabia	1991	Diagnostic	FIAS conducted a diagnostic study of the investment climate.
Tunisia	1996	Implementation	FIAS assisted in implementing earlier recommendations for the establishment of a new investment promotion institution.
Tunisia	1995	Institutions, promotion strategy	FIAS conducted a competitiveness study of selected manufacturing sectors and assisted in the design of an investment promotion strategy.
Tunisia	1992	Promotion strategy	FIAS developed a foreign investment promotion strategy.
UMA	1996	Investment policy, incentives	FIAS conducted a study on the desirability and feasibility of harmonization of investment incentives among countries constituting the UMA (Algeria, Libya, Mauritania, and Tunisia).
United Arab Emirates	1993	Diagnostic	FIAS conducted a diagnostic study of the investment climate.

Country	Fiscal year	Type of project	Description
Uzbekistan	1997	Diagnostic	FIAS conducted a diagnostic review of foreign direct investment environment.
West Bank and Gaza	1997	Investment policy	FIAS provided assistance in developing the basic regulatory and institutional framework for private sector activities.
West Bank and Gaza	1996	Implementation	FIAS provided assistance in revising a draft investment law based on its earlier recommendations.
West Bank and Gaza	1995	Diagnostic	FIAS reviewed the policy and legal framework for foreign direct investment.
Yemen	1997	Diagnostic	FIAS conducted a diagnostic review of the investment climate and an investor survey identifying major impediments to foreign direct investment.
Yemen	1992	Institutions	FIAS conducted a study on the structure and operations of the General Investment Authority and made recommendations.

EUROPE

Country	Fiscal year	Type of project	Description
Belarus	1996	Diagnostic	FIAS conducted a diagnostic review of the investment climate.
Bulgaria	1996	Investment policy	FIAS conducted a review of impediments to the formation of joint ventures between foreign investors and Bulgarian state enterprises.
Bulgaria	1994	Diagnostic	FIAS conducted a diagnostic study of the investment climate.
Central and Eastern Europe	1992	Investment promotion	FIAS prepared a report on the impact that EEC corporate income tax regimes have on the profitability of foreign investments in five taxation EEC countries. The results were presented in a workshop sponsored by FIAS at the UNIDO Center in Vienna.
Croatia	1997	Institutions	FIAS helped in the development of the mandate, organizational structure, and the work program of the investment promotion agency.
Croatia	1996	Investment policy	FIAS provided assistance in drafting an investment policy statement.
Croatia	1995	Diagnostic	FIAS reviewed the legal and regulatory environment for foreign investment and helped develop an institutional framework for investment promotion.
Czechoslovakia	1991	Diagnostic (with World Bank)	FIAS conducted a diagnostic study of the investment climate.
Czechoslovakia	1991	Investment policy, institutions	FIAS reviewed the legal framework for foreign investment and the investment promotion agencies and made recommendations.
Estonia	1997	Diagnostic II	FIAS conducted a diagnostic review of the investment climate.
Estonia	1993	Diagnostic	FIAS conducted a diagnostic review of the investment climate.
Georgia	1997	Investment policy, law	FIAS reviewed the draft of a new foreign direct investment law.
Georgia	1997	Institutions	FIAS provided advice on the structure, design and strategy of an investment promotion agency.
Georgia	1996	Diagnostic	FIAS conducted a diagnostic review of the investment climate.
Hungary	1991	Investment policy, laws	FIAS conducted a review of screening and approval procedures, taxation and the legal framework for foreign investment.
Hungary	1990	Diagnostic	FIAS reviewed incentives, screening and the role of foreign direct investment in the privatization of state-owned enterprises.
Latvia	1996	Investment policy	FIAS reviewed policies and procedures affecting FDI, as well as the ongoing privatization program, from the strategic investors' point of view.
Latvia	1993	Diagnostic	FIAS conducted a diagnostic review of the investment climate.
Lithuania	1993	Diagnostic	FIAS conducted a diagnostic review of the investment climate.
Poland	1990	Diagnostic, institutions	FIAS conducted a diagnostic study of the investment climate and prepared a review of the role and organization of the Foreign Investment Agency.
Romania	1991	Diagnostic	FIAS conducted a diagnostic review of the investment climate.

Country	Fiscal year	Type of project	Description
Russian Federation	1997	Diagnostic	FIAS conducted a review of the investment climate in Novgorod Oblast in Russia.
Russian Federation	1994	Investment policy, law	FIAS advised on amendments to Russia's Foreign Investment Law.
Russian Federation	1993	Institutions	FIAS developed a technical assistance proposal for the promotion and regulation of foreign direct investment.
Russian Federation	1993	Diagnostic	FIAS conducted a diagnostic review of the investment climate.
Slovakia	1994	Diagnostic	FIAS conducted a diagnostic study of the investment climate.
Ukraine	1994	Diagnostic	FIAS conducted a diagnostic study of the investment climate.
Yugoslavia	1990	Investment policy, swaps	FIAS assisted in the design of regulations and procedures to implement a debt-equity swap program.
Yugoslavia	1989	Investment policy	FIAS prepared a review of obstacles to increased flows of foreign investment and commented on the draft of the new foreign investment law.

LATIN AMERICA AND THE CARIBBEAN

Country	Fiscal year	Type of project	Description
Argentina	1994	Institutions	FIAS assisted in the institutional development of the Investment Promotion Agency.
Bahamas	1993	Investment policy	Following the diagnosis of policy issues in FY92, FIAS helped the Government draft an Investment Policy Statement.
Bahamas	1992	Investment policy, institutions	FIAS reviewed the screening and approval procedures for investment applications, with special attention to the regulatory and institutional dimensions of the process.
Bolivia	1996	Implementation	FIAS assisted in implementing earlier recommendations for the creation of a new investment promotion institution.
Bolivia	1995	Institutions	FIAS assisted in the institutional development of the Investment Promotion Agency.
Brazil	1996	Institutions	FIAS developed a proposal for the creation of a national-level institution to promote inward FDI.
Costa Rica	1997	Investment policy	FIAS assisted in developing a national strategy for strengthening the country's electronics sector.
Dominican Republic	1994	Investment policy, laws	FIAS reviewed the legal framework for foreign investment and made recommendations on formulating a promotion strategy.
El Salvador	1997	Investment policy	FIAS assisted in drafting a new investment law.
El Salvador	1997	Institutions, promotion strategy	FIAS assisted in strengthening the role of the investment agency and developing a national promotion strategy.
El Salvador	1994	Investment policy, laws	FIAS prepared a report on legal obstacles to lending to private firms, including foreign investors.
El Salvador	1993	Investment policy, institutions	FIAS reviewed the approval procedures and regulation of private investment and suggested recommendations for the reform of the investment bureaucracy.
Guyana	1995	Diagnostic	FIAS reviewed policies impeding foreign direct investment and helped the national investment authority to develop its institutional capacity.
Honduras	1992	Investment policy, laws	FIAS examined the investment climate and the legal framework for foreign investment and made recommendations for reforming the legal structure for foreign investments.
Mexico	1996	Investment policy	FIAS reviewed the policy and institutional aspects of increasing backward linkages between foreign and domestic firms.
Panama	1996	Institutions	FIAS assisted in developing the structure and defining the functions of a new investment promotion agency.
Paraguay	1996	Institutions, promotion strategy	FIAS assisted in developing a strategy and a three-year business plan for the investment promotion agency.
Paraguay	1995	Investment policy	FIAS helped the cabinet to prepare an Investment Policy Statement.
Paraguay	1994	Promotion strategy	FIAS helped in the development of legal, policy and institutional changes, after identifying the opportunities for foreign investment.

Country	Fiscal year	Type of project	Description
Paraguay	1993	Diagnostic	FIAS conducted a diagnostic review of the investment climate.
Peru	1995	Institutions	FIAS helped in the development of institutional capacities for promoting foreign investment.
St. Lucia	1997	Institutions	FIAS assisted in defining an institutional framework and exploring strategic options for investment promotion.
Trinidad and Tobago	1996	Investment policy	FIAS conducted a detailed study emphasizing the implementation of previously recommended reforms in incentive regime, foreign investment law, and entry procedures and restrictions.
Trinidad and Tobago	1995	Investment policy	FIAS reviewed the corporate taxation system.
Trinidad and Tobago	1994	Diagnostic	FIAS conducted a diagnostic study of the investment climate.
Uruguay	1991	Diagnostic	FIAS conducted a diagnostic review of the investment climate.
Venezuela	1995	Implementation, institutions	FIAS reviewed the functioning of the promotion agency.
Venezuela	1993	Promotion strategy	FIAS assisted the National Investment Promotion Council (CONAPRI) to develop a comprehensive strategy for promoting foreign investment.
Venezuela	1991	Promotion strategy	FIAS provided assistance to the National Investment Promotion Council in formulating a promotion strategy.

SUB-SAHARAN AFRICA

Country	Fiscal year	Type of project	Description
Angola	1992	Diagnostic	FIAS conducted a diagnostic study of the investment climate.
Benin	1992	Diagnostic	FIAS conducted a diagnostic study of the investment climate.
Burkina Faso	1992	Diagnostic	FIAS conducted a diagnostic study of the investment climate.
Cameroon	1995	Diagnostic	FIAS conducted a diagnostic study of the investment climate.
Cameroon	1990	Investment policy	FIAS assisted in the revision of the investment code.
Cameroon	1990	Diagnostic	FIAS prepared a diagnostic review of the investment climate.
Cape Verde	1995	Institutions	FIAS assisted in the evaluation of the investment promotion agency.
Congo, Republic of	1991	Diagnostic	FIAS conducted a diagnostic study of the investment climate.
Côte d'Ivoire	1993	Institutions	FIAS conducted an evaluation of procedures used to implement the Investment Code of 1984.
Equatorial Guinea	1993	Investment policy, regulations	FIAS assisted the government in drafting a new foreign investment law in FY1992 and was subsequently asked to help draft implementing regulations.
Equatorial Guinea	1992	Investment policy, investment code	FIAS assisted the government in drafting a new foreign investment law.
Ethiopia	1997	Diagnostic	FIAS reviewed the investment climate and the approval process for foreign direct investment.
Gambia	1995	Diagnostic	FIAS conducted a diagnostic study of the investment climate.
Ghana	1996	Promotion strategy	FIAS assisted in the development of a strategic plan for investment promotion.
Ghana	1995	Investment policy, barriers	FIAS conducted a regulatory review of barriers to FDI.
Ghana	1994	Institutions	FIAS helped in the restructuring of the investment institution.
Ghana	1993	Investment policy, investment code	FIAS helped the government formulate a new set of investment incentives that would be administered automatically through the tax system and helped redefine the internal structure and functions of the Ghana Investment Center following the changes.
Ghana	1987	Institutions	FIAS provided assistance to the Ghana Investment Center in implementing the country's 1985 investment code, focusing primarily on organization and management.
Guinea	1996	Investment policy	FIAS assisted in the implementation of its earlier advice on improvements to the investment code.
Guinea	1989	Diagnostic	FIAS undertook a diagnostic review of the investment climate.
Guinea-Bissau	1991	Investment policy	FIAS assisted in the revision of a new investment code.

Country	Fiscal year	Type of project	Description
Kenya	1992	Investment policy, backward linkages	FIAS conducted a study on the environment for backward linkages in Kenya, focusing on policy and administrative issues.
Kenya	1991	Investment policy	FIAS assisted in the preparation of an investment policy statement.
Kenya	1991	Promotion strategy	FIAS assisted in the preparation of an investment promotion strategy.
Kenya	1990	Investment policy	FIAS conducted a seminar in Washington for Kenya's Ministry of Finance and the Investment Promotion Center for the preparation of an investment policy statement.
Kenya	1988	Diagnostic	FIAS conducted a diagnostic review of the investment climate.
Lesotho	1997	Investment policy	FIAS conducted a detailed review of administrative barriers to private investment, as well as the investment legislation.
Lesotho	1991	Promotion strategy	FIAS assisted in the preparation of an investment promotion strategy.
Lesotho	1990	Diagnostic	FIAS prepared a diagnostic review of the investment climate.
Madagascar	1992	Promotion	FIAS developed a strategic plan for investment promotion following an earlier diagnostic study of the investment climate.
Madagascar	1990	Investment policy	FIAS assisted in the revision of the 1985 investment code and the preparation of a draft of new legislation for the creation of export-processing zones.
Madagascar	1989	Diagnostic	FIAS undertook a diagnostic review of the investment climate.
Malawi	1995	Promotion strategy	FIAS assisted in the design of an investment promotion strategy.
Malawi	1994	Institutions Investor tracking software	FIAS installed the software developed for foreign investment tracking in the investment promotion agency.
Malawi	1992	Investment policy, investment code	FIAS assisted the government in redefining its approach to private investment through deregulation, a new approach to investor servicing through the creation of an IPA, an Investment Policy Statement and, inter alia, an Investor's Guide.
Malawi	1991	Diagnostic	FIAS conducted a diagnostic review of the investment climate and assisted in the preparation of an investment policy statement, investor's guide and statute establishing an investment promotion agency.
Mali	1997	Institutions	FIAS assisted in developing the capacity of the investment promotion institution.
Mali	1992	Diagnostic	FIAS prepared a study in which previously identified obstacles to investment would be compiled in a single document. This study helped provide background material to a revision of the investment code.
Mauritania	1996	Investment policy, barriers	FIAS developed detailed recommendations for the short term improvements in the investment environment.
Mauritania	1993	Diagnostic	FIAS conducted a diagnostic review of the investment climate.
Mozambique	1996	Investment policy, barriers	FIAS conducted a detailed review of specific barriers to private investment.
Mozambique	1994	Institutions	FIAS assisted in the institutional development of the investment promotion agency.
Mozambique	1993	Diagnostic	FIAS conducted a diagnostic review of the investment climate.
Mozambique	1991	Investment policy, swaps	FIAS conducted a review of the debt equity conversion program.
Namibia	1997	Investment policy, incentives	FIAS recommended strategies for improving the investment incentives framework.
Namibia	1996	Investment policy, barriers	FIAS conducted a detailed review of specific barriers to private investment.
Namibia	1996	Investment policy, incentives	FIAS conducted a review of the investment incentives regime.
Namibia	1993	Diagnostic	FIAS conducted a diagnostic review of the investment climate.
Namibia	1992	Investment policy, investment code	FIAS helped develop a new Investment Promotion Act.

Country	Fiscal year	Type of project	Description
Senegal	1996	Investment policy	FIAS reviewed the investment incentives and the EPZ regime as well as custom procedures affecting foreign direct investment.
Senegal	1994	Investment policy, incentives	FIAS assisted in the rationalization of the investment incentive framework.
Senegal	1989	Sector, agriculture	FIAS helped formulate a promotion strategy for foreign investment in the Senegal River Basin.
Sierra Leone	1997	Investment policy, law	FIAS reviewed the foreign investment law.
Sudan	1993	Diagnostic	FIAS conducted a diagnostic review of the investment climate.
Swaziland	1997	Investment policy	FIAS reviewed the investment legislation.
Swaziland	1994	Diagnostic	FIAS conducted a diagnostic study of the investment climate.
Tanzania	1993	Investment Policy, swaps/forex	FIAS reviewed policies to encourage foreign direct investment with special attention to exchange controls and debt-equity swaps.
Togo	1990	Promotion strategy	FIAS helped to develop a short to medium term strategic plan for foreign investment promotion.
Togo	1989	Investment policy	FIAS assisted in the revision of the investment code and the preparation of implementing regulations.
Uganda	1997	Investment policy, barriers	FIAS conducted a detailed review of administrative barriers to private investment.
Uganda	1995	Institutions, investor tracking software	FIAS installed the software developed for foreign investment tracking in the Investment Promotion Agency.
Uganda	1990	Diagnostic	FIAS prepared a diagnostic review of the investment climate.
Zambia	1993	Diagnostic	FIAS conducted a diagnostic review of the investment climate.
Zambia	1993	Investment policy, investment code	FIAS conducted a diagnostic study of the investment environment and proposed amendments to the existing Investment Act.
Zimbabwe	1997	Sector, infrastructure	FIAS completed the work on improving the policy environment for private investment in infrastructure.
Zimbabwe	1995	Promotion strategy	FIAS organized a series of corporate planning workshops to facilitate the preparation of a strategic plan for investment promotion.
Zimbabwe	1994	Institutions	FIAS assisted in the institutional development of the investment promotion agency.
Zimbabwe	1994	Institutions	FIAS assisted the Investment Center in the preparation of a policy initiative paper.
Zimbabwe	1993	Diagnostic	FIAS conducted a diagnostic review of the investment climate.
Zimbabwe	1990	Diagnostic	FIAS prepared a diagnostic review of the investment climate.

ASEAN	Association of South East Asian Nations
BOT	Build Operate Transfer
EPZ	Export Processing Zone
FIAS	Foreign Investment Advisory Service
UMA	Union du Maghreb Arabe